Library Services for Hispanic Children

A Guide for Public and School Librarians

Edited by Adela Artola Allen

ORYX PRESS
1987

Copyright © 1987 by The Oryx Press
2214 North Central at Encanto
Phoenix, Arizona 85004-1483

Published simultaneously in Canada

Printed and Bound in the United States of America

∞ The paper used in this publication meets the minimum requirements of American National Standard for Information Science—Permanence of Paper for Printed Library Materials, ANSI Z39.48, 1984.

Library of Congress Cataloging-in-Publication Data

Library services for Hispanic children.

Bibliography: p.
Includes index.
1. Hispanic Americans and libraries. 2. Hispanic American children—Books and reading. 3. Hispanic American children—Education. 4. Libraries, Children's—United States. 5. School libraries—United States. 6. Public libraries—United States—Services to Hispanic Americans. I. Allen, Adela Artola.
Z711.8.L526   1987   027.6′3   86-42788
ISBN 0-89774-371-7

To my loving husband,
Judge John Fitzgerald Molloy

Table of Contents

Contributors

ADELA ARTOLA ALLEN is Head of the Division of Language, Reading and Culture at the University of Arizona. She teaches courses in reading, bilingual reading, and children's literature. She has a Ph.D. in Spanish and Portuguese literature from the University of Arizona.

FRANCISCO AVALOS is the Foreign and International Law Librarian at the College of Law of the University of Arizona

GILDA BAEZA is currently a Mexican-American Studies Librarian at the Benson Latin American Collection at the University of Texas, El Paso, and was formerly Head of Mexican-American Services at the El Paso Public Library.

SARAH BARCHAS is a children's librarian for Tucson Unified School District and teaches courses in storytelling and children's literature at the University of Arizona.

STEPHEN DIAZ is a Research Psychologist at the Laboratory of Comparative Human Cognition at the University of California, San Diego. His research interests include education and child development

F. LANCE HOOPES combines many years of computer experience with his interest in Hispanic youth developed during 39 years in Arizona. He has been Principal of Superior High School in Superior, Arizona, and is currently Assistant Principal of Doolen Middle School in Tucson. Hoopes has selected computer software as his dissertation topic for the Ph.D. he is currently pursuing at the University of Arizona.

MARY FRANCES JOHNSON is a bilingual branch librarian in the Redwood City (California) Public Library, specializing in Spanish children's literature. She was educated in Latin America, Canada, and the Caribbean, and is completing work on an Ed.D. in Multicultural Education at the University of San Francisco.

R. CECILIA KNIGHT is the Acting Principal Cataloger at the University of Arizona Library, where she is also responsible for cataloging the Spanish-language juvenile collection.

LIZ RODRIGUEZ MILLER is the Regional Manager of the Tucson Public Library, Main Library. She is the recipient of a GLISA (Graduate Library Institute for Spanish-Speaking Americans) fellowship.

JUDY NICHOLS MITCHELL is Associate Professor of Reading at the University of Arizona. She has a Ph.D. in Linguistics from Northwestern University. Her research interests include text characteristics, reading comprehension, and early reading.

LUIS C. MOLL is Associate Professor in the Division of Language, Reading and Culture at the University of Arizona. His research interests include child development and education.

NITA NORMAN is a branch librarian at the Phoenix Public Library, Harmon Branch. In 1980 she received the Librarian of the Year Award from the Friends of the Chicago Public Library for her services to the Hispanic community, and in 1985 she received an award from the City of Phoenix for her work with minorities.

ISABEL SCHON is Professor of Library Science at Arizona State University and has published numerous books on Hispanic literature for children and young adults. She received the Grolier Award from the American Library Association in 1986.

MARIA SEGURA is a reference librarian at the University of Arizona in Tucson. Segura, who was born in Mexico and is a native Spanish speaker, has been a teacher of Spanish and a children's librarian in Tucson schools. Her chapter here is a culmination of a long held interest in language, books, and children's literature.

Acknowledgments

There are several people without whom this book would not have been possible. The editorial board—Sarah Barchas, Isabel Schon, and Maria Segura—helped determine the shape and content of the book and provided many hours of their time to support this endeavor.

Sandra Wilde provided invaluable editorial assistance. Graciela Osterberg spent many long hours typing the manuscript. I am deeply grateful to all of them.

Adela Artola Allen

Introduction

Ethnic groups constitute the unique and rich tapestry of our multicultural society, with each group bringing its history and experience to enrich the fabric with a distinct and novel flair. Perhaps no other group has influenced the American lifestyle with such a vast assortment of cultural contributions as the Hispanics. We see and feel the force of their culture at every turn—in architecture, food, clothing, music, and art. The rapidly increasing Hispanic population now constitutes one of the largest minority groups in this country. The ethnic pride of this population has recently emerged, partly as the result of the civil rights movement of the 1960s, and has stimulated a significant interest in developing university courses to teach students more about the Hispanic cultural heritage. As a result, the development of Hispanic library collections has increased. Only recently have libraries begun to serve ethnic minority groups and become sources of information for those in search of their roots. Library services to Hispanic children have lagged even behind the belated services to adult Hispanics. This book is long overdue. It represents a groundbreaking and challenging publication that will aid school and public librarians, specialists, and teachers who are seeking assistance to develop libraries and to evaluate and select materials for the diverse and heterogeneous population of Hispanic children that they serve.

For professionals involved in bringing children together with their heritage, as represented in print and nonprint library materials, this book offers a wealth of information to make the experience of literature a rewarding one. Hispanic children, neglected in their library needs for much too long, want to see and read images and stories in their strongest language, and in the context of their own culture. Through the library they can meet people like themselves and learn to appreciate the beauty of the Hispanic and of all people. In this way, children can grow aesthetically, as well as in self-image, by discovering through literature the roots and accomplishments of their own people.

The book begins with Gilda Baeza's discussion of the evolution of educational and public library services to the Spanish-speaking community. She presents a historical overview of library services to

Hispanics and discusses relevant professional organizations. A description of exemplary library programs covers policies of recruitment, cataloging, acquisition of materials, and special programs. These library services for Hispanic children are discussed with particular emphasis on the sociological, economic, geographic, and cultural issues that must be addressed to serve the needs of Hispanic children.

The reader is next given an overview of a socio-cultural approach to the study of Hispanic children, as presented by Luis C. Moll and Stephen Diaz. This article deals with issues of cognitive style and bilingualism and illustrates the point that understanding of Hispanic children must be based on actual knowledge of their lives rather than preconceptions about their culture. The article provides rich background knowledge for teachers and librarians, especially those not of Hispanic origin.

Several articles discuss professional issues related to library services for the Hispanic child. Judy Nichols Mitchell writes about language issues: the relationship between language and reading, and how it affects the matching of reader to books. Since some Hispanic children do not speak English, some do not speak Spanish, and others speak language which is a mixture of both, a working knowledge of the linguistic characteristics of Hispanic children is a must for librarians to function successfully in a Spanish-English setting. Mitchell describes some of the factors that teachers and librarians must consider in evaluating suitability of materials for particular children.

Next, Liz Rodriguez Miller discusses methods for the identification of a particular community's needs and various ways in which libraries, schools, and communities can cooperate to create or develop an effective program. Suggestions are given on how to plan and implement programs and how to select the personnel to manage them.

Mary Frances Johnson describes guidelines for selection and acquisition of materials in Spanish, including quality of print and binding, readability, special considerations when purchasing from foreign publishers, and sources of bibliographical information. Appendices to Johnson's article include extensive lists of sources of bibliographic information and of series and collections of books. It is followed by Cecilia Knight's practical guide to identifying and solving the cataloging problems presented by Spanish-language materials.

Sarah Barchas discusses strategies for involving children in reading literature, with special attention to reading aloud, storytelling, dramatization, booktalks, and displays. The use of poetry, music, chants, and syntactic pattern materials for motivating children to read are presented, with examples in both English and Spanish. Many specific suggestions about how to use particular books are provided, as well as an extensive bibliography of both professional and children's books. Adela Artola Allen's bilingual list of literary terminology gives additional support to those wishing to involve children in literature.

Adela Artola Allen and Sarah Barchas provide guidelines for the non-Spanish-speaking librarian serving Hispanic children in the form of a list of requests, instructions, and general library management expressions in both English and Spanish. This article is followed by an English-Spanish library-related vocabulary list by Francisco Avalos. Library-related terms are listed here with their Spanish equivalents. Librarians can avail themselves of this list to label locations in the library or in communicating library information to non-English-speaking patrons. Classroom teachers can use the list when helping their students to develop library skills. The Avalos vocabulary list is completed by an appendix showing the Dewey Decimal system in Spanish.

The last section of the book is bibliographic. Isabel Schon has provided two extensive, annotated bibliographies, one of books about Hispanics in English, the other of books in Spanish. These are supplemented by Nita Norman's bibliography of nonprint bilingual materials and Lance Hoopes' listing of computer software for Spanish-speaking students.

Finally, Maria Segura provides an extensive bibliography of resources for librarians about Hispanic culture. It includes sources of information on library services to Hispanics as well as resource books that deal generally with historical and cultural information about the different Hispanic populations and with such specific topics of interest as holidays, customs, dance, music, art, folklore, and history. This article can be used by professionals to expand their knowledge of the population they serve and by librarians or classroom teachers for background or when preparing a specific unit. This article also includes a list of publishers and distributors of Hispanic-oriented material.

Part I

Serving Hispanic Children: History and Approach

The Evolution of Educational and Public Library Services to Spanish-Speaking Children

Gilda Baeza

The evolution of library services to Hispanic children in school and public libraries is currently at a stage comparable to life on earth during the Ice Age. That is, library services to Spanish-speaking children are available in limited and local forms but are in embryological stage nationwide. Many strides were made during the 1970s when the critical need for such services was initially recognized by the library and information science profession. This recognition coincided with the era in which Hispanics began articulating their concern over their benign neglect by libraries. The historical development of services focusing on Hispanic children since that era will be explored in this article. It is based on both the literature in the field and personal observations and experiences.

In researching the history of library services to Hispanics in general, one is struck by the lack of documentation in the literature prior to 1970. Duran (1979) noted that library literature as early as the nineteenth century addressed the development of services to non-English-speaking European immigrants. Yet sources of information about library services to the Hispanic population are virtually nonexistent, despite the fact that a major component of that population (Mexican Americans) predates the arrival of English speakers to the southwestern United States. According to Duran, "the American public library has a disappointingly poor history of service to the nation's largest non-English-speaking group, the Spanish-speaking people" (p. 22). He cites the singular case of the New York Public Library's response to serving Puerto Rican immigrants in the 1920s and comments that library literature does not consider native Mexican Americans of the Southwest until the 1960s.

EDUCATING LIBRARIANS

In addition to overlooking the Hispanic user group in the literature, the library profession historically neglected to provide appropriate academic programs to prepare librarians for serving the
Spanish-speaking. To compensate for the lack of formal programs, it
became necessary to hold continuing education workshops. One of
the first workshops in which a substantial number of school and
public librarians participated was a joint effort of three state libraries
and the Western Interstate Commission for Higher Education in 1970
(Vadala, 1970). About 70 school and public librarians attended the
three-day workshop held in Santa Fe, New Mexico. This meeting was
significant, for it brought together concerned librarians from Arizona,
Colorado, and New Mexico in order to address the fact that large
segments of their state populations were left largely unserved. The
state libraries were, in effect, publicly acknowledging the dire need for
improvement in the quality of services provided. The Hispanic population was no longer being ignored; its needs were being acted upon.
One of the keynote speakers was Dr. Horacio Ulibarri, an educator
from the University of New Mexico. He applauded the historical and
cultural heritage of Southwest Chicanos. Ulibarri spoke of the failure
of educational and library systems to incorporate Hispanic values in
their approach to children, thus depriving them of the opportunity to
reach their full potential. He called for the elimination of tokenism
by teachers and librarians alike. At the conclusion of the workshop,
three major ideas had been discussed as essential for improving
library services to Hispanics: the need for community involvement,
the selection of relevant materials free of stereotypes, and the implementation of bilingual programs and services. More than 15 years
after the workshop, these ideas are still valid.

Continuing education programs in library services to Hispanics
were a reflection of the increasing social consciousness of the 1960s
and 1970s. The programs were accompanied by a proliferation of
literature that prompted librarians to be more critical of library
collections and services for Hispanics. Previously, many public and
school library programs involved unexamined assumptions about the
Spanish-speaking. Librarians, like other members of society, may
have been influenced by stereotypes about Hispanics perpetuated in
books, the cinema, and the mass media, where Hispanics were often
characterized as illiterate, lazy, fatalistic, and emotionally unstable
products of a poverty-stricken peasant society. In cases where librarians assumed that Hispanic culture made library use unlikely, little
would have been done to attract potential users. Ironically, many
Hispanic leaders and scholars speak of having been fascinated by
libraries as children. One example is Rudolfo Anaya, author of the
classic novel *Bless Me, Ultima,* which is considered one of the finest

works of Chicano literature. In an interview several years ago, Anaya recalled that he preferred to spend Saturday mornings in the library rather than roaming the barrio streets of his childhood. He credited the librarian for nurturing his interest in books and the wonderful world of discovery (Bruce-Novoa, 1980).

In the case of school libraries, a federal mandate acted as a catalyst for action in improving library services to Hispanic children, although this was not always accompanied by appropriate education for the librarians involved. Martha Cotera (1978, p. 101), librarian and educator, observed:

> The advent of bilingual education legislation and program imple-mentation has changed the face of school library services....The nature of school library service has been altered in schools with bilingual education programs because large amounts of funds have been allocated to the purchase of materials and because many of these materials are in languages other than English. In the early seventies, the impact was not immediately felt, but as the program grew in size and sophistication, more and more of these materials have found their way into regular school library collections. As a result, school librarians have found themselves progressively more involved with bilingual education materials. Unfortunately, their involvement has not been rewarded with the specialized training and technical assistance available to bilingual education personnel.

Happily for school librarians, individual school systems are now facing the challenge of the 1980s by providing the necessary training. Also in response to this need, *Catholic Library World* (1981) has produced a thematic issue on bilingual library programs.

The recruitment policies of school and public libraries certainly affect the quality of services to Hispanic children; there is a critical lack of qualified librarians who are properly prepared to provide quality service to these children. The shortage can be attributed both to the small numbers of Hispanics who enter the library and informa-tion science profession, and to the paucity of appropriate courses in graduate library programs. Two programs in the 1970s were commit-ted to training qualified students to provide library services to Hispanics: the Mexican American Institute of Library Science at the California State University at Fullerton (1972–1974) and the Tucson-based Graduate Library Institute for Spanish-speaking Americans (GLISA) at the University of Arizona (1976–1979). Both programs were responsible for recruiting, training, and placing an impressive number of library professionals, many of whom now work with Hispanic children. In 1978, it was reported that the Chula Vista School District near San Diego, California, had the highest number of Hispanic librarians and the best bilingual library services for children. Most of the librarians of the system were graduates of the Fullerton program (Haro & Smith, 1978). The GLISA program, on the other hand, produced most of the librarians serving the Hispanic population in El Paso, Texas. The majority of the latter are now affiliated with the El Paso Public Library or El Paso Community College. Sadly, neither the Fullerton program nor GLISA are currently operating due to budget cuts.

Affirmative action policies have expanded employment opportunities for qualified candidates, not only in entry-level positions but also in management-level slots. Among the public library systems that make conscientious efforts to recruit Hispanic librarians in middle management are the San Diego, El Paso, and Long Beach Public Libraries. These library systems have accepted the necessity of having properly trained and sensitive individuals in administrative positions to make long-term policy decisions. This is not to say, however, that sufficient numbers of Hispanics have been placed in these critical positions in those cities. Hispanic librarians still lag behind in proportion to the percentage of the Spanish-speaking population in these communities.

PROFESSIONAL ORGANIZATIONS

Professional library organizations and committees have played a definite role in the evolution of library services to Hispanic children, either directly or indirectly. The largest and the most established of these professional groups is REFORMA, the National Association of Spanish-speaking Librarians. Founded as an ALA affiliate in 1971, REFORMA began primarily as a public library oriented group. Its activities and concerns were focused on the library needs of Mexican Americans in the Southwest and California. Since then, the organization has expanded geographically throughout the nation and includes Cuban Americans, Puerto Ricans, and other Hispanic groups. The organization works to promote and improve library services to Hispanics, and serves as a professional network for the dissemination of information. For example, the El Paso Chapter of REFORMA has been active in securing equitable representation of Hispanics on the El Paso Public Library Board. The result has been more effective policy development which keeps Hispanic interests in mind. Consequently, recent figures indicate an increase in library use by Hispanics, who constitute 62 percent of the city's population.

In another instance, the Los Angeles Chapter of REFORMA was instrumental in negotiating the donation of 1,500 Spanish-language books from Mexican President Luis Echeverría while he was in office. The books were designated for inclusion in the Lincoln Heights Branch, which, at the time, housed the most extensive collection of materials relevant to Mexican Americans (Taylor, 1978).

Other professional organizations that have been created to improve library services to Hispanics include the California-based

Asociación de Bibliotecarios Chicanos (ABC), and Bibliotecas Para La Gente, which started in the San Francisco Bay area in 1978. ALA has established the Chicano Task Force of the Social Responsibilities Roundtable, and the Committee on Services to the Spanish-speaking of the Reference and Adult Services Division (Caballero, 1984). Another group is the Ethnic Materials Information Exchange Roundtable, also an affiliate of ALA.

These organizations are effective catalysts for change. In addition to proposing remedial solutions to problems and promoting library services, members of these organizations serve as excellent role models for children and young adults, particularly potential librarians. These organizations have played an active role in identifying candidates for library and information science graduate programs. Prospective employers have targeted these groups for recruitment purposes as well.

EXEMPLARY LIBRARY PROGRAMS

Innovative changes and outreach programs have been successfully implemented by many public library systems. These include the Albuquerque Model Cities Library and Cultural Centers, El Centro Library in Chicago, the Miami-Dade Public Library, the South Bronx Project in New York City, the Los Angeles Public Library, and the Inglewood (CA) Public Library. Detailed descriptions of these programs, and others, are cited in the bibliography. I will elaborate on the program with which I am most familiar, the El Paso Public Library, highlighting general principles that could be followed elsewhere.

Selection and Ordering of Materials

Juvenile materials for Hispanic children are selected by the children's librarian at the El Paso Public Library. When the position is not held by a bilingual librarian, the responsibility is delegated to another professional staff member who has the appropriate background. The selector compiles a monthly list of titles to be acquired and includes a citation from a review source for each title. When a published review is not available (which is often the case), the review is done in-house by a staff committee of bilingual librarians. (The criteria for review are described below.) The list is then distributed to the branch heads who make their selections from the choices provided.

The acquisition and processing of materials is handled centrally by the Technical Services Section of the Main Library. Multiple copies of selected titles are ordered through a contract jobber when possible. When the items are received, unbound materials are sent to an external book bindery; recognizing that most Spanish-language juvenile materials are available only in softcover, the El Paso Public Library has allocated funds to be used for binding of materials. This has eliminated the need for selectors to be concerned with format. The cataloging of juvenile materials is done by a bilingual librarian who does original cataloging when necessary. Access to materials is through the card catalog, which utilizes Library of Congress subject headings supplemented by Spanish-language headings. As is the case with most public libraries, the Dewey Decimal system is used.

The library's Spanish-language review committee assumes the task of evaluating materials to determine their appropriateness for inclusion in the collection. The committee is chaired by the head of the Mexican American Services section and includes all bilingual librarians. Consequently, there is adequate representation of management, extension services, and librarians from both public and technical services.

The criteria for the evaluation of Spanish-language materials is as follows:

1. **Applicability to the Library's Mission and Goals Statement**—Materials selected are to comply with the Mission and Goals Statement set by the Library Board. Self-education and self-improvement materials are a priority for selection.

2. **Accuracy and Timeliness**—Materials are to be authoritative, preferably from publishers known for their quality. Dated materials are scrutinized carefully before being accepted for inclusion. This is especially true for materials in science and technology that were originally released several years ago, but translated into Spanish only recently.

3. **Language**—Materials should reflect the language standards set by local usage. Language level is checked for appropriateness for the grade level intended. In the case of translated works, the quality of the translation is noted. Too often, translations are literal or otherwise poor in quality. For original Spanish-language works, care is taken that the vocabulary and syntax are comprehensible to children who speak the border dialect of the El Paso-Juarez area.

4 **Characterization, Illustrations, and Story Development**—Only materials portraying positive images of Hispanics are accepted. Material must be presented in a nonsexist, nonracist manner. Illustrations, settings, and characters are to be presented in a way that a Hispanic child can relate to positively.

5. **Value System**—Materials should incorporate Hispanic values. For example, books on sex education, treatment of the elderly, and social etiquette are more closely evaluated than others. Any item that violates the value system is rejected.

Bibliographic Services

As mentioned previously, few juvenile materials for Hispanics are routinely reviewed in standard reviewing sources. The El Paso Public Library has responded by publishing *La Lista*, which is compiled 10 times a year. Each issue contains over 100 Spanish-language titles that have been selected for inclusion in the library's collection. Although the emphasis is on adult materials, *La Lista* frequently includes Spanish-language juvenile materials as well. A brief annotation, complete bibliographic information, and prices are provided for each entry.

Special Programs

Children's programs are designed in relation to the community's interests, with special attention given to Hispanic children since they constitute a major sector of the user group. Routine programs include bilingual story hours, puppet shows, film viewings, and arts and crafts workshops. Important regional holidays such as Cinco de Mayo and Dia de las Madres (Mother's Day, celebrated on May 10th in Mexico) are commemorated, as are the Fourth of July and other American holidays. The El Paso Public Library understands that the area's Mexican-American children are products of a dual culture; therefore, neither is emphasized at the expense of the other.

To increase visibility within the Hispanic community, the Library produces bilingual flyers and a monthly calendar of events. These are readily available at the Main Library and branches. Publicity for programs is done through local newspapers and other news media. To promote summer activities, the librarians who work with children pay visits to the schools in their respective service areas. All promotional materials are done bilingually to maximize participation and cooperation from the schools.

The El Paso Public Library's approach to reaching Hispanic children is consistent with the "Guidelines for Library Service to Spanish-speaking Americans" developed by Cuesta and Tarin (1978). Most other library programs described in library literature also follow the guidelines to some extent. While these efforts are certainly welcomed by the Hispanic community at large, quality library services are still not provided on a sufficiently large scale. Also, some of these efforts are finite in nature rather than continuing. Although the El Paso Public Library and other libraries have at least instituted library services to Hispanics, these isolated cases can barely begin to fill the needs of the nearly 15 million Hispanics estimated by the Census Bureau to reside currently in the United States (*Hispanic Almanac*, 1984, p. 22).

CONCLUSION

Urban planner Leobardo F. Estrada of UCLA (1984) reports that the Hispanic population is the most youthful in the nation and has the highest fertility rate of any American ethnic group. Supplemented by immigration from Spanish-speaking countries, this group will continue its dramatic increase in numbers and will continue to require more from the library and information science profession. The 1970s were marked by an upsurge in the provision of services to Hispanics due largely to the efforts of vocal educators, particularly those interested in bilingual education, and of the handful of library professionals active in the field at the time. The 1980s, however, have shown little more than nominal progress. Despite repeated calls for action in the library literature and by Hispanic interest groups, library services to Hispanic children are beginning to show a decline. Programs that had set a hopeful precedent have fallen victim to fiscal constraints and an apparent lack of concern on the part of decision makers. During a time when an increasing need for services is predicted by experts, the evolution of delivery of those services is threatened. Public and school library administrations have an obligation to society to assure that quality library services to Hispanic children do not fade to a memory from the 1970s and become extinct.

REFERENCES

The Albuquerque Model Cities Library and Cultural Centers. (1971, December). *New Mexico Business, 24.*

Beck, L. (1974, July-August). El cuarto de los libros: Kenosha's service to the Latin American community. *Wisconsin Library Bulletin, 70* (4), 161–162.

Bruce-Novoa, J. (1980). *Chicano authors: Inquiry by interview.* Austin, TX: University of Texas Press.

Bucy, F.A. (1970). Denver, Colorado: El numero cinco. *Wilson Library Bulletin, 44*(7), 765–766.

Caballero, C. (1984). Chicano librarianship: Collective intellectual processes and professional organizations. In F. Garcia-Ayvens & R.F. Chabran, (Eds.) *Biblio-politica: Chicano perspectives on library service in the United States* (pp. 197–206). Berkeley, CA: University of California Chicano Studies Library Publications Unit.

Catholic Library World. (1981, April). Special issue on bilingual library programs.

Cotera, M. (1978). The impact of bilingual education on school library services: Some problems and recommendations. In R. Urzua, M.P. Cotera, & E. Gonzalez Strupp, *Library services to Mexican Americans: Policies, practices and prospects* (pp. 100–118). Las Cruces, NM: ERIC CRESS.

Cuesta, Yolanda, & Patricia Tarin. (1978). Guidelines for library services to Spanish-speaking Americans. *Library Journal, 103*(13), 1350–1355.

Duran, D.F. (1979). Library service to Latinos. In D.F. Duran, (Ed.) *Latino materials: A multimedia guide for children and young adults* (pp. 19–22). Santa Barbara, CA: American Bibliographic Center in association with Neal-Schuman Publishers, Inc.

Estrada, L.F. (1984). The importance of demographic data for information providers: An illustration of the latino population. In F. Garcia-Ayvens and R.F. Chabran, (Eds.) *Biblio-politica: Chicano perspectives on library service in the United States* (pp. 9–22). Berkeley, CA: University of California Chicano Studies Library Publications Unit.

Godoy, A. (1978). Miami: Two decades of Latin accent. *Wilson Library Bulletin, 53*(3), 236–237.

Haro, R.P. (1981). Library services for children of Hispanic origin. In *Developing library and information services for Americans of Hispanic origin* (pp. 104–121). Metuchen, NJ: The Scarecrow Press.

Haro, R.P., & E.M. Smith. (1978). Si, Se Puede! Yes, It can be done. *Wilson Library Bulletin, 53* (3), 229.

Hispanic Almanac. (1984). Washington, DC: Hispanic Policy Development Project.

Lopez, W. (1970). New York: The South Bronx project. *Wilson Library Bulletin, 44*(7), 757–763.

Michael, M.E., & L. Encarnacion. (1973). *An evaluation of the El Centro de la Causa Library and Information Center: August 1973 through July 1974. Final Report.* Urbana, IL: University of Illinois Library Research Center. ED 107291.

Peterson, R. (1977). *Library service to the Spanish-speaking.* Inglewood, CA: Inglewood Public Library.

San Bernardino Public Library. (1979). San Bernardino Chicanos, a service priority. *Library Journal, 104,* 2610.

Taylor, J.G. (1978). The profession and services to the Spanish- speaking: Library reform sought by bilingual group (REFORMA). In R. Urzua, M. P. Cotera, & E. Gonzalez Stupp, (Eds.) *Library services to Mexican Americans: Policies, practices and prospects* (pp. 63–73). Las Cruces, NM: ERIC CRESS.

Vadala, J. (Ed.) (1970, April-May). *Hispano library services for Arizona, Colorado and New Mexico: A workshop held in Santa Fe, New Mexico.* Boulder, CO: Western Interstate Commission for Higher Education.

A Socio-Cultural Approach to the Study of Hispanic Children

Luis C. Moll
Stephen Diaz

It is the special emphasis of a socio-cultural approach to examine the links between individuals and social history. From this perspective, human beings are thoroughly social beings. That is the essence of being human. From the moment of birth we enter into specific social relationships with caretakers who shape and mold us, relationships that make us complex and dynamic *social* individuals. Our world emerges and develops through the activities these social relationships facilitate. And it is, in turn, through social relationships that we influence and change others.

All of our learning, then, is socio-cultural learning; it occurs by engaging in social activities with the help of other human beings, such as parents, teachers, and friends. Most of these activities are mediated through the use of cultural inventions, such as literacy (Scribner & Cole, 1981; Vygotsky, 1978; Wertsch, 1985). Without in any way denying our biological inheritance, which provides all human groups with remarkable uniformity (Gould, 1985), entering into specific and constantly changing socio-cultural activities provides us with the astounding diversity that characterizes human beings.

From this perspective, the study of Hispanics must be contextualized in the specific socio-cultural conditions and practices of each group. It is obviously beyond the scope of this chapter to examine the implications of this approach for all of the groups that make up the Hispanic population. Our examples are taken from studies of a Puerto Rican community in New York and from a Mexican-American community in California. In no way are our examples intended to be representative of the entire Hispanic population in this country. On the contrary, as we point out throughout this chapter, regardless of presumed or actual similarities among

Hispanics, studies with children from the different Hispanic groups must be contextualized in the specific socio-historical circumstances of each group.

In this chapter we will examine the implications of this view for the study of Hispanic children in the United States. We will start by examining what has been called a cognitive styles approach to the study of cultural patterns and psychological characteristics. We will go into detail here not only because investigators within this framework have made important contributions to the study of Hispanic children, but because this perspective, with its emphasis on using tests to label children as possessing certain pervasive "styles" of learning and thinking, represents a major line of research with Hispanic groups. We will then point out what we believe is the main weakness of this framework, namely its inability to deal with the diversity of socio-cultural practices that characterize Hispanics. As illustrations of an alternative approach that deals directly with social life, we provide examples of recent ethnographic studies that address two of the most important issues facing the Hispanic population, its bilingualism and its education.

THE IDEA OF GENERAL THINKING STYLES

One of the better known psychological models for explaining the behavior of Hispanic students is the so-called "cognitive styles" approach. This model, based largely on the extensive research of Witkin and his colleagues (Witkin & Berry, 1975; Witkin, Dyk, Faterson, Goodenough, & Karp, 1962), posits that there are individual differences in the way in which people go about solving perceptual and cognitive tasks. These differences, labelled "cognitive styles," are described as characteristic modes of functioning that exert their influence on all of the individual's perceptual and intellectual activities in a consistent and pervasive manner. This claim of uniformity, that the styles manifest themselves in all areas of a person's psychological functioning, is central to this line of research. In general, this approach includes the following assumptions: (a) the kinds of cultural activities that can be engaged in are constrained by physical ecology; b) cultures elaborate different kinds of social organization to deal with the basic life predicaments that their members have encountered; c) cultures transmit their acquired patterns of adaptation to their children in ways that are shaped by the ecology and necessary maintenance activities of adults; d) all of these influences, separately and in concert, affect the development of cognitive skills, as well as other psychological characteristics (see Laboratory of Comparative Human Cognition [LCHC], 1983, for a detailed discussion of these issues).

Witkin and his colleagues (Witkin et al., 1962) began their studies on cognitive styles by attempting to discover why it was that some pilots lost their sense of uprightness when flying through clouds and emerged upside down or disoriented while other pilots did not. The researchers noted that these behaviors remained consistent among the pilots and developed several tests to study the phenomenon. All of these tests shared an underlying common denominator in that each essentially measured the extent to which a person is able to deal with a part of the field separately from the field as a whole.

On the basis of experiments with various tests, Witkin et al. (1962) concluded that differences existed in the ways individuals approached perceptual and cognitive tasks. Two cognitive styles were identified by Witkin. A "field dependent" cognitive style is one in which perception is strongly dominated by the overall organization of the field and parts of the field are experienced as "fused." A "field independent" mode of perceiving is one in which parts of the field are experienced as discrete from the organized background. These modes of operating remain remarkably stable across time and manifest themselves in behavior by a variety of other indicators. These indicators pervade the entire organization of an individual, from perception and intellectual activities to personality, psychopathology, and sex differences.

CULTURAL DIFFERENCES AND COGNITIVE STYLES

The most comprehensive research on the origin of cognitive styles is concentrated on studies showing child rearing and cultural practices to play a very important role in the development of field dependence-independence. Research on cognitive styles across different cultural groups has compared groups that differ in regard to social arrangement and standards relevant to the development of self/nonself segregation, that is, directly related to field dependent-independent cognitive styles (Witkin & Berry, 1975). This work has supported expectations that members of cultures and subcultures that are "tight" in their social organization and stress social conformity would be more field dependent than members of cultures and subcultures that have a loose organization and place less stress on conformity.

Ramirez and Castañeda (1974), for example, in an extensive study of Mexican-American values, and the beliefs of three communities, found that socialization practices associated with traditional Mexican values were more highly correlated with field dependence (also see, Buriel, 1975; Kagan, 1981; Ramirez & Price-Williams, 1974a, 1974b). These types of practices are similar to those belonging to social organizations defined by Witkin et al. (1962) as "tight."

Traditional Mexican-American communities foster strong identification with the family and establish close personal ties to community members. They are taught to respect convention, exercise self-control, and demonstrate respect for others. Additional support for the influence of socialization practices on cognitive style was provided by the finding that field dependence decreased as Mexican Americans moved away from traditional values and took on the values of the dominant culture. That is, as Mexican Americans became more acculturated, there was a concomitant shift in the way in which individuals approached learning and communicated with others, and in their manifestation of cognitive style. It is noteworthy, however, that despite increased acculturation, Mexican-American field independence never reaches the levels of their Anglo-American peers.

SEARCHING FOR COGNITIVE STYLES IN SOCIO-CULTURAL PRACTICES

A study by Jackson and Espino (1979) sought to trace the sociocultural antecedents of cognitive style (in addition to other factors) in Mexican-American children. In an impressively rigorous study, the researchers collected ethnographic observations of children's behavior in home/community settings and in the classroom in an attempt to trace the manner in which familial and community values were related to cognitive style. They expected that certain cultural experiences would discriminate between children of differing cognitive styles. Their findings did not support this expectation.

The difficulty in matching cognitive style with actual behavior can be seen in some examples from this study. Results often ran counter to what was hypothesized on the basis of previous research with other cultural groups. Below we provide a description of some of Jackson and Espino's findings.

After having conducted extensive ethnographic observations of a young girl, Nancy, the authors proceeded to make predictions about whether the girl would be field independent or dependent. Their rationale was based on the socio-cultural practices that they had observed. Their observations and predictions—coded as FI for field independent and FD for field dependent—were as follows:

Nancy's parents, particularly her mother, stress independence, autonomy, and responsibility for taking care of herself, her possessions, and her share of the household duties (washing dishes, vacuuming, cleaning the kitchen, keeping her room orderly); these traits are linked to field independence. (FI)

Nancy is pretty much a "loner," even among her friends. She says she would rather have a lot of friends than a few close friends, because then "if we fight, I'll still have some left." (FI)

Nancy is generally "external" in her motivation, rather than "internal" as would be expected of a psychologically differentiated individual. This tendency is related to field dependence. (FD)

Nancy scored as a field dependent, but the majority of the observations would lead one to predict field independence. According to Jackson and Espino (1979), "the accuracy of the predicted scores for Nancy is decidedly mixed, calling for a questioning of the hypothesized links between culture and test performance in some cases" (p. 48).

Although the researchers were able to make some predictions accurately, they nevertheless concluded that "the predicted scores for FD/I vary considerably from the test results."

Social and community antecedents are undoubtedly major antecedents of ways of thinking and behaving. But simply knowing this is insufficient. Socio-cultural variables proved very weak predictors of *tested* cognitive style. In the Jackson and Espino study (1979), only 3 out of 23 cultural and behavioral variables showed even a weak predictive power, and even then the most striking aspect was the lack of any definite pattern between the variables and cognitive style. As Jackson and Espino note:

> ...there is apparently little support for most of the child rearing or socialization practices which have been cited in previous research to explain differences in [cognitive style] between groups of children. [As others have indicated]...differences between *groups* (their emphasis) may be significant, but correlations between parents' socialization patterns and childrens' scores [on cognitive styles measures] is not generally significant (pp. 146–147).

Jackson and Espino concluded that it is poor policy to assume that Mexican-American children are homogeneous in terms of language background, home experiences, interaction styles, or cognitive styles. They commented, "the degree of intra-cultural diversity documented in this study indicates that Mexican American students, as with students of any cultural group, must be seen as individuals" (1979, p. 152).

We can draw several implications concerning the utility of psychological models that posit "general, characteristic modes of functioning" as explanations for the performance or behavior of Hispanic children. First, the psychological construct that explains behavior may be too broad to encompass the complexity of individuals as they interact with socio-cultural environments. Characteristics that may manifest themselves when performance is assessed for groups of people cannot be generalized to individual performance, nor can they be directly linked to specific factors in the socio-cultural environment of that individual. Second, diversity is the hallmark of all groups, irrespective of how homogeneous they may appear (or how homogeneously they are treated) in the research literature. Psychological models that use general constructs to explain performance mask this diversity and may promote stereotypes of cultural groups that are counterproductive in efforts aimed at, for example, fostering academic learning.

Culture clearly has a strong impact on the manner in which individuals interact with the world; there *are* cultural differences. But cultural differences are made manifest by interactions in social contexts. The individual is not a carrier of culture as if culture were a flu virus; it is rather the individual, with a certain history of socialization and education, in dynamic interaction with other people, that creates a sense of "culture." It is this sense of mutual creativity, captured in the study described below, that is missing from such psychological models, and that is the critical flaw that restricts their utility in trying to understand and work with people from different cultures or subcultures.

LANGUAGE AS SOCIO-CULTURAL PRACTICE

Perhaps no other issue is associated more closely with Hispanics than language. Yet the language characteristics of the different Hispanic groups in the United States are difficult to describe because of the scarcity of data sources that would facilitate comparative analysis (Macias, 1982). Nevertheless, it seems safe to conclude that there is an intergenerational shift to English, as claimed by Lopez (1978). This pattern is similar to that found with other non-English languages in the United States, in that the first generation acquires some English, their offspring become bilingual, and the third generation becomes English monolingual. What is dissimilar about Hispanics, and controversial, is that the acquisition of English may not be accompanied by a concomitant loss of Spanish (see Arce, 1982; Flores, Attinasi, & Pedraza, 1981).

Regardless of individual language abilities, Hispanics are overwhelmingly members of bilingual communities. It is in dynamic, changing community contexts that social and individual factors converge to shape individual language characteristics. As Macias (1982) has indicated, the great majority of individuals in Hispanic communities "come into contact with both Spanish and English over their lifetimes, whether through contact with monolingual and bilingual members of the communities or monolingual persons outside of the communities" and this "community bilinguality is a salient characteristic that distinguishes Latinos as a group from the majority of the dominant monolingual population" (p. 117).

It is this "community bilinguality" that has been studied by Pedro Pedraza and his colleagues from the Language Policy Task Force (LPTF) of the Centro de Estudios Puertorriqueños at Hunter College. For the past decade they have been studying the bilingual language behavior of members of a Puerto Rican working-class community in East Harlem, New York, known locally as El Barrio. Their ethnographic research represents the most complete and sophisticated analysis of the relationship between social life and language practices available in the literature (see, for example, LPTF, 1980, 1982, 1984; also see Duran, 1981; Heath, 1986; Sanchez, 1983). Here we will concentrate on depicting how variations in the social organization of children's social environments within the community lead to different linguistic characteristics for individual children (for details, see LPTF, 1982). The LPTF data make clear that language use or development cannot be explained solely in terms of individual psychology, differences or preferences; any individual's behavior must be understood in the context of the concrete and dynamic social conditions of life, and in the context of the individual's responses to those conditions.

The study was conducted in a city block in El Barrio. The 16 children selected for study (from 13 families) "embody in their activities, family situations, and interests the broad range of experiences available to children raised in an urban ethnic neighborhood" (LPTF, 1982, p. 92). The families were working-class poor, and only one parent had finished high school. All of the parents claimed Spanish as their first language. Although several caretakers learned English in early childhood or early adolescence, half of them spoke little or no English. A combination of factors made the home an important influence on the language choice of the children. Attitudinally, the parents wanted the children to become bilingual. The need to learn English, the language of the broader society, was obvious to them. Equally desirable, however, was the need to maintain and develop Spanish; the parents cited the "possibility of moving back to Puerto Rico, the world importance of Spanish, the identification of Puerto Ricans with Spanish, and the intrinsic value of knowing more than one [language]" (LPTF, 1982, p. 96) as reasons for retaining Spanish. And they saw the school, as well as the home, as a legitimate place to develop either language.

In general, however, the results show that the home plays an important role in Spanish maintenance. One reason is that children, out of respect (*respeto*), are generally required to accommodate their speech to the language used by elders, particularly in the family environment. Children, especially infants, are usually addressed in Spanish and asked to address parents, grandparents, or other elders in Spanish. The home is, therefore, a relatively stable Spanish-speaking environment.

In contrast, the street or the block is an environment for English. The greater the exposure to the block, the greater the preference for English. Therefore it turns out that the parents' most powerful role, especially as the children get older and want to play outside with peers, is in controlling access to the block; that is, access to sociolinguistic environments outside the home. The extent to which parents give children the freedom to come and go outside the home determines the extent to which sociolinguistic factors other than the home influence the children's speech. In short, access to linguistic environments outside the home is a key determinant of the children's linguistic repertoire.

It must be pointed out that it is not simply a case of Spanish at home, English in the streets. Very few settings in the community require the exclusive use of Spanish or English. The community is characterized by widespread, stable bilingualism with very little separation of languages by social domain. It is the case, however, that community norms require the children, under specific circumstances, to separate language by social domain. As Pedraza has written,

> ...children know that when approached by older Spanish monolingual speakers, when running errands at either of the *bodegas* (as opposed to the supermarket, the Korean fruit store, or the Greek shoe repair shop), or when relaying the winning numbers along the block, Spanish is the appropriate and expected language. On the other hand, when participating in activities organized by the Protestant church (which is run by Anglos), or when playing certain games such as baseball or stickball that use English terminology, English is required (LPTF, 1982, p. 99).

Although access to the streets is associated with English speech, it is by no means a uniform phenomenon. It is variable and context-specific; it is common to hear conversations by children carried out solely in English, in Spanish, or in both, depending on the composition of the group and the needs and goals of the moment. Access to domains outside the home also does not necessarily represent a diminishing role for Spanish, because plenty of social networks in the community require the use of Spanish for communication. Thus, individual (linguistic/psychological) characteristics must be understood as emerging and changing through the socio-cultural practices available to the individual. And this relationship between social activity and individual development is dynamic: similar social activities may lead to diverse individual outcomes; similar outcomes may result from diverse activities.

As the LPTF researchers (1982) point out, although "we cannot determine a priori the 'dominance' or language preference of a given child in a given setting any more than we can predict the site of a given codeswitch, we can assess the relative strength of the different influences upon his [or her] behavior at a given stage and with given

interactions, and make a general prediction of the likely outcomes"
(p. 166).

EDUCATION AS SOCIO-CULTURAL PRACTICE

A similar perspective applies to the study of Hispanic children's
schooling. Instead of perceiving problems of education in terms of
general, internal properties of children or teachers, a socio-cultural
approach investigates the concrete conditions under which children
are asked to learn and perform and how these conditions are created
by extra-curricular (societal) or instructional (interactional) factors
(e.g., Diaz, Moll, & Mehan, 1986; Heath, 1983; for a provocative
social analysis of Hispanics' problems in education, see Ogbu &
Matute-Bianchi, 1986). From a socio-cultural perspective, learning is
as much a social as a cognitive activity (Cole & Griffin, 1983).

In the example presented here, we will limit our discussion to
how changing the social context of learning leads to very different
evaluations of children's individual capabilities. The example is taken
from a study in which we explored ways of using community data to
inform classroom practice (for details, see Moll & Diaz, in press;
Trueba, Moll, Diaz, & Diaz, 1982). We conducted the study in a
predominantly Mexican-American, working-class community in San
Diego, California. To facilitate the study, we situated our research
operations in a local residence in the heart of the community; from
this "home base" we hired students, residents, and teachers to help us
conduct observations on the uses of literacy in homes and other
community locations. While the community study was taking place,
we worked with 12 teachers from local schools to start exploring ways
of improving writing instruction, especially for Hispanic, limited-
English proficient (LEP) children. These children have one of the
highest dropout rates in the country (Steinberg, Blinde, & Chan,
1984).

Like the other community-based studies reviewed above, our
field observations revealed the diversity that characterizes Hispanic
community life. Several factors, especially immigration, constantly
mold the social configuration of the community. This diversity was
most evident in the different arrangements that families adopted in
their attempts to adjust to social and economic realities. For example,
these arrangements ranged from the so-called "traditional" families,
with clearly demarcated roles and responsibilities for family members,
to families where the father is missing and the offspring must assume
adult roles. Often, depending on the families' English-language fluency, the children took responsibility for transactions with important
social institutions (e.g., paying bills or answering school-related in-
quiries). In short, the social, economic, and linguistic demands of life

in the community were met with familial flexibility, adjusting roles and responsibilities as necessary for survival.

Our home observations showed that most literacy events in the homes were organized around school matters; homework created opportunitis for literacy to occur. Parents repeatedly expressed their belief in the value of education and viewed writing as an essential element of "being educated." There was also broad concern about community issues, such as immigration, unemployment, and the need to learn English. As we proceeded with the project, we began to view the teaching of writing in the context of the community and organized writing lessons to address important social issues.

The schools' curricula were in English, with few attempts to capitalize on the students' Spanish oral language and literacy skills as a way of developing their English language skills. Formal writing instruction was an infrequent classroom activity. This was particularly true with limited English-speaking children, because it was generally assumed that their low level of oral English skills precluded their writing. Most classroom writing was limited to tests or homework assignments; writing was not used to communicate opinions or ideas, or to analyze and explore social issues.

As part of the project, we used the above findings to suggest changes in the social organization of writing lessons. In one such change we asked the teachers to use social and community issues as topics for writing. We felt that making social life the content of writing would provide the students with a very different *motive* for writing than simply responding to worksheets. At the same time we asked the teachers to emphasize writing for communication as the goal of their lessons. That is, whether or not students were fluent in English, we had teachers engage them in the same basic educational activity: writing for communication. Given their English-language difficulties, we expected that LEP students would contribute differently to the completion of the activity than did regular students, and that the teachers might have to provide them more assistance, but we wanted both groups of students to participate in *comparable, demanding intellectual activities*. Regardless of language differences, elaboration of thinking through communication became the higher order goal of classroom writing; the mechanics of writing were taught in the service of this goal (Graves, 1983).

Another change in instructional practice was having teachers keep a detailed journal on how they went about reorganizing instruction and the consequences of their changes. This was an attempt not only to get teachers writing, but to make them conscious and, we hoped, critical observers of how they routinely created environments for thinking. Finally, taking advantage of our observations about the important role of homework in creating writing at home, we used homework assignments as a vehicle to involve the parents with the students' classroom writing. That is, we had the students interview their parents and others about a particular community issue and then had the students include this information to transform their original drafts (see Moll & Diaz, in press).

The teachers implemented these changes in various ways. One of the most successful teachers, for instance, converted her English oral language lessons into a "pre-writing" discussion of opinions about bilingualism. On the basis of the class discussion, she had the students write a first draft, encouraging them to write freely, without concern for punctuation or spelling. She then helped them create a brief questionnaire to survey opinions about bilingualism among people in the school, home, or elsewhere. Once the students collected this information, she helped them tabulate some of the results and taught them how to include some of their findings to expand and revise their first drafts.

This teacher wrote in her journal about the interest generated by the students interviewing adult respondents:

> The students were buzzing when they came in and they buzzed all along! Some had never had occasion to speak to adults other than their teachers here and a few...were itching to show me [the adults'] responses....I instructed that all future entries must be in students' own handwriting and that they were to ask the questions orally, explicating if necessary since a few answers were not directed appropriately. The students didn't even moan at that; they thought that was logical for practicing oral English.

At each step of the way the teacher made sure that the students stayed in contact with the goal of the lesson. That is, the tasks necessary to complete the assignment were done to accomplish a specified and mutually understood goal; at no time were the students relegated to doing writing exercises unrelated to the purpose of the writing activity. Soon thereafter, the students showed signs of taking over the activity without the need for highly structured supervision. Noticing this change, the teacher decided to be less directive and have the students assume most of the responsibility for completing the necessary tasks. This shift in the control of the task was very important; it indicated to the teacher and to the students that they were indeed capable of writing in English, regardless of oral language limitations. Of general importance, it made clear to all concerned that a "watered down" curriculum was unnecessary and unwarranted.

Below is an *unedited* example of a student's writing in his second language.

> I found that people in our community feel good about bilingualism for several good reasons. They think it very important because they can communicate with other people. The people I asked are 60% students, 40% adults, 70% are Spanish speakers, 20% were English speakers, 70% can write and read English, 20% can write and read Spanish well. Most of the people told me that in there house can

speak English and Spanish. The people I ask the questions, answers me very polite and they said the questions were very interesting. Some person said that these project was very good for me and interesting for him. When he said that I feel very good about the work I was doing. The most interesting thing that I found wat that the people like the project. Most of the people said that they were willing to take classes to become totally belingual because it could help them right now and in the future. The students I ask said that they have only friends that speak only Spanish and English not othey language. The adults I ask said that been belingual is very important for them because they can communicate with more people and they can have more opportunitis for some jobs that othey people do I feel very good about the way people answer me.

The teacher was successful in organizing lessons that minimized the constraining influence of the students' lack of oral language fluency, while maximizing the use of the student's knowledge of the topic and other experiences. This goal was accomplished by using information collected from the students' community to help them become active writers in their second language. Regardless of obvious mistakes in the students' writing, producing this amount of coherent text gave the teacher opportunities to teach writing that previously did not exist.

Our example illustrates that teaching and learning must be studied as a distinct socio-cultural practice. Doing so shows just how thoroughly what we call lessons are social constructions; they are developed, implemented, manipulated, and changed through the social actions of teachers (and other adults) and students. Our work suggests also how easy it is within current practices to seriously underestimate the capabilities of Hispanic children. A teacher's representation of an educational activity such as writing—what it is used for, its goals, what it can accomplish—can make a critical difference not only in whether children learn, but in how and what they learn. It is here that students' backgrounds and lifestyles become important pedagogical assets. Connecting lessons to life allows the teacher as well as the students to discover valuable resources in their social environment to enhance instruction.

CONCLUSION

The approach presented in this paper emphasizes the importance of social context as a major determinant of human behavior. Our examples portrayed specific social contexts as dynamic, changing environments and human beings as active agents within them. Instead of relying on indicators that "measure" a general, pervasive characteristic or attribute of children independent of social context, as does much of the current work, our approach shows that Hispanic children cannot be defined in static, homogeneous terms; their diversity defies any such stereotyping. Hispanic children's characteristics must be studied not as fixed traits, but as characteristics of "children-in-interaction" with specific (and changing) socio-cultural circumstances.

Examining such socio-cultural circumstances reveals the multiple factors that influence Hispanic children's behavior. As noted by the LPTF researchers (1982), "It was due to our being physically on the spot and seeking the interconnections among the often seemingly unrelated behaviors we observed on a daily basis that we were able to see how such factors as the youthfulness of the community, its high population density, contact with blacks and other Hispanics, diversity of migration experience, and economic history could help explain both the linguistic variability and continuity of the community" (p. 443). Hispanics are neither "resistant" to acquiring English (they are doing so at a rapid pace), nor "romantically attached" to Spanish, as is sometimes claimed in the popular press. Whether Hispanics acquire, retain, lose, or regain a language depends on what social environments they have available for language development at any given time (Sanchez, 1983).

Our research in education points to a similar conclusion. Our attempts at incorporating features of the students' language, culture, and community into learning activities show that there is nothing about Hispanic children's language or culture that impedes academic achievement. We locate the children's problems and the solutions in the social organization of schooling. Our results suggest the need to create flexible and varying instructional circumstances that take full advantage of the children's ample resources (Diaz, Moll, & Mehan, 1986). It is possible to connect strategically what occurs in the classroom with what occurs outside the classroom to reorganize teaching and learning situations. To do so we need to view Hispanic students in their full diversity, possessing the social, linguistic, and cognitive capabilities to succeed. And we need to view classrooms for what they are: institutions that socially constrain progress or socially create success.

REFERENCES

Anyon, J. (1980). Social class and the hidden curriculum of work. *Journal of Education, 162*, 67–92.

Arce, C. (1982). Language shift among Chicanos: Strategies for measuring and assessing direction and rate. *Social Science Journal, 19*(2), 121–132.

Buriel, R. (1975). Cognitive style among three generations of Mexican-American children. *Journal of Cross-Cultural Psychology, 6*, 417–429.

Cole, M., & P. Griffin. (1983). A socio-historical approach to remediation. *Quarterly Newsletter of the Laboratory of Comparative Human Cognition,* 5(4), 69–74.

Diaz, S., L. C. Moll, & H. Mehan. (1986). Socio-cultural resources in instruction: A context-specific approach. In *Beyond language: Social and cultural factors in schooling language minority students* (pp. 187–230). Los Angeles, CA: California State University at Los Angeles, Evaluation, Dissemination, and Assessment Center.

Duran, R. (Ed.) (1981). *Latino language and communicative behavior.* Norwood, NJ: Ablex.

Flores, J., J. Attinasi, & P. Pedraza. (1981, Spring). La carreta made a U-turn: Puerto Rican language and culture in the United States. *Daedalus,* 193–217.

Gould, S. (1985). Human equality is a contingent fact of history. In S. Gould, *The Flamingo's Smile* (pp. 185–198). New York: Norton.

Graves, D. (1983). *Writing: Teachers and students at work.* Exeter, NH: Heinemann.

Heath, S. (1983). *Ways with words: Ethnography of communication in communities and classrooms.* New York: Cambridge University Press.

Heath, S. (1986). Sociocultural contexts of language development. In *Beyond language: Social and cultural factors in schooling language minority students* (pp. 143–186). Los Angeles, CA: California State University at Los Angeles, Evaluation, Dissemination, and Assessment Center.

Holtzman, W., R. Diaz-Guerrero, & J. Swartz. (1975). *Personality development in two cultures.* Austin, TX: University of Texas Press.

Jackson, S., & L. Espino. (1979). *Cultural antecedents of language proficiency, intellectual development, and achievement in Mexican-American children. Final Report.* Austin, TX: Southwest Education Development Laboratory.

Kagan, S. (1981). Ecology and the acculturation of cognitive and social styles among Mexican-American children. *Hispanic Journal of Behavioral Sciences,* 23(2), 111–144.

Laboratory of Comparative Human Cognition. (1983). Culture and cognitive development. In W. Kessen, (Ed.) *Mussen handbook of child psychology,* (Vol. 1), 295–356. New York: Wiley.

Laboratory of Comparative Human Cognition. (in press). The contributions of cross-cultural research to educational practice. *American Psychologist.*

Language Policy Task Force. (1980). *Social dimensions of language in East Harlem.* (Working paper No. 7). New York: Hunter College, Centro de Estudios Puertorriqueños.

Language Policy Task Force. (1982). *Intergenerational perspectives on bilingualism: From community to classroom.* New York: Hunter College, Centro de Estudios Puertorriqueños.

Language Policy Task Force. (1984). *Speech and ways of speaking in a bilingual Puerto Rican community.* (Report No. NIE-G-81-054). Washington, DC: National Institute of Education.

Lopez, D. (1978). Chicano language loyalty in an urban setting. *Sociology and Social Research,* 62, 267–278.

Macias, R. (1982). Language diversity among United States Hispanics. In J. Spielberg, (Ed.) *Proceedings—Invitational symposium on Hispanic-American diversity* (pp. 110-136). Lansing, MI: Department of Education, Special Education Services.

Moll, L. C., & R. Diaz. (in press). Teaching writing as communication: The use of ethnographic findings in classroom practice. In D. Bloome, (Ed.) *Language, literacy and schooling.* Norwood, NJ: Ablex.

Ogbu, J., & M. E. Matute-Bianchi. (1986). Understanding sociocultural factors: Knowledge, identity, and school adjustment. In *Beyond language: Social and cultural factors in schooling language minority students* (pp. 73-142). Los Angeles, CA: California State University at Los Angeles, Evaluation, Dissemination, and Assessment Center.

Ramirez, M., & A. Castañeda. (1974). *Cultural democracy, bicognitive development, and education.* New York: Academic Press.

Ramirez, M., & D. Price-Williams. (1974a). Cognitive styles in children: Two Mexican-American communities. *Intramerican Journal of Psychology, 8,* 93-100.

Ramirez, M., & D. Price-Williams. (1974b). Cognitive styles in children: Two Mexican American communities. *Journal of Cross-Cultural Psychology, 5,* 212-219.

Sanchez, R. (1983). *Chicano discourse: Socio-historic perspectives.* Rowley, MA: Newbury.

Scribner, S., & M. Cole. (1981). *The psychology of literacy.* Cambridge, MA: Harvard University Press.

Steinberg, L., P. L. Blinde, & K. S. Chan. (1984). Dropping out among language minority youth. *Review of Educational Research, 54*(1), 113-132.

Trueba, H., L.C. Moll, S. Diaz, & R. Diaz. (1982). *Improving the functional writing of bilingual secondary school students.* (Cont. No. 400-81-0023). Washington, DC: National Institute of Education.

Vygotsky, L.S. (1978). *Mind in society.* Cambridge, MA: Harvard University Press.

Wertsch, J.W. (1985). *Vygotsky and the social formation of mind.* Cambridge, MA: Harvard University Press.

Witkin, H., & J. Berry. (1975). Psychological differentiation in cross-cultural perspective. *Journal of Cross-cultural Psychology, 26*(1).

Witkin, H., R.B. Dyk, H.F. Faterson, D.R. Goodenough, & S. Karp. (1962). *Psychological differentiation.* New York: Wiley.

Part II

Professional Issues Related to Library Services for the Hispanic Child

Language, Reading, and Hispanic Children

Judy Nichols Mitchell

According to Torres (1986), "'Hispanic' is an umbrella term that refers to Spanish-speaking populations that come from 21 different countries" (p. 429). It should not be surprising, then, that the backgrounds of Hispanic children may actually be quite diverse linguistically as well as culturally. Some children are bilingual, proficient to varying degrees in both Spanish and English. Other groups of children speak only Spanish or only English. Still other children use language that is a mixture of both Spanish and English; they are not as proficient in either language as are monolingual speakers (del Prado, 1975). All of these children have distinctly different linguistic experiences and needs, yet they tend to be considered as one group with the same needs.

Because reading is essentially a language process like speaking and listening, the influence of children's oral language development on reading is considerable. In fact, the relationship of oral language and reading achievement at all grade levels is well documented in the literature (Loban, 1963). Children with good oral language backgrounds have many strengths which help them become good readers. Among these strengths are:

1. **Vocabulary Knowledge.** Children who know the meanings of many words readily understand these concepts when they meet them in reading materials. For such children, the job of reading is simply to learn the correspondences between the printed word forms they do not know and the concepts they already have from their oral language.

   Children who do not have rich oral language vocabularies in a particular language have more work to do when they read in that language; they must decode the words and, at the same time, try to make sense of what the words mean. Often such children can learn to sound out the words, but their lack of vocabulary knowledge leads to reading comprehension problems.

2. **Knowledge of Syntax.** Children with good oral proficiency in a language also have mastered most of the syntactic patterns of that language. They know the various forms of sentences, as well as the various slots within a sentence that can be occupied by nouns, verbs, adjectives, and other parts of speech. This understanding of the syntax of oral language helps children in reading, because the written language they read utilizes many of these same syntactic patterns as the language they speak. Children can use their syntactic knowledge to make and verify predictions as they read, accommodating the semantic information into familiar structural patterns.

On the other hand, children who have only limited oral language proficiency in a particular language lack the cues that these syntactic patterns provide during reading. The syntax used in reading is more formal than that of oral language; children who are not highly fluent in the language in question must bridge an even greater gap in apprehending such language patterns. Further, the situational and nonverbal cues of oral language are not available to readers to help compensate for their lack of syntactic knowledge (DiStefano, Dole, & Marzano, 1984).

3. **Listening Skills.** Children with good oral language backgrounds are proficient listeners as well as speakers. They have acquired oral language fluency by observing language as used by others around them. Additionally, they have participated in meaningful linguistic exchanges through conversation, discussion, question asking and answering, and story reading. If children have oral language fluency, it means that they have been good listeners all their lives. These listening skills are helpful in development of reading abilities, because reading is similar to listening in many ways: both processes involve the recognition and comprehension of information. Further, listeners and readers use some of the same cognitive and linguistic strategies to comprehend oral and written language respectively.

However, a child who has good listening skills, but is not fluent in the language of the school or library, may still run into problems, since listening comprehension skills are necessary for purposes of attending and following directions. Children who lack fluency in the language of the school or library may miss out in reading instructional situations or library experiences because they cannot pick out the important information for learning.

4. Ability to Discriminate Speech Sounds in the Language.
Children with good oral language proficiency have learned
all the sounds of their language. They can readily identify
similar sounds and discriminate between dissimilar sounds.
This knowledge can be important in reading, because many
teaching methods rely on children's ability to use
letter/sound correspondence as a strategy to identify words.
Children whose oral language proficiency is in a language
other than the language of instruction, or in two languages,
may have difficulty identifying, discriminating, generalizing,
and talking about speech sounds since their phonological
system is different or more complex than that of the
school's curriculum.

Besides factors associated with oral language proficiency, the
reading ability of Hispanic children is also affected by how and when
reading was introduced, and in what language. The legal requirements
of bilingual education state that reading instruction must be conducted in the child's home or dominant language. Children therefore
receive reading instruction in the language in which they are most
proficient until they can conceptually function in the second language. Many bilingual children learn to read in Spanish, and then
transfer their reading skills to English when they have internalized the
reading process and built up their oral language proficiency in English.

Other children who speak Spanish may have learned to read in
English, with or without concurrently developing their oral English
skills. It is difficult for some of these children to be successful in
reading English because their English-language base has not been fully
developed.

Bilingual children have strengths in both languages, and can
usually become biliterate, or able to read materials in either language.
Children who, on the other hand, speak a mixture of Spanish and
English may have difficulty becoming literate in either language, since
neither written language matches their own oral language very closely.

Language preferences may also affect Hispanic children's developing reading abilities. Many parents of Hispanic children have
strong preferences concerning the language their children learn to
read. Some parents, while interested in English for their children,
want strongly for them to learn to read in Spanish, in order to
maintain their oral language fluency as well as to foster other ties to
their ethnic heritage. Other parents are especially concerned that their
children learn to read in English for economic and social reasons,
regardless of the children's linguistic background or proficiency in
English.

Thus Hispanic children may, particularly at early stages, read in
Spanish only, in English only, in both languages at about the same

level of proficiency, or in both languages at widely differing proficiency levels. Children's reading proficiencies also have been influenced by the development of educational programs designed to meet a variety of mandates, including state laws, local customs, school board directives, and/or enrollment constraints.

As a group, Hispanic children may have some special reading problems. If they have been exposed to two languages, these children may have limited oral language fluency in any one language since their knowledge is divided between two languages. That is, children may know some expressions and vocabulary only in Spanish but not in English, and vice versa. Thus their vocabulary range and linguistic fluency may be somewhat restricted in both languages. These knowledge gaps can be quite considerable in the case of children who speak a mixture of Spanish and English.

Another problem for some Hispanic children is the confusion of the sound system of English and Spanish. Since they have knowledge of two phonological systems and may not be able to abstract out the differences between them, such children may have difficulty in matching like sounds, in distinguishing unlike sounds, and in making generalizations about letter/sound relationships.

Finally, some Hispanic children, like all children, have self-concept problems related to reading. If Hispanic children are not proficient in oral Spanish or in oral English, they may have considerable difficulty learning to read Spanish or English respectively. These children may find themselves trapped in a vicious cycle: they don't read very well, leading to a lack of motivation and interest in reading and a negative attitude about reading; at the same time, those affective factors influence the children's willingness to read and to try hard to learn more about reading. Consequently, such children may not read very much and may continue to have difficulty reading because of the cumulative effects of lack of success.

It is obvious, then, that Hispanic children as a group are not homogeneous regarding linguistic or literacy levels. These children vary widely with respect to oral language background, degree of linguistic proficiency in both Spanish and English, exposure to Spanish and/or English in initial reading instruction, and reading ability in both Spanish and English.

In order to serve Hispanic children's reading needs well, therefore, two special concerns need to be addressed by libraries and schools. First, school and public libraries should have a wide variety of books and other materials available in both Spanish and English at several levels of reading difficulty. The collection should encompass a wide variety of topics to allow for varying interests and cultural perspectives. Special attention should be given to the notion of text difficulty. Standard readability formulas are generally inadequate as an index of true difficulty, because they only measure artificial surface text characteristics such as vocabulary frequency and sentence length. Better indications of difficulty are compatibility of reading material to children's oral language patterns, concept load or number of new ideas per sentence or paragraph of the text, and the degree of fit between the background of experience of prospective readers and the text content. When a child is reading in a less familiar languge, it is especially important that the content of that reading be interesting and culturally relevant.

A second concern is for librarians and teachers to be sensitive to children's present and developing linguistic competencies, as well as to the language attitudes of children and parents within the community. Adults who work with Hispanic children should become more aware of cultural differences in order to value diversity and to create a climate of acceptance and understanding for these children. Further, teachers and librarians should encourage all children by having high expectations for their success and by realizing that the reading needs and interests of Hispanic children are just as diverse as those of the dominant population.

REFERENCES

del Prado, Y. (1975). Bilingual-multicultural education: A definition. In M. P. Douglass (Ed.) *Claremont Reading Conference, Thirty-ninth Yearbook* (pp. 101–106). Claremont, CA: Claremont Graduate School.

DiStefano, P., J. Dole, & R. Marzano. (1984). *Elementary language arts.* New York: John Wiley and Sons.

Loban, W. (1963). *The language of elementary school children.* Champaign, IL: National Council of Teachers of English.

Torres, M. (1986). Special language issues. In G. G. Duffy & L. R. Roehler, *Improving classroom reading instruction* (pp. 423-450). New York: Random House.

Management of Library Programs and Services for Hispanic Children: Some Practical Considerations

Liz Rodriguez Miller

Libraries serving communities with Hispanic populations should be very eager to institute programs and services for Hispanic children. Providing such services and programs can be seen as the library's affirmation of its commitment to serve all segments of its constituency. These services and programs can be viewed as promoting the advantages of cultural diversity. They can be pointed to as investments in the future growth and development of the community.

These services and programs can take different forms. They can be aimed at filling specific needs, or they can foster certain interests. They can begin modestly and evolve, or they can start with a major infusion of funds and new staff. Regardless of their original intent or size, they should always be seen as positive forces, benefiting Hispanic and non-Hispanic children alike. They should never be seen as strictly remedial. They should make long-lasting contributions to a library and its patrons rather than have a beginning and ending period of usefulness. The ultimate goal should be to make these services and programs an integral part of the overall library picture, so much so that the library would seem incomplete without them.

Managers and administrators can make use of certain practical ideas to assure that effective, quality programs and services for Hispanic children exist in their libraries.

COMMITMENT

The single most important element necessary for the success of library programs and services for Hispanic children is commitment on the part of administrators, decision makers, and staff.

Commitment begins with an understanding of why programs and services for Hispanic children are beneficial. Statistics are blended with thought-provoking arguments for such programs in the article "Hispanics in the U.S.: Implications for Library Service" (Dyer & Robertson-Kozan, 1983). This is recommended reading for those considering new programs and services for Hispanic children, or those who need reinforcement for current efforts in this area.

The next step inherent in a strong commitment is a pledge of material support to ensure adequate funding and staffing. Alternative strategies to attain these needed resources are mentioned in a later section.

Encouragement, endorsement, and recognition on the part of administrators and managers also signify commitment. Reiterating the importance of the programs in communications to all staff members, involving personnel at all levels in orientation and training sessions for these services, and publicizing the library's efforts on behalf of Hispanic children are all examples of how this level of commitment can be demonstrated. Overall, administrators and managers should be eager and willing to use management skills and knowledge they have acquired from past library experiences to assure the success of these important programs and services.

AGREEMENT ON GOALS AND OBJECTIVES

Defining the intent of the library's programs and services for Hispanic children is a very important first step. Regardless of the size or scope of the programs and services, before anything is begun a discussion of desired outcomes and the resources needed to attain these outcomes is indispensable. Managers, administrators, and line staff who will be involved in carrying out the day-to-day operations should take part in this discussion. Involvement of children, parents, community members, and related professionals can be very beneficial after the basic parameters have been set. Research into the operation of similar programs and services can also be helpful. This can be accomplished by searching the professional literature; contacting staff at other libraries; or communicating with local, regional, or national library agencies and organizations.

After these discussions and research, a statement of goals and objectives should be drawn up. This statement should include specific timelines; the resources needed to achieve the goals; where these resources are to be obtained; and who will be responsible for implementing, monitoring, and evaluating the services and programs. The manager or administrators should play an important role in this process by interjecting realistic expectations based on their knowledge and understanding of the overall organizational picture. The document that emerges from this process should serve as the foundation on which the success of services and programs for Hispanic children will be based.

FINDING RESOURCES TO SUPPORT NEW PROGRAMS AND SERVICES

Any library, regardless of size, can undertake some form of service or program for Hispanic children. Of course, ideally an institution should provide full support in the form of specially-trained bilingual/bicultural professional staff and all other resources required for successful implementation. Other options open to managers and administrators looking for ways to institute programs and services without the luxury of full funding are:

- Assigning responsibility for these programs and services to existing staff, be they professionals or paraprofessionals, and providing them with necessary training and guidance.

- Entering into a cooperative agreement with other schools or libraries in the area with similar goals in regard to programs and services for Hispanic children.

- Seeking help from nonlibrary professionals. Faculty or even students from nearby universities or community colleges are but two examples of potential resource people.

- Turning to lay people from the community concerned with the needs and interests of Hispanic children. This can include parents, grandparents, community activists, or any others willing to donate time, talent, or resources to help achieve the library's goals.

- Soliciting help from state, regional, or national agencies and organizations. This can involve submitting a grant proposal for funding to the state library, taking advantage of consultant services offered by various entities, or seeking advice from national professional groups such as REFORMA, the National Association to Promote Library Services to the Spanish-Speaking.

SUMMARY

The foregoing epitomizes the most basic, practical thinking that needs to take place from a management perspective when dealing with programs and services for Hispanic children. A more detailed analysis for implementing such programs and services can be found in the classic "Guidelines for Library Services to the Spanish-Speaking" (Cuesta & Tarin, 1978), which for many years has served as a guide for libraries serious about fulfilling their obligation to serve Hispanic children. The present publication, we hope, will provide a more recent standard to measure such efforts.

It is exciting to think about the advances many libraries have made in their efforts to serve Hispanics. It is also challenging to think about how much still needs to be done. If we as librarians are successful in capturing the interest and attention of Hispanic children through programs and services tailored to meet their needs, we will have established a basis for library use that can last a lifetime. Is there any better reason to put our full support behind these important programs?

REFERENCES

Cuesta, Y., & P. Tarin. (1978, July). Guidelines for library services to the Spanish-speaking. *Library Journal*, 1350–1355.

Dyer, E., & C. Robertson-Kozan. (1983, April). Hispanics in the U.S.: Implications for library service. *School Library Journal*, 27–29.

Guidelines for Selection and Acquisition of Materials for School and Public Libraries

Mary Frances Johnson

THE NEED FOR EDUCATION IN HISPANIC CULTURE

The major role of public school librarians is to provide a collection of educational materials to support the school curriculum. Librarians in children's departments of public libraries have a somewhat different role: to support the recreational reading pleasure of children by providing them with interesting books that are fun to read and informational books that satisfy their intellectual curiosity. Books for parents are also provided, as are books for preschool children and nonprint materials.

In order to prepare both of these types of children's librarians, library schools provide specialized courses in children's literature and in areas such as folklore, storytelling, and the reading habits of English-speaking children. But very few library schools have any courses in Spanish-language children's literature, the cultural differences of Spanish-speaking children, or the historical influence of Spanish culture on U.S. history. Children's literature courses deal mainly with English-language children's books, classic and modern, and the mythology and fables covered are largely Roman and Greek. The non-English classics that are included, such as Andersen, Collodi, De Brunhoff, and Lionni, are so ingrained in English children's literature that their foreign provenance is almost overlooked.

Children's librarians learn about *Bre'r Rabbit, Uncle Remus,* and maybe *La Cucarachita Martina,* but seldom hear about *Tio Conejo* or *Jaboti,* who are the Latin American counterparts of Bre'r Rabbit. They study Aesop's fables, but never learn about Iriarte's and Samaniego's versions of the same fables. They study Anglo-Saxon nursery rhymes, but know nothing of Pomob's or Galarza's Latin American versions of the same rhymes. A book titled *Mother Goose in Spanish* (Reid & Kerrigan, 1968), was widely publicized in the

United States, but few librarians know of the W.P.A. bilingual collection of nursery rhymes, games, and songs from New Mexico (*Spanish-American Song and Game Book*, 1942; recently republished but unfortunately out of print again). They learn about Grimm's and Perrault's fairy tales, but are not exposed to the Spanish variants of many of the same stories, which were recently collected in New Mexico. (In some of the Spanish versions of Cinderella, she meets Prince Charming at Mass, or at a bullfight.) Many non-Hispanic librarians avoid children's literature with themes centering on death, being unaware of the central part religion, death, and life after death play in Latin cultures based on Catholicism or pre-Columbian mythologies. Books that are culturally relevant for the Spanish-speaking child in the United States should certainly be the foundation of Spanish-language children's book collections.

HOW TO ACQUIRE NECESSARY INFORMATION

Individual librarians who wish to increase their knowledge of Hispanic culture in order to better serve children of that background might wish to consider the following courses of action.

- Take a course in Spanish literature at your local college or university, preferably one that includes the literature of Spain, Latin America, and Central America.

- Become acquainted with the names of the best and most famous authors in the Spanish language, since many of them have written for children, or had works adapted for children.

- Contact some of the publishers and organizations specializing in Hispanic children's literature to obtain their catalogs, bibliographies, and newsletters. (See Appendix A to this chapter)

- Read some of the available material about Spanish-language children's books. For those who read Spanish, you may wish to explore books written by Spanish-speaking authors in the field. Some examples are Bravo-Villasante (1983), Almendros (1971), and Salgado Corral (1982), whose book contains a recommended list of literature for classroom use.

- Talk to your local library school and community college about the possibility of providing courses in this field.

- Build up your library's professional collection of books covering Spanish-language children's literature.

SPANISH-LANGUAGE MATERIALS

Language Issues

When the Spanish explorers arrived in the Americas, they found completely new flora, fauna, and foods, for which they had no equivalent words in their languages. In order to speak about their surroundings, they had either to apply existing Spanish words to similar items (Piña, pine cone = Piña, pineapple; tortilla, pancake = tortilla, maize pancake) or to adopt words from the Native American languages spoken by the local inhabitants (e.g., maize, banana, aguacate, mecate, cacahuate, bohio, tiburon, pampa, papaya, nopal, gaucho, llama, tapir, yucca).

The first conquistadores were predominantly male and frequently married Native American women. Since words having to do with food, clothing, household items, and rearing children were often those from these women's own languages, such words often differ widely from area to area in Latin America. As a consequence, the vocabularies of elementary school children vary widely depending on which Native American language (Nahuatl, Quechua, Tupi-Guarani, Arahuaco-Caribe, Maya) was originally spoken in their country, more so than does the language used by adult speakers. Consequently, the books available for younger children from Puerto Rico or various Latin American countries use many local indigenous words that cannot be understood by children from other Spanish-speaking countries. It should be understood that although Latin American countries start their children with primers containing local indigenous words (just as our primers often use the speaking vocabulary of our English-speaking children), as Latin American children progress in grade level, their textbooks expand their vocabulary, just as our English-language ones do. Books published in Spain would be equivalent to books published in England in terms of language differences. Since we do not deprive English-speaking children of British books, neither should we deprive Spanish-speaking children of books from countries other than their own.

The subject of what type of Spanish to use in books for young Spanish-speaking children in the United States is a controversial one. There is no one correct answer, since every locality has to choose books that will best suit its children. This, however, creates a problem for publishers. No U.S. publishers want to publish Spanish books until they know what type of Spanish to use; since U.S. publishers deal in huge quantities of English-language children's books, they don't want to bother with small quantities of Spanish children's books. Many Spanish-language juvenile books published in the United States don't sell well; prospective purchasers reject them because the language is slightly different from what they know.

Children in the United States, including immigrant children, mature early, and Spanish-language books from abroad often do not match the interest or age ranges of U.S. Spanish-speaking children. Spanish-speaking children learning English are often pushed to advance in English at the expense of their Spanish, which is allowed to stagnate. Thus their level of Spanish dominance is lower than that of children of similar ages in Spanish-speaking countries, although their interest levels are more mature. They often use much simpler language constructions, and smaller and different vocabulary, and thus feel uncomfortable with many books written for children of their own age in Spain, Argentina, or Mexico.

Appropriateness of Spanish-Language Books

Children's librarians choose books that are different from the textbooks purchased by schools. For instance, librarians may look for books to help children understand math, or have fun with math, or learn interesting things about math (like Babylonian cuneiform, math puzzles, biographies of mathematicians, and the history of mathematical discoveries), but would not really purchase many books about how to *do* math problems—since the children would learn this in the classroom. The library would also have basic counting books, and mathematical concept books for parents to read to preschool children to prepare them for school.

The Spanish-language book industry makes no clear distinction between textbooks and trade books (those published for libraries). This is because there are proportionately fewer public libraries serving children in the Hispanic world, and most of the books bought for Spanish-speaking children are to support school curricula. Even when the books are not bought for school purposes, the Hispanic culture until recently has highly valued the didactic purposes of recreational reading (as English-speaking culture did during the Victorian era). This complicates U.S. library Spanish-language book collection development, since children's librarians have great difficulty finding Spanish-language books that fit our criteria. However, the demand for Spanish-language books that meet our library standards has given rise to newer types of Spanish-language children's books.

Issues Concerning the Types of Books Available in Spanish in Spain, Latin America, and the United States

- **Content.** Librarians often waste much time looking for books that do not really exist in Spanish—such as books about U.S. history at an elementary grade level, juvenile biographies of

U.S. historical personages, books abut U.S. holidays and customs, fiction about Mexican-American life in the United
States, and up-to-date juvenile encyclopedias with complete
indexes and geographical and historical coverage of the United
States. With regard to fiction, U.S. librarians look for interesting plots that will appeal to modern children, and that are not
didactic, religious, or moralistic.

- **Format.** Librarians are spoiled by the physical quality of
English-language children's books—binding, paper, clarity of
type, and abundance of color illustrations. When purchasing
Spanish-language books, they often refuse to purchase quality
literature because of its unattractive physical format or lack of
durability, and sometimes purchase poor quality books just
because they have good bindings.

- **Binding.** Due to the lack of sturdy bindings on most Spanish
children's books, it is necessary to spend extra money to bind
most Spanish-language children's books before circulating them
to the public. When this is done, the book loses its attractive
covers, and is less appealing to its prospective readers. In fact,
many children feel that books bound with buckram covers are
second-class ones compared to more attractive English-
language books; Spanish books that circulated well with new,
colorful covers seem much less read once they've been sent to
the bindery.

- **Language.** Although the majority of American Spanish speakers
are of Mexican descent, there are considerable numbers of
Puerto Rican, Cuban, Central American, and other Latin
American immigrants. Teachers, librarians, and parents all
want children to use books in their local version of Spanish.
Although many parents and teachers have an aversion to using
books from Spain, thinking that Castilian Spanish will be more
difficult for young children, the opposite may be true. Since it
contains fewer non-Spanish indigenous words, although some
of the words may be unfamiliar to some of the children, they
will be learning universal Spanish vocabulary understood by all
Spanish speakers, rather than learning vocabulary understood
in only one section of the Americas. For example, the basic
preschool "Vocabulario Minimo" (for Spanish preschoolers) in
Brocal (1981), includes only 2 words (out of the basic list of
161) not in common use in Latin American Spanish. In any
case, U.S. librarians are looking for books written in Spanish
that their juvenile patrons can understand.

- **Standards of Library Schools.** Library schools emphasize specific standards for collection development, and librarians serving the Spanish speaking have to learn to compromise on these

standards if they are going to have a sizeable Spanish-language children's collection.

- **Selection Points.** Goodman (1985–86) and the Council on Interracial Books for Children (n.d.) have published pamphlets providing lists of criteria for evaluating children's books dealing with Hispanics. Addresses for both are included in Appendix A to this chapter.

SOURCES OF INFORMATION

Bibliographic and review information about Spanish-language books does not exist to the extent that it does for English books. Librarians in charge of English-language children's book collections have many specialized periodicals available to them that publish continuing book reviews, and they can join organizations that send them prepublication reviews of books. Also, publishers send out free sample copies in the thousands to book reviewers, as well as preview copies to prospective volume purchasers such as library systems. These resources are not usually available for Spanish-language books.

There have been several attempts in the United States to make information about Spanish-language children's books available. Several of these are listed in Appendix A to this chapter. One further resource is Proyecto Leer, which published several issues of a bibliographic bulletin. Bulletin Number 17 was a special issue devoted to reviews of books about Hispanic American heritage listed by countries, periodicals and organizations reviewing Spanish-language materials, and lists of publishers and distributors of these materials in both the United States and Hispanic countries. Although Proyecto Leer no longer exists, its bulletins still contain valuable information and may exist in some corner of your library system.

In addition, library journals such as *The Horn Book, Booklist, School Library Journal,* and *Wilson Library Bulletin* publish both articles about and reviews of Spanish-language children's literature on a regular basis.

A BALANCED COLLECTION

American children's librarians place a good deal of importance on "balancing" the English-language materials collection. This means having sufficient numbers of books in many different subject areas to cover the children's reading interests. It also means replacing lost or damaged titles to maintain coverage of the subject. When dealing with Spanish-language books, compromises have to be made since books go out of print so rapidly. Books may have to be bought from reviews alone in order to acquire them before they go out of print. (Runs of 3,000 books are large for Mexican publishers!).

The *OAS Humanities Curriculum for Hispanic Culture* (1983; see Appendix A to this chapter) contains a recommended list of representative authors and subjects for a core Spanish-language children's book collection. The list gives general series names, authors' names, and types of folklore to look for rather than particular editions of books.

A library collection should include Spanish-language comic books, records of games and songs, and preschool educational games and puzzles in addition to just books. *Abecedarios, vocabularios,* and illustrated dictionaries from as many different Spanish-speaking countries as possible should be included to give the young children a wide exposure to many different varieties of Spanish. In particular, books that develop vocabulary are especially necessary to help children function as fully as possible in Spanish.

Since children who read only Spanish translations of English-language books have had too limited an experience, an attempt should be made to include the following in library collections serving Spanish-speaking children:

- The same subject areas that are available in the English book collection.
- All of the important Spanish-language children's authors.
- Hispanic, Latin American, and indigenous mythology and art.
- Hispanic nursery rhymes and songs.
- Latin American and Mexican-American culture and customs.
- Translations made in Spanish-speaking countries of children's "classics."

Appendix B to this chapter lists various series and collections that are sources of such material.

SUMMARY

All of the many differences and difficulties cited above complicate the development of a Spanish-language children's book collection in the United States, add to the cost of providing Spanish services, and are so time-consuming that they may take up librarians' time more than does English-language collection development. But if librarians in the United States are to fulfill their professional goals of providing free books for the children in their service areas in order to strengthen the educational development of our future society, the extra effort involved in providing a balanced Spanish-language children's book collection is worth the time and money involved. Fortunately, as such collections multiply in Spanish-speaking areas, the tools needed for managing them become available, and professional library organizations facilitate the spread of the expertise acquired by the pioneers in the field.

This increase in professional tools can mean improved service if librarians will apply themselves to acquiring the expertise necessary to fulfill their obligations to their Spanish-speaking juvenile patrons. It is up to the librarian in the field to see that the regular library review media include reviews of Spanish books on a regular basis, that library budgets for Spanish-language books are proportionate to the number of Spanish readers, that material collections be culturally relevant to the local patrons, and that Spanish-speaking library personnel are available to serve the patrons who need them.

REFERENCES

Almendros, H. (1971). *Estudio sobre literatura infantil.* (Col. Nueva Biblioteca Pedagógica). México: Oasis.

Bravo-Villasante, C. (1983). *Historia de la literatura infantil española.* Madrid: Doncel. ISBN 84-325-0391-6.

Brocal Vocabulario básico ilustrado. (1981). Elaborado por Chelo Caballero, Dirección: Arturo Medina. Barcelona, Spain: La Galera. ISBN 84-246-0590-X.
This book is highly recommended.

Goodman, L. (1985-86). *How to select children's books in Spanish.* New York: Bilingual Publications.

Reid, A., & A. Kerrigan. (1968). *Mother goose in Spanish.* Illustrated by Barbara Cooney. New York: Crowell.

Salgado Corral, R. (1982). *La literatura infantil en la escuela primaria.* México: Editorial Patria. ISBN 968-6054-25-1.

Spanish-American song and game book. (1942). Washington, DC: Works Progress Administration.

Ten quick ways to analyze children's books for racism and sexism. (n.d.). New York: The Council on Interracial Books for Children.

Appendix A
Sources of Information on Spanish-Language Juvenile Books

The sources of information listed in this appendix include both published sources and organizations or businesses involved in some aspect of producing or publishing Spanish-language books for children.

Adoption bibliography and multiethnic sourcebook. (1977). Compiled and annotated by Elizabeth Wharton Van Why. Open Door Society of Connecticut, Inc. 320p. (PO Box 478, Hartford, CT, 06101). ISBN 0-918416-02-7.
> Compiled in response to needs of families who had adopted children of other races. The title is misleading, since the interracial theme of the items included is an equally important focus of the book. Contains listings for many small presses that are otherwise difficult to locate. Includes several indexes.

Asociación Española de amigos de IBBY. Ministerio de Cultura, I.N.L.E., Santiago Rusiñol 8, Madrid-3, España.
> Publishes a bulletin with articles about Spanish children's literature, prizes, awards, authors, meetings, and conferences. Publication began in January 1983.

El Barrio Communications Project. PO Box 31004, Los Angeles, CA, 90031.
> Distributor, annotated catalog.

Bibliotecas para la Gente. CLA Chapter. c/o Mission Branch, San Francisco Public Library, 3359 24th Street, San Francisco, CA, 94110.
> Membership provides an informative newsletter sharing useful information, book reviews, and sources for purchasing. Institutional or individual memberships available to public or school librarians, distributors, booksellers, and authors. Conducts workshops and participates in ALA, CABE, CLA, and other conferences. Produces subject bibliographies for sale; e.g., a Spanish film bibliography, a bibliography of Spanish children's books, and *Revista* (a bibliography of recommended Spanish magazines).

Bilingual Educational Services. 1603 Hope Street, PO Box 669, South Pasadena, CA, 91030. (213) 682-3445.
> Distributor, catalog.

Bilingual Publications Company. 1966 Broadway, New York, NY, 10023. (212) 873-2067.
> Annotated, classified catalogs. Distributor. Very valuable set of purchasing guidelines included in children's catalogs.

Boletín Bibliográfico. Centro Regional para el Fomento del Libro en América Latina y el Caribe (CERLAL). Apartado Aéreo 17438, Bogotá, Colombia. Tel. 2-49-41/2-55-45-94.
Bulletin with news and bibliographic supplements. Funded by UNESCO. Official attempt at organizing Latin American bibliographical information. Available direct, surface mail, or air mail (extra cost).

Bookbird: Literature for children and young people. International Board of Books for Young People (IBBY).
Magazine from Austria about international children's literature. Available from magazine jobbers. Contains information about translation of books into Spanish and other languages, or from Spanish into English or other languages.

Children's Music Center. 5373 West Pico Blvd., Los Angeles, CA, 90019. (213) 937-1825.
Distributor of books and records.

Claudia's Caravan. PO Box 5582, Berkeley, CA 94705. (415) 843-2030.
New distributor. Multicultural, multilingual materials. Mimeographed annotated catalog.

Comision Católica Española de la Infancia. (C.C.E.I.).
This organization is a chapter of the Bureau International Catholique de L'Enfance. It has a section called Secretariado de Prensa y Literatura, which sponsors studies of children's literature, and publishes its results in a monograph series titled: "Cuadernos para Educar". Published *Literatura actual infantil y juvenil en España 1970–1977.* (1979). Madrid: Sm Ediciones (General Tabanera 39, Madrid-25). ISBN 84-348-0731-9.

Council on Interracial Books for Children. 1841 Broadway, New York, NY, 10023.
Organization that publishes an informational *Interracial Books for Children Bulletin* on multicultural children's literature. Includes book reviews, bibliographies, recommended lists, not-recommended lists, and biographical information on ethnic authors and illustrators.

Cuentacuentos, una colección de cuentos para poder contar. (1982). Collected by Nuria Ventura and Teresa Durán. Madrid: Siglo XXI de España. ISBN 84-323-0449-2.
First published by Pablo del Río Editor, S.A., 1980. A storytelling sourcebook with theoretical background on history and techniques of storytelling, how to use stories in the classroom, criteria for suitable stories, an index by ages, and a bibliography of Spanish-language books useful as sources for storytelling. Sixteen stories are included, ranging from "Zeralda's Ogre" (Ungerer), through Catalonian, Russian, and Blackfoot folktales to "Petronilla" (Williams).

Dale, Doris Cruger. (1985). *Bilingual books in Spanish and English for children.* Littleton, CO: Libraries Unlimited (PO Box 263, Littleton, CO, 80160-0263). ISBN 0-87287-477-x.
A comprehensive, historical coverage of all bilingual Spanish/English books available for children in the U.S. Includes lists of readings, jour-

nals that review books, tables of numbers of books published, and several indexes.

A directory of ethnic publishers and resource organizations. (1979). Second Edition, compiled by Marjorie K. Joramo. Chicago: American Library Association. 102p. ISBN 0-8389-3223-1.
An annotated bibliography of publishers, distributors, and resources in the ethnic publishing field. Includes several indexes.

Donars Spanish Books. PO Box 24, Loveland, CO, 80539-0024. (303) 669-0586.
Distributor. Annotated catalog. Newsletter.

Durán, Daniel Flores. (1979). *Latino materials. A multimedia guide for children and young adults.* New York & Santa Barbara, CA: Neal-Schuman; ABC Clio.
An annotated bibliography, with lists of suppliers, and indexes by subject areas and types of materials.

Espan-Dura Libros. PO Box 767, Muskogee, OK, 74401.
New distributor, presenting prebound books from Spanish publishers, bound in library binding in the United States. Twenty-three "colecciones" offered in first catalog.

Exposición Itinerante de Libros Infantiles y Juveniles. (1983). *Catálogo.* Ministerio de Cultura, Dirección General del Libro y Bibliotecas. Madrid: Ministerio de Cultura, (Paseo de la Castellana 109). ISBN 84-7483-298-5.
Catalog arranged by subject areas of book included in model Spanish library established in 1982 by Ministerio de Cultura in Spain. Bibliographical information is included, but no ISBN numbers, translator, or original titles information.

Fondo Cultural Latinoamericano. PO Box 1784, San Diego, CA, 92112. (213) 562-1400.
Distributor, mimeo lists.

Bernard H. Hamel Spanish Books. 2326 Westwood Blvd., Los Angeles, CA, 90064. (213) 475-0453.
Bibliographies, catalogs. Distributor.

Humanities Curriculum for Hispanic Culture. Dean, School of Library Science, Texas Women's University, PO Box 22905, TWU Station, Denton, TX, 76204.
Highly recommended course designed for teachers and librarians working with Spanish-speaking children. Contains bibliography of recommended library core collection children's books.

Iaconi Book Imports. 300 Pennsylvania Avenue, San Francisco, CA, 94107. (415) 285-7393.
Call for appointment. Specializes in children's books. Distributor. Annotated catalog.

Imported Books. PO Box 4414, Dallas, TX, 75208. (214) 941-6497.
Distributor, annotated mimeographed catalogs.

INLE. Instituto Nacional del Libro Español. Ministerio de Cultura, INLE, Santiago Rusinol 8, Madrid-3, España.
Publishes a complete listing of all children's books printed in Spain, titled *Libros Infantiles y Juveniles.* This list appears every few years. Includes an alphabetical list of Spanish juvenile publishers, and an alphabetical title list with complete bibliographic data on the publication (which might be a comic book or coloring book), and an author index listing all the titles in the catalog under that particular author's name. A few Latin American books are included, but the emphasis is on Spanish publications. Official publication of the Spanish Ministry of Culture.

I.S.B.N., INLE, Santiago Rusinol 8, Madrid-3, España.
Catalog similar to *Books in Print,* for books published in Spain; it contains no measurable coverage of Latin American publications. Includes an index of Spanish publishers by ISBN numbers. Issued on a yearly basis.

La Latina Bookstore. 2417 Mission, San Francisco, CA, 94110. (415) 824-0327.
Annotated monthly listing and mailing list. Bookstore. Newsletter. Weekly book reviews on local radio.

Lector. The Review Journal for Spanish language and bilingual materials.
A review magazine published in English, with an emphasis on materials suitable for American public and academic libraries. The magazine includes regular reviews of Spanish-language and bilingual children's books available in the United States.

Lectorum Publications, Inc. 137 West 14th Street, New York, NY, 10011. (212) 929-2833.
Annotated catalog. Distributor.

Lectura y Vida, Revista Latinoamericana de Lectura. International Reading Association, PO Box 8139, Newark, DE, 19714. ISBN 0325-8637.
The Spanish-language journal published by the International Reading Association includes research articles about reading instruction theory in addition to reviews of books of interest to teachers and children. Some of the articles originate in Spain or Latin America, especially Argentina, although others are translations of articles originally published in English. This journal is useful in aiding the U.S. librarian to focus on the cultural differences between the U.S. and Hispanic educational establishment's attitudes towards the definition of "good" children's literature.

Librería México. 2631 Mission, San Francisco, CA, 94110. (415) 647-0329.
Spanish-speaking only. In person purchase advised. Bookstore, Mexican chain.

Multicultural, multilingual resources, a vendor directory. (1979). California Ethnic Services Task Force (California State Library).
Directory. Out of print but available in California library systems. Contains annotated lists of vendors of material by language, with comments as to quality of service. It is not limited to Spanish-language vendors,

incudes Vietnamese, Chinese, etc. Any copies located should be marked "Do Not Discard." Microfiche copies available through ERIC.

National Clearinghouse for Bilingual Education. *Forum.*
Agency is moving. No address available at this time. Toll free number: (800) 647-0123. Newsletter about events occurring in the bilingual education field. Includes reviews of research publications, announcements of changes in the law, requests for proposals. Will provide low-cost computerized database searches.

Parapara, Revista de literatura infantil. Banco del Libro. Apartado 5893, Caracas 1010-A, Venezuela.
A Spanish-language magazine on children's literature with theoretical articles, historical essays, book reviews, and biographies of authors and artists. Bound into center of magazine are 3 x 5 perforated cards with bibliographical data and book annotations that can be filed directly into an order file.

Pelegrín, Ana. (1982). *La Aventura de Oír. Cuentos y memorias de tradición oral.* Illustrated by Mario Lacoma. Madrid: Editorial Cincel (Col. Expresión y Escuela). ISBN 84-7046-287-3.
How to tell stories, what kinds of stories to choose, voice techniques, selected folklore, and useful stories.

La Red/The Net. Newsletter of the National Chicano Council on Higher Education. 600 West 78th Street, Suite 201, Austin, TX, 78705. (512) 479-8497.
Published 16 times a year, no charge. Reports on networking activity in scholarship of or about Hispanics. Newsletter.

Rio Grande Book Company. PO Box 2795, McAllen, TX, 78501. (512) 682-7531.
Distributor. Catalog.

Rizzoli International Publications, Inc. 712 Fifth Avenue, New York, NY, 10019. (212) 397-3700.
Distributor. Catalog.

Schmidt, Velma E., & Earldene McNeill, (1978). *Cultural awareness: A resource bibliography.* Washington, DC: National Association for the Education of Young Children.
Lists of names and addresses of over 800 sources of the materials cited in this bibliography: books, records, AV materials (film, filmstrips, slides, dolls), museums, catalogs, periodicals, festivals, fairs, and celebrations. Includes a preface giving "Ten Quick Ways to Analyze Children's Books for Racism and Sexism" (taken from an Interracial Books for Children publication). Due to its recent publication, this bibliography includes proportionately larger amounts of newer material that is usually less offensive than some of the older items that abound in older bibliographies.

Appendix B
Sample Series or Collecciones

Col. A favor de las niñas. Barcelona, Spain: Lumen, 1980s.
Colorful illustrated picture storybooks translated from Italian; specifically feminist nontraditional fairytales designed to present young girls with positive images. Full-page color illustrations, very good graphic layout. Has a subseries "Las Aventuras de Asolina." Good translations, credited to "Humpty Dumpty." Some titles better than others. Grades 4 and up.

Col. Agata. Madrid: Susaeta, n.d.
A collection of Spanish fairy tales in picture storybook format. Stapled paperbacks, oversize, bright color illustrations on every page. Fairy tales from the Latin culture. Grades 3–5.

Col. Albumes de Herge. Barcelona, Spain: Juventud, 1970s.
Oversized picture books based on the movie versions of Tintin stories. The illustrations are photos from the films. Translated from French. Paper over board binding. Grades 5–7.

Col. Alicia. Barcelona, Madrid, Buenos Aires: Ediciones Toray, 1980s.
Oversized picture storybook adaptations of such classic juvenile titles as *The Wizard of Oz* and *Pinocchio.* The color illustrations on nearly every page are not the original ones. Paper over boards binding. Good size type, children will enjoy reading.

Col. Altea mascota. Madrid: Altea, 1980s.
Reader-sized paperbacks, with abundant illustrations on every page; translations of contemporary children's literature from outside of Spain, using the original illustrations.

Col. Así vivimos. Caracas, Venezuela: Ekaré-Banco del Libro.
Stapled paperback picture books on contemporary themes of daily life in Latin America. Illustrated by Venezuelan artists. Caribbean vocabulary. Grades 4–6.

Col. Austral juvenil. Madrid: Espasa-Calpe, 1980s.
Paperbacks for young readers (pocket book size and style, glued spines). Approximately 143 pages. Over 100 titles in print. Spanish translations of literary classics for young people from all over the world and many different languages. Excellent translations. Editor of the series is Felicidad Orquin Lerin (Directora del Depto. Juvenil), who is well known in Spain as a specialist in children's literature. Good for Jr. High supplementary reading, or younger readers who have been educated in Spanish-speaking countries. Grades 6 and up. Sample authors: C.T. Hoffman, William Steig, and Roald Dahl.

Col. Babar. Barcelona, Spain: Bruguera, 1970s.
The every popular Babar series, translated beautifully into Spanish from the original French. (May be difficult for American Spanish-speaking children to read.) Some bindings are better than others, with no obvious

pattern. Many books will have to be rebound for long-term use in school libraries. Oversize picture story books, very popular with children and parents, for storytelling and for reading by third and fourth graders.

Col. Barbapapa. Barcelona, Spain: Juventud, 1970s.
The famous Barbapapa books by Annette Tison and Talus Taylor, available in hardback and paperback, but not all titles available in both formats. Delightful fantasy, with bright attractive colorful illustrations, picture book style, about a family of animals of assorted shapes, sizes, and colors. Human style attributes and foibles exist in their liberated society, which does not discriminate because of the various colors, shapes, or sex of the individuals in the stories. Exciting adventure stories that are very attractive to young readers. Preschool–3.

Col. Barbapapa-historietas.
More Barbapapa, in comic book illustration style. Grades 3–5.

Col. Barco de papel, el. Barcelona, Spain: Editorial Labor, 1960s, 1970s.
Full-size color illustrations every other page. Most of the titles in this series are translations. The amount of text varies in different titles. Paper over boards binding. K–5.

Col. Baúl de cuentos. Barcelona, Spain: HYMSA, 1980s.
Oversize picture books, fullpage bright color illustrations. Paper over boards binding. Original Catalonian literary creations and universal folktales in beautiful settings. Grades 5 and up.

Col. Biblioteca educativa infantil. Barcelona, Spain: Molino, 1970s.
Small-size nonfiction picture books, translated from English. Each book on a single subject, many titles in the series. Color illustrations alternate with monochrome illustrations. English versions are rather old, some contents are now outdated, but these are still popular for introducing children to the world that surrounds them, including such things as trains, cars, planes, birds, and animals. Some distributors have these available in prebound library binding. K–4.

Biblioteca temática para niños. México: Fernández Editores, 1984.
Paperback translations of nonfiction books from the MacDonald and Company Series from England. Many color illustrations and controlled vocabulary makes these books easy reading and very popular. Sample subseries: Ciencia, Historia, Matematicas, Paises, Personajes.

Col. La brújula. México: CIDCLI, S.C. (Centro de Información y Desarollo de la Comunicación y la Literatura Infantiles), 1980s.
A new series of thin paperbacks, with beautiful glossy paper, color illustrations plus diagrams, line drawings, and maps. The emphasis is on the sciences, including ecology. Very well done, with the scientific part of the text contributed by scientists. In the Hispanic style, includes additional small doses of fantasy to "appeal" to the children, but in this series it does not detract from the real text, since the two different aspects are set off by different type styles. Grades 3 and up.

Col. Cada día aprendo algo. Barcelona, Spain: Editorial Molino, 1976.
Oversize picture books translated from English; concept books teach children about their surroundings and develop their vocabulary. Color illustrations. Good for extending vocabulary and thinking processes. K–3.

Clásicos infantiles ilustrados. México: Promexa, 1982.
These elegant editions were supported by the "Fomento Cultural Banamex." Oversize picture story books of universal classic fairytales illustrated by well-known artists and translated by authors known for their literary prominence. The collection includes some Mexican folktales illustrated by Mexican artists.

Col. Las cosas de cada día. Barcelona, Spain: La Galera, 1970s.
Illustrated by Fina Rifa. Paper over boards. These picture books about daily life, designed to extend the vocabulary of Spanish children, are part of a larger series called *Coleccion Ya se leer* and are intended for beginning readers. Color illustrations. Their small size make them popular with parents and beginning readers who can handle Spanish-style script. Preschool–2.

Col. Cuadrada. Barcelona, Spain: Juventud, 1970s, 1980s.
Oversize square picture storybooks for younger readers with brightly colored illustrations. Well-known authors and illustrators. Some books are original Hispanic works; others are translations. Bibliographic data on inside rear cover. Paper over boards binding. K–4.

Col. Las cuatro estaciones. Barcelona, Spain: Instituto Parramón, 1982.
Unpaged (30p.) with color illustrations. Paper over boards binding. Four picture books about the seasons of the year for preschoolers and primary grades illustrated by some of Spain's foremost illustrators. Each book has an explanatory text for the teacher to aid in discussion of the simple story. Preschool–2.

Col. Cuéntame por favor. Buenos Aires, Argentina: Sigmar, 1970s.
Oversize picture books translated from English titles by Jack Kent.

Col. Cuentos a dos voces. Buenos Aires, Argentina: Editorial Estrada.
An Argentine series, by Argentine authors for non-readers. Designed to be shared by an older and a younger reader. There are questions to elicit the child's participation at the end of the text on each page. The older reader should then weave these answers into the story on the next page. Paperback picture books with color illustrations for preschool or beginning first or second graders. There are six titles in both the first and second series. K–3. (Children's books from Argentina are difficult to locate at present.)

Col. Cuentos criollos. Caracas, Venezuela: Ekaré-Banco del Libro, 1970s.
Stapled paperback picture books based on indigenous folklore. Illustrations reflect native fauna, dress, geography. Vocabulary uses local animal names. Black-and-white illustrations by Venezuelan artists on every other page. 24p. Grades 3–5.

Col. Cuentos de hadas en color. Barcelona, Spain: Molino, 1970s.
The color illustrations in this series are large, fullpage size (oversize books). The Carruth titles are translations from English versions. One title contains Spanish folktales.

Col. Cuentos para sonreír. Buenos Aires, Argentina: Kapelusz, 1970s.
Stapled paperback picture book series of stories in rhyme for beginning readers. Color illustrations on every page. Preschool–3.

Col. Cuentos populares. Barcelona, Spain: La Galera, 1974.
Part of larger series *Colección Ya sé leer.* Spanish folktales for beginning readers translated from Catalan. Some are more difficult than others; some are slightly bowdlerized; all are genuine Latin folklore. Medium-sized stapled paperback picture storybooks for the middle grades. Some of the titles in this series have text in Spanish-style script; one should specify that script editions are not wanted when ordering.

Col. Cumiche. San José, Costa Rica: Editorial EDUCA (Editorial Universitaria CentroAmericana), 1980s.
Small thin stapled paperbacks based on Central American folklore, mythology, and children's literature. Poetry by Claudia Lars, stories about Tio Conejo, an adaptation for children of the *Popol Vuh*, all in colorfully illustrated (sometimes primitive) versions. Grades 4 and up.

Col. Dick Bruna. Madrid: Aguilar, 1970s.
The Dick Bruna books are very popular translations. Small-size picture books with large primary color illustrations and little text (in large print). The Spanish translation is very good, but the original texts themselves are not very literary; sentences are short and stilted in some cases. In the case of fairy tale "adaptations," the plots are very truncated. Matching English-language versions are available in some cases. Very good for vocabulary development in beginning readers. Popular with parents and children. Preschool–2.

Col. Duende. Valladolid, Spain: Miñon, 1970s.
Paper over board binding, picture books for preschool or lower grades. Fullpage color illustrations. Contains award winning titles. Some titles have bibliographic data on inside covers. 32p. K–4.

Col. Edad de oro. Perú: Editorial Arica, n.d.
Anthologies of children's poetry, folklore, nursery rhymes, adaptations of classical Spanish drama, etc. by Alma Flor Ada and Ma. Pilar de Olave. Small paperbacks, with brightly colored illustrations, very popular with children. Grades 3–5.

Col. Ekaré. (No series named in catalog). Caracas, Venezuela: Ekaré-Banco del Libro, 1980s.
Medium-sized stapled paperback and/or hardback picture books for preschool and elementary school age children, with emphasis on Latin American culture. Color illustrations. Good paper. Paperback and hardback versions. Some titles are original Latin American works, others are translations.

Col. Elige tu propia aventura. Barcelona, Spain: Timun Mas, 1983, 1984.
Translations by Carles Alier i Aixala of the popular English-language "Choose Your Own Adventure" books. Paperback format and illustrations match the English originals. The Spanish editions include a teacher's guide explaining how valuable the technique of letting the reader choose the path of the plot can be. Approximately 100p. Grades 4 and up.

El joven científico. Madrid: Plesa, 1978.
Originally published in English by Usborne Publishing Co., in England. Nonfiction books lavishly illustrated in color with a minimum amount of text. Oversize paperbacks. 31p. plus index. Grades 4 and up.

Col. El joven ingeniero. Madrid: Ediciones Plesa, 1978.
Originally published in English by Usborne Publishing Co., in England. English author Jonathan Rutland. Translated into Spanish by Antonio Zorita Garcia. Oversize paperbacks illustrating the history and the mechanisms of trains, motorcycles, and cars. Many color illustrations, diagrams, schematics. 32p. including index. Grades 4–8.

Col. En busca de palabras. Barcelona, Spain: Editorial Molino, 1970s.
Originally published by Hampton House Productions Ltd. in 1978. Wordbooks in picture book format, items are labelled and identified. Bright colorful illustrations make these books very popular and useful. Preschool–3.

Col. Estrella. Buenos Aires, Argentina: Editorial Sigmar, 1960s.
Oversize picture storybook versions of classical children's literature: Esopo, Fedro, La Fontaine, Samaniego, Iriarte, Andersen, Grimm. Paper over boards binding with color illustrations on every page. Grades 3–5.

Col. Fábulas. Barcelona, Spain: La Galera, 1970s.
The familiar La Fontaine fables in picture book format for beginning readers or storytelling. The adaptations by Catalonian specialists give us a different, Hispanic view of La Fontaine. Color illustrations on every other page, facing a page of text. Easy-to-read text, though some titles printed in Spanish-style script. Very popular, need to be bound to last. Medium-size books. Middle grades, 3 and up, but can be read by younger children.

Col. Fábulas de ahora mismo. Madrid: Ediciones Altea, 1976.
Authored by a team composed of J.L. Garcia-Sanchez and M.A. Pacheco. Modern "fables" designed to teach the modern child about today's world. Didactic stories, with beautiful illustrations, written to formula. Very Spanish in style, in keeping with the Spanish tradition of didactic children's literature, usually fables. Some of the plots are better than others; some are merely designed to teach. Sample subjects of the stories are: housing, transportation, industry, hygiene, demography, careers, and professions. The books are in hardback, and the illustrations are modern contemporary art. The books are very attractive, but lack real literary quality. Middle grades, 4 and up. Can be useful to support social science.

Fifth world tales/Cuentos del quinto mundo. San Francisco, CA: Children's Book Press, 1970s.
Bilingual paperback picture storybooks with brightly colored illustrations by contemporary artists, many of them in the muralist tradition. The stories represent different folk traditions from Latin America and the Spanish U.S. heritage. The series covers Maya, Philippine, Aztec, Spanish Colonial, Inca, Cuna, and Taino mythology, among others. Grades 5–8.

Col. Galera de oro. Barcelona, Spain: La Galera, 1960s, 1970s.
Translated from Catalan by Carola Soler, under the pedagogical direction of Marta Mata, these supplementary readers from Spain are designed for Spanish school children, and include a vocabulary based on the text to explain the new words in the story. Each story in the series is designed to interest readers while educating them about some facet of life in this world. Very useful to show Spanish-speaking American children that all Spanish-speaking children have to develop a school vocabulary in addition to their home vocabulary. Questions and answers about the text are also included. Grades 3 and up in United States.

Col. Globo de colores. Madrid: Aguilar, 1970s.
This series has several sub-series with individual names. A collection of picture books designed for preschool or primary grade children is called *Libros Para Mirar*. These picture books are designed to expand the Spanish child's vocabulary, and present different aspects of Spanish daily life that reflect Spanish culture.

Col. Grandes álbumes Babar. Barcelona, Spain: Ayma, 1965.
Written by Laurent de Brunhoff, this series of Babar picture books has Spanish-style script letters that are difficult for American Spanish-speaking children to read. (See also *Col. Babar.*) Grades 3–5.

Col. Grandes libros en color. Barcelona, Spain: Molino, 1970s.
Oversized picture books about the contemporary world, everyday life, real animals, etc. for preschoolers. Translated from English. Very popular with children and their parents. Good vocabulary development, interesting for young beginning readers to peruse. Middle grades for reading, younger for being read to. Preschool–3.

Col. Grandes libros de oro. México: Novaro, 1970s.
Oversize picture books (32 cm.). Translated from English. Bright colors, match English versions by Golden Books except for binding. Grades 3–5.

Col. El Hongo mágico. Barcelona, Spain: HYMSA, 1980s.
Oversize picture books of folktales, many Catalonian or Spanish. Fullpage color illustrations. Paper over boards binding. Has a fairy tale with a female hero. Middle grades and up.

Col. I can read series in Spanish. New York: Harper & Row, assorted dates.
Spanish translations of English-language, easy-to-read books in Harper's *I Can Read* series. Very popular with children in bilingual classes because they are identical in format to the English-language titles. The Spanish is such a literal translation, that it uses English syntax; English and Spanish sentences have identical page locations. Children who will not read books

published in Mexico or Spain will often read these because they are familiar with the English title. Grades 3 and up.

La Imagen y la palabra. Madrid: Ediciones Plesa, 1981.
Oversize picture books for concept development, basic understanding of society, and word recognition. Many color illustrations on each page, each identified with its name. A short sentence sets the scene. Designed to encourage discussion between preschoolers and adults and to start children on their way to reading. Translated from English titles published by Usborne Publishing, 1980.

Col. Imágenes. Barcelona, Spain: Juventud, 1970s.
Large, oversize, brightly colored illustrated wordbooks specifically designed for vocabulary development. The pictures are labelled with the names of the objects found in the area of the title. These books are also useful for helping both parents and teachers increase their Spanish vocabulary. Translated by Herminia Dauer. Paper over boards binding. Preschool–2.

Col. Infantil Alfaguara. Madrid: Ediciones Alfaguara, 1978.
Medium-size, paperback, picture book translations of quality children's literature from various non-Spanish-speaking countries. Excellent translations. Art matches that in English originals. Good paper, but paperback binding will not withstand library use. Grades 3–5.

Col. Infantimágenes. Barcelona, Spain: Instituto Parramón Ediciones, 1979, 1980s.
Attractive small-sized books for intermediate readers, paper over boards, illustrated. Includes biographical data about author and illustrator. Most titles are international juvenile classics, such as Grimm, Aesop, and Andersen.

Col. Jardín de Infancia. Barcelona, Spain: Editorial Juventud, 1960s.
Paperback, stapled picture books, small size. For preschool and first grade children. Simple stories about everyday life, folklore, or fantasy. Illustrations on every page. The ABC book is especially popular with children and parents. Preschool–4.

Col. Juvenil Alfaguara. Madrid: Ediciones Alfaguara, 1978–1985.
Reader-sized paperbacks, good paper, nicely sized type, very attractive layout. Lots of black-and-white illustrations. On a higher reading level than *Col. Infantil Alfaguara*. Prices range from $5.00 to $9.00 depending on number of pages. Evidently intended for Spanish teenage readers; U.S. reading level ranges from Grade 5 to adult. Sample authors: Maria Gripe, Francoise Sautereau, Mary Norton, Upton Sinclar, Gerald Durrell, Ruben Caba, Richard Hughes, Tove Jansson, Robert Graves, Roald Dahl, Peter Hartling, and Michael Ende.

Col. Kukurukú. Barcelona, Spain: Editorial Juventud, 1970s.
Picture books for children, attractive illustrations on every page, assorted styles. Varying types of texts, some easy to read, some longer, to be read to children. Simple children's adventures or folktales for preschool storytelling, or third or fourth grade readers. Requires fluency in Spanish, as the vocabulary is not watered down. Paper over boards, Spanish-style binding. Full color illustrations. Grades K–4.

Col. Letras. México: Editorial Terra Nova, 1982.
Paperback anthologies of literature for children by Hispanic authors. The Mexican volume contains poems, nursery rhymes, folklore, and folktales, in addition to short stories. The Latin American volume consists of short stories, and includes a glossary of Latin American words not usual in Mexican usage. Illustrated with black-and-white drawings, one per story. Good for supplementary reading for older children in bilingual classes, or for recreational reading. Attractive full color covers, approximately 142p., good paper, glued spines. Will probably need binding. Grade 5 and up.

Col. Let's read about science books in Spanish. New York: Crowell, 1960s.
Fairly good translations, books match the English books in format and binding. Library binding available. third or fourth grade level. Nonfiction science book for beginners translated from the English *Let's Read and Find Out Science Books* series.

Col. Leyendas Mexicanas. Mexico: Novaro, 1980s.
This series of folktales, myths, and legends from Mexico has no official series name from the publisher, but all the books are published in the same format and are being advertised by some distributors as a series. Published in conjunction with CONAP, under the patronage of the former first lady of Mexico, this is an official effort to provide Mexican children with beautiful editions of their cultural and folkloric heritage. Many of the titles contain stories collected early in the century by early Mexican folklorists and have been out of print since the 1930s; others are historical fiction set in the previous century in Colonial Mexico. In spite of some English or other European sounding author names, all of the titles are original Spanish works. The illustrations are for the most part by illustrious Mexican artists, the paper is good, and the binding is done in the United States. Oversize picture storybook style. Grade 4 and up.

Col. Un libro de la fresa. Barcelona, Spain: Juventud, 1970s.
Translated from Richard Hefter's popular English "Strawberry" books. Good translations, paperback format, bright colors, identical to English editions except for binding. For preschoolers or beginning grades.

Un libro de imaginación. Caracas, Venezuela: Litexsa Venezolana, 1981.
The illustrations by Pam Adams in this series of preschool picture books are cut-outs that imply one thing from one side of the brightly colored page, but reveal something else when the page is turned. (Similar to her version of *I Know an Old Lady*). Very popular with young children. The cut-outs need to be covered with transparent tape to survive library use. Translated from English-language originals. 30–32p.

Col. Los libros de los colores. Barcelona, Spain: La Galera, 1970s.
Translated from Catalan with illustrations by various artists. Each individual book centers on one of the primary colors, or on black and white (with references to skin colors in that book). Spanish binding (paper over boards). Beautiful books covering the concept and artistic

applications of color. Very good concept books for preschool children. Grades 3–5.

Col. Libros de la florecita. Buenos Aires, Argentina: Ediciones de la Flor, S.R.L., 1970s, 1980s.

Small-size paperback picture books and picture storybooks, illustrated in color by Juan Marchesi. The works published are either translations of international classics or by local Argentine authors. Some titles are better than others; those by Argentine or Latin authors are culturally relevant. The others have good translations, but some don't fit in with U.S. children's reading habits. Grades 4 and up.

Col. Libros de oro del saber. Mexico, Editorial Novaro, 1970s.

Spanish translations of *Golden Books of Knowledge* (Western Publishing Co., U.S.A.). Some titles are by Dr. Herbert Zim, some are adaptations from Time-Life paperbacks. Good translations. Many color illustrations and indexes are included. Grades 4–6.

Col. Lumen series of juvenile picture books. Barcelona, Spain: Lumen, 1970s.

This series lacks a formal name, but is usually advertised in distributors' catalogs as a series. Oversize picture books translated from established European authors of children's literature. Very high quality illustrations. The sizes and prices of the individual titles vary and the illustrations vary in style, but the artistic and literary quality of these books remains constant. Picture storybooks to be read to primary grade children, or to be read by third or fourth graders. Some are available in identical English versions (by different publishers).

Serie Margarita cuenta cuentos. México: Editorial Trillas, 1983.

Medium-sized square paperback picture books for young children, ranging from preschool to third or fourth grade. Stapled, 24 pages, color illustrations. Age recommendations given on each book. Texts by Margarita Heuer, the Mexican author and official library storyteller for the Mexican Ministry of Education. Illustrated by various Mexican artists.

Mi primera biblioteca básica. Barcelona, Spain: Molino, 1971.

Small non-fiction introductory books for lower grade children. Translated from the MacDonald & Company series. Paper over boards binding, 31 pages with color illustrations. Very popular with children, but some of the scientific data may be out of date by now.

Col. Mini-libros. San Jose, CA: Editorial Almaden (Col. Mini-libros), 1970s.

Written and published locally by Ernesto Galarza. Small paperback books written especially for California's Spanish-speaking children. Humorous poetry that blends the Anglo and Latin cultures. Very good for language and vocabulary development. Format is not as attractive as some mass produced books; one must look beyond the format to see the real value of the contents. Best titles are the nursery rhyme and poetry ones (some bilingual), some of which are based on familiar English Mother Goose rhymes, while preserving the rhythm of the Spanish language. (Much better than *Mother Goose in Spanish.*) Preschool–4.

Mis primeros libros de imágenes. Barcelona, Spain: Juventud, 1983.
Text and illustration by Helen Oxenbury. Small picture books translated
from the English titles published by Walker Books. Paper over boards
binding with color illustrations. Preschool–1 or 2.

Col. Naraciones Indígenas. Caracas, Venezuela: Ekaré-Banco del
Libro, 1978, 1980s.
A beautiful collection of genuine native folktales from Venezuela, with
bright, attractive illustrations on every page that bring the stories to life
with all the local features that make them interestingly different. Trick-
ster tales and local nature myths. Caribbean vocabulary. Color and
black-and-white illustrations.

Col. Nuestro barrio. Madrid: Ediciones Altea, 1980.
A new series of concept books in picture book style, specifically designed
to sell to the American market. The stories are written to formula; some
of the children go to public school, some to private school. Each of the
families portrayed represents a different lifestyle (single parent family,
working class family, extended family, etc.) The children encompass
different races; one child has a physical handicap. The educational
background of the families also varies (a laborer, a biologist, a press
photographer, a professional sports figure, a nurse, etc.) "The purpose of
this series is to help the young reader integrate himself into the real
world in which he lives, which presupposes acceptance, respect and
understanding of others." The plots are rather slim and could not be
considered "literature," but the books could be used to support social
studies concepts. Also published in English in England. Grades 3–5.

Col. Panorama. Barcelona, Spain: Juventud, 1980s.
Translated from French. A series of picture books intended to develop
the child's vocabulary by covering individual themes in depth; the sea,
shops, transportation, forests, nature, plants, and animals are all covered.
Much detail, good for vocabulary development. Items discussed are
named and identified in the illustrations. Grades 3–5.

Col. Piñata. México: Editorial Patria. [Uruguay 25-2 piso, México,
D.F.], 1981.
10,000 copies printed. A nonfiction picture book series for beginning
readers. Includes several subseries: "El Medio Ambiente," "Las Artes,"
and "La Flora." Paper over boards, full-page color illustrations based on
Aztec motifs. Bibliographic data on end papers in some titles. Illustrations are by well-known Mexican artists, reflecting Mexican culture and
history. Texts are all based on themes in Mexican life, such as crafts,
foods, and clothing. (One title, *El Universo,* is scientifically inaccurate
and not recommended.) Grades 3–4. Series is highly recommended.

Col. Ponte poronte. Caracas, Venezuela: Ekaré-Banco del Libro,
1980s.
Paperback picture books based on Latin American children's daily life,
or on folklore. Some titles have miniature copy of book as toy. Well
illustrated, attractive layout, color illustrations. Grades 3–6.

Col. "El Por qué." Madrid: Plesa, 1982.
Oversize nonfiction books for middle grade children. Translated from English versions published by Usborne Publishing Co., England, in 1981. Basic introductions to the world around us through many color illustrations and including one paragraph of text per picture. Paperback, 32p., index. Grades 4 and up.

Col. Prism press books. Detroit, MI: Blaine-Ethridge Books.
Bilingual children's books published in the U.S. Translations are not idiomatic Spanish. Format of binding is superior, but type is photocopied typewriter print. Illustrations are inferior, plots quite bad. A few titles are acceptable, but most are poor. Designed for middle grade and upper grade children. Best title is *Alberto and His Missing Sock.*

Col. Rimas y Adivinanzas. Caracas, Venezuela: Ekaré-Banco del Libro, 1980.
Small picture books with rhyming texts, some paperback, some paper-over-boards hardback. Some titles better than others. Texts are Hispanic-related folklore or classics of juvenile literature. Nice layout and illustrations, including an emphasis on having culturally relevant skin colors.

Col. La ruta del sol. Barcelona, Spain: La Galera, 1970s.
An excellent introduction to the seasons of the year for lower grade children. These books are available in two editions, one with individual books for each season, and one with the four seasons together. Preschool–3.

Scholastic Books in Spanish. New York: Scholastic Book Services, 1970, 1980.
Popular English-language picture books translated into very good Spanish by Argentina Palacios. Preschool–3.

Col. Una series de libros para niños a partir de 3 años. Madrid: Interduc-Schroedel, 1978.
Small-size concept books for preschool children. Simply illustrated with bright primary colors, one or two lines of text per page. Develops vocabulary and ideas about self and surroundings, including anatomically correct body image. Very poor bindings should be treated as paperbacks. Translated by Arturo Ruiz from Swedish. Preschool–K.

Col. Sorpresas. Barcelona, Spain: Juventud, 1980s.
Katy y Martin, 32p., hardback. Small-sized humorous concept books for preschoolers. Very attractive simple colored drawings with text to encourage vocabulary and concept development. Preschool–2.

Col. Teo descubre el mundo. Barcelona, Spain: Editorial Timun Mas, 1970s, 1980.
Large-size picture books, double spread illustrations with one paragraph of text to each double spread. Two pages at end of book are a "Guia Didactica para padres y educadores" that explains the principal points of interest of each of the illustrations. Both preschool and kindergarten levels of difficulty. Attractive books to expand a child's vocabulary and understanding of the world. Grades 3–5.

Col. Tina Ton. Barcelona, Spain: Juventud, 1980s.
Eleven small paperbacks for 3- to 6-year-olds, written and illustrated by Pia Vilarrubias. Textless picture books encourage thinking processes and vocabulary development, a first step in learning to read and write. Each book includes a vocabulary development game to cut out, with instructions to the adult (parent or teacher) for using the book and game with the child. Teacher's manual *Orientacion pedagogica para padres y maestros* also available. Paperback, 28p. Preschool–2.

Col. Títeres. Barcelona, Spain: Juventud, 1970s.
Spanish versions of Catalan originals. Small-size, colorful pictures on every other page, small amounts of easy-to-read text. Stories based on everyday children's adventures, or fantasy. Well liked by young children who are beginning readers in Spanish. Grades 1–3.

Col. Tom e Irene. Barcelona, Spain: Juventud, 1970s.
Translated from Alain Gree's French. Series based on a boy and a girl's discoveries in the world around them, introduces children to science, math, measurement, etc. Grades 3–5.

Col. Vela Mayor. Barcelona, Spain: La Galera, 1978.
Texts by Ricardo Alcantara Sgarb. NOT RECOMMENDED DUE TO STEREOTYPED PLOTS, CHARACTERIZATIONS, AND CULTURAL REPRESENTATIONS. (See review in *Lector*, 1, (4), June 1983, p. 18.) This series, an attempt to expose Spanish children to ethnic diversity, is an example of subconscious stereotyped views expressing themselves in otherwise beautiful picture books.

Col. Ya sé leer. Barcelona, Spain: La Galera.
Small-sized hardback easy-to-read books for beginning readers. Text is in Spanish-style script. Nicely illustrated. Concept books, folktales, nursery rhymes. Good for storytelling for preschoolers and primary grade children. K–6.

Col. Zafiro. Barcelona, Spain: Ediciones Susaeta, n.d.
Large, thin oversize paperbacks, lavishly illustrated, of favorite fairy tales in Spanish versions. No authors, compilers, or sources named. In some of the books the artist is named. Attractive to children because of the colorful, bright illustrations. May be out of print. Grades 4–6. Sample titles: *Aladino, La Bella Durmiente, La Casita de Chocolate (Hansel and Gretel), Pulgarcito.*

Classification and Cataloging of Spanish-Language Children's Materials

R. Cecilia Knight

With the move towards collecting more Spanish-language juvenile materials comes the need to provide access to these materials through cataloging and classification. This chapter provides a brief description of some of the special problems involved and how to resolve them.

CLASSIFICATION

In the Library of Congress Classification System, Spanish-language juvenile *belles lettres* are classed in the PZ70s. More subject-specific works are classed with the subject area. In the Dewey Decimal Classification System such works are classed as fiction where appropriate, or by subject.

Many libraries choose to use separate children's literature classifications in order to separate these works from the rest of the collection and keep them in one location. Since in most libraries the classification number serves largely as a location device, almost any designation that will group these items so as to give ready access to them is acceptable.

DESCRIPTIVE CATALOGING

The same difficulties faced in cataloging any Spanish-language materials are faced in cataloging Spanish-language juvenile materials. A number of basic technical problems are involved.

1. **Establishing Edition and Dates.** Often edition statements are actually printing statements. When it is clearly printed inside the book that eight editions have been published over a two-year time span, it is fairly easy to decide that these are really separate printings rather than actual new editions. When the only information appearing on the piece is a reference to its being the fifth edition, along with either a single date or the date of legal deposit, then it is a bit more difficult to determine the relationship of the item to any other "edicion" of the same work. ISBNs are often lacking, but when included usually remain constant through all of the editions/printings, even though these may otherwise appear to be new editions.

2. **Establishing Names and Responsibility.** It is helpful to determine the author's nationality and the place of publication before deciding on the proper form of his or her name, since spellings are changed from country to country; e.g., Josep vs. Jose, and Wensel vs. Wensell. When in doubt or confused, check to see if the work has been published elsewhere or if the author has published other books. Also, abbreviations may be used, such as Ma. for Maria. As with any language, certain names have standard abbreviations. Authors will also on occasion latinize their names when publishing works in Spanish to make them more recognizable and acceptable to a Spanish-speaking audience. This is quite difficult to recognize unless there is an indication that the work is a translation.

   Authors (or publishers) are sometimes inconsistent about the form of name used; e.g., Monserrat del Amo vs. Monserrat del Amo y Gili. The first challenge is determining whether the same person is being referred to; the second is in deciding on the correct form of the name in accordance with AACR2. Most of the popular children's authors and illustrators are in the Library of Congress' Name Authority List and in the On-Line Name Authority files.

3. **Choice of Access Points.** This is more a problem of children's books in general, rather than a difficulty faced specifically in Spanish-language cataloging. Some children's literature publishers feel that the title graphics and the cover and title page illustrations are more important for marketing purposes than is the name of the author. Therefore, authors' names are often placed in inconspicuous locations on the item. Their names, along with the illustrator's, may be found at the bottom corner of the cover or on the verso of the title page above the publisher's information. It is quite clear in most cases that a person whose name appears in such a location, even if in small print, is responsible for a

particular work of literature. The rules in AACR2 stating that statements of responsibility must appear prominently must sometimes be stretched. If the verso of the title page states: "Idea y texto de Ulises Wensel," then, even though it is in very small type, it is quite clear that this is the author.

4. **Series.** Almost every Spanish-language book is published within some series; juvenile books are no exception. Items may be published by different publishers in their own series; a children's book may also be published by the same publisher in more than one series at different times. When collecting series sets it is therefore important to ascertain that the titles have not already been ordered or obtained as part of other series. In cataloging, it is important to be aware that the numbering of a book within a series is often located only on the spine of the book. The decision to trace (cross-reference books within a series) varies from library to library. The Library of Congress has not dealt with many of these series; guidance for cataloging is therefore not available from that source.

5. **Subject Access.** Juvenile cataloging requires a summary of the item. The summary is written in English, so the cataloger/summarizer need not be fluent in Spanish. (This can, however, certainly be seen as a disadvantage for primarily Spanish-literate consumers choosing reading material for themselves or their children.). Much information can be picked up from the illustrations. However, the moral or other central aspects of the story can be missed or misinterpreted using this method. One instance of this was a book that had been translated from Dutch to Spanish, and the Dutch name of a character, unpronounceable in Spanish, had been changed to "Miffy." The book had very little text, but the illustrations were clearly about a birthday. The character was a rabbit and its sex was not readily apparent from visual information about its appearance or the gifts it received. The summarizer, coming from an English-language perspective, wrote about a little girl rabbit (since the name "Miffy" sounded female), but from the text it was clear that Miffy was a little boy rabbit.

Subject headings are also primarily in English. One provision in the Library of Congress Subject Headings for Children's Literature is: *Spanish language materials*, a heading to be used for basic children's reading materials in Spanish. *Spanish language materials—Bilingual* is to be used when the item is in Spanish and another language. Also, a source is available to aid in establishing Spanish-language headings if desired. The Library of Congress has approved the use of Spanish-language subject headings from *Bilindex:*

A Bilingual Spanish-English Subject Heading List: Spanish Equivalents to Library of Congress Subject Headings (Oakland, CA: California Spanish Language Data Base, 1984). This book includes a section on "Library of Congress Subject Headings for Children's Literature with Spanish Equivalents." (This work also provides some guidance on name authority work.) *Bilindex* is aimed at the English-language-speaking cataloguer of Spanish-language materials.

The problems described here are situations commonly faced by catalogers. As the emphasis on Spanish-language juvenile materials increases and individual libraries feel the need for better access, the problems of English-language summaries and subject headings should decrease. These issues are being recognized and addressed by such tools as *Bilindex*. The rest of the difficulties mentioned here are part of the challenge of cataloging; trying to solve the puzzle of who wrote and/or published what, when, and where.

Strategies for Involving Children in Reading Literature

Sarah Barchas

How can we involve children in reading literature? The answer is basically simple and twofold. First, we must make literature come alive for young people by making it so inviting, enticing, and exciting that they will not want to resist it. Second, we must offer a rich variety of literature meeting the full range of interest and ability needs, and provide access to effectively utilize the literature through an inviting, attractive physical environment, and a welcoming, vibrant, stimulating emotional and intellectual climate.

If young people's association with literature is that of work and frustration, if reading is penalized with never-ending reports, a profusion of questions and answers, lack of choice, and tests, tests, tests, then how can one expect them to seek out literature and make reading a lifetime habit? Literature can and must be associated with enjoyment, pleasure, and vitality. Sharing literature can be a genuine means of reinforcing sense of self and sense of community with others.

In order for children to become involved in reading literature, certain strategies evolve as a natural focus. There must be modeling of enthusiasm by a significant adult. Effective reading aloud by an adult should be part of every day. Storytelling can create magic, motivation, and memorability. Dramatization can bring the reading to life and help children create personal connectedness with literature. Booktalks can meet and extend interests and broaden acquaintance with literature. Use of syntactic pattern materials—poetry, songs and stories with repeated language patterns—can ensure predictability and success. Time, interest, and effort must be given to help individuals make the "right match." Enticing displays can activate interest. Resource speakers can stretch interests with tie-ins to literature. First, last, and throughout must be creation of a positive climate for sharing.

MODELING OF ENTHUSIASM

Most learning is acquired through imitation. Children imitate and acquire the attitudes, habits, and values of those adults who are important to them; who are, in Sullivan's terms (1947), "significant others." We as teachers and librarians should seek to be significant others to the young people with whom we have contact. If our interactions with them are genuinely caring, nurturing, and mutually respecting, we can become significant others for them. When that is so, our attitudes can have a very real impact on their lives.

As librarians and as teachers we must model a love of reading. We must show genuine excitement and delight in books that we share with children. We must read aloud or tell stories or do booktalks that we truly enjoy ourselves, motivating our young people by the genuine enthusiasm we feel.

Enthusiasm is contagious. When we share stories, books, poems, and songs that we and the children can enjoy, that are *fun*, that stimulate our thinking, stretch our awareness, and touch our wellspring of deep feelings, the enthusiasm engendered is a most positive source of contagion. It is indeed well worth catching and passing on!

No matter what pedagogical technique is used, it is the teacher—his or her attitude, enthusiasm, and interaction—that is most important. It stands to reason that if literature is exciting to you, and if the children find you a person of interest and value who matters to them, you will transmit your love of literature to them by your modeling of the enthusiasm you show.

READING ALOUD TO CHILDREN

Reading aloud to children every day is the most helpful thing that librarians and teachers can do to instill the love of reading in them. That is true not only for young children. It is true for *all* children.

Trelease (1985, p. 6), in his acclaimed *Read-Aloud Handbook*, writes: "In concentrating exclusively on teaching the child *how* to read, we have forgotten to teach him to *want* to read. There is the key: desire. It is the prime mover, the magic ingredient....Somehow we lost sight of the teaching precept: What you make a child love and desire is more important than what you make him learn."

Sharing literature aloud brings delight not only to the children, but to the librarian or teacher as well. It is one of the most enjoyable and fulfilling aspects of being a librarian. Together you have shared group experiences that can provide warmth and enjoyment, as well as respect for each other and for the written word and the language of literature. You entice children to step into the shoes of others, leading them to respond to adventure, suspense, excitement, humor, fear, sadness, struggle, and triumph evoked by characters and events in the story. Together you explore the multifaceted sounds and shapes and imagery of language, the rich vocabulary, the visual images, the turns of phrase, and the implied structures of stories. Together you participate in stories that have repeated patterns of language that children can anticipate and naturally want to say with you. Together you can find that one book leads to another in an endless linking of enjoyment, exploration, and growth.

Attractive illustrated picture story books have tremendous appeal for young children. How can they resist the grotesque enchantment of *Where the Wild Things Are* (Sendak, 1963), and the warmth of *Mother, Mother, I Want Another* (Polushkin, 1978). They delight in the sounds of language evoked in *Tikki Tikki Tembo* (Mosel, 1968), and bring laughter to the ridiculous in *The Stupids Die* (Allard, 1981). Yet many picture story books are for a wide span of ages. Older children will enjoy humor and anticipation in *The Riddle of the Drum* (Aardema, 1979), imagination and rich imagery in *The Unicorn and the Lake* (Mayer, 1982), intriguing sophistication in *Jumanji* (Van Allsburg, 1981), and surprise in *Do Not Open* (Turkle, 1981). They will be touched by the distressing possibility of truth in *The Last Free Bird* (Stone, 1967).

The reading aloud of longer books can have much impact. Children are charmed by the humor of *Ramona the Pest* (Cleary, 1968), *Tales of a Fourth Grade Nothing* (Blume, 1972), and *Sideways Stories of Wayside School* (Sachar, 1978). They delight in the intriguing predicaments of *How to Eat Fried Worms* (Rockwell, 1973) and *Freaky Friday* (Rodgers, 1972). They are entranced by the fantasy worlds of *Charlotte's Web* (White, 1952), *The Lion, The Witch and the Wardrobe* (Lewis, 1968), and *Crystal Child* (Wersba, 1982). They are much moved by the real inner struggles and growth in *The Pinballs* (Byars, 1977), *Bridge to Terabithia* (Paterson, 1977) and *Stone Fox* (Gardiner, 1980).

Reading aloud is important for *all* children of all ages and backgrounds. Yet for children who might be perceived by some as "reluctant readers" because of lack of language fluency and lack of motivation due to lack of success, reading aloud is crucial. It sparks interest; extends language fluency in vocabulary, syntax and sentence structure; invites participation and involvement; and promotes a community of sharing that helps build a climate of success.

The sharing of English-language literature even for non-English-speaking children can be aided by extra expressiveness on the part of the teacher in showing excitement, anger, fear, suspense, humor, and joy. Using hand and body expressiveness to dramatize the reading aloud can add to understanding of vocabulary, concepts, and expressions. Reading aloud can help change reluctance into willingness because a particular book can so captivate particular children that they need to make it their own by reading it themselves after the adult has shared it.

The librarian/teacher reading aloud must model effective reading aloud techniques. There must be expressiveness and animation in the voice, with variety and range in tone and volume. The voice must project well so that all can hear, and the pace should be comfortable and natural, neither too fast nor too slow. There must be familiarity with the material and commitment to it. There must be effective handling of the book, showing pictures when appropriate, and good eye contact with the listeners. Timing is important, using effective pauses and knowing when to stop to build suspense for the next reading. Reading aloud can be a joyful time for the children and the librarian or teacher, and a sure way to involve children in reading literature.

STORYTELLING

Storytelling can create an atmosphere of magic with children. It is the oldest art of communication and entertainment. That art need not and must not be lost. The attention of the children is riveted on the storyteller through direct eye contact and expressiveness. The child listener enters the world of the story as the storyteller internalizes it, personalizes it, and brings it to life through voice, facial, and hand expressiveness. Very often children become directly involved in the telling by participating in repeated phrases and actions, and even dramatization afterwards. Storytelling is an extraordinarily effective tool for leading children to literature.

If possible, the storyteller should always share or show the source of the story before telling it. Afterward, when interest is so keenly whetted, a written version of that story, or others related in some way to it, should be made available to children so that they can be involved in further literature.

The story "Soap, Soap, Soap" is a delightfully humorous Appalachian folk story of a boy who copied what was said by others and got himself into trouble when that inappropriate copying was applied to each new situation. Exaggerating his foolishness with facial expressions and body language in the telling is sure to bring laughter and enjoyment. The storytelling can then lead to children's involvement in more literature in the reading of that story and others in *Grandfather Tales* (Chase, 1948), the reading of other Appalachian stories and other stories collected by the same author, and the reading of other stories in which a character does not use his head.

The Mexican folktale of "The Giant and the Rabbit" is ideal for telling. A man's wife is kidnapped by a giant, but who threatens to eat her. Several strong and fearsome animals try to help the man by fighting the giant, but to no avail; yet a tiny rabbit, by using his wits and humor, wins the woman's safety. Children of a wide span of ages can enjoy that story and then be led to read it and other stories from its source, *Tales the People Tell in Mexico* (Lyons, 1972). They can read other stories from Mexico and Hispanic culture; and other stories about giants or about rabbits; other stories about how a powerful force for evil is outwitted by a seemingly weak yet clever creature; and other stories about unusual ways of using one's head.

Through storytelling, children can become involved in seeing how stories change in many variants, and explore the differences between them. *The Riddle of the Drum* (Aardema, 1979) and "The Prince" (Hayes, 1982) are both stories of Hispanic culture which have many aspects in common yet some distinct differences in details. Children can become fascinated by both tellings and discuss the differences and similarities. They then can become involved in reading more literature of stories that have changed, with variants in different cultures, as with the more than 300 variants of the Cinderella theme.

Storytelling is such an important means of involving children in literature that it must not be neglected. The librarian or teacher should feel that a story need not be memorized, but only visualized in sequence, with strategic patterns of language and vivid or important phrases memorized. One must love the story and read it aloud to oneself many times to make it one's own. Then it becomes a gift to share with group after group, class after class, year after year. Often those stories told are the ones children want to hear time and time again for listening enjoyment, participation, dramatization, and becoming involved in further reading of literature.

DRAMATIZATION OF LITERATURE

Dramatization often follows as a spontaneous natural outgrowth of the sharing aloud of many simple picture story books and the storytelling of folktales. When children love a story, they often ask to be able to "act it out." Story dramatization can take many forms. During a first reading aloud by the adult, young children will often want to pantomime a story. If the dialogue is simple and has repeated phrases, they will want to act it out, saying the repeated spoken dialogue. Older children will enjoy drawing from a story and improvising dialogue to personalize it.

What more natural way is there to share a story like "The Enormous Turnip" than for young children to help pantomime it with the first reading or telling, with everyone pretending to help pull on the turnip? Afterward, children can be chosen to each take a part and improvise dialogue, following in cumulative sequence as grandfather calls on grandmother who calls on the boy, girl, dog, cat, mouse, and perhaps even a little beetle to help pull the turnip from the ground. All pull together and finally fall down on top of each other, to child laughter and delight. Many other stories for young children, like "Little Red Hen" and *Caps for Sale* (Slobodkina, 1947) beg for dramatization.

What more delightful way is there to follow up a story like "Soap, Soap, Soap" (Chase, 1948) or *Master of all Masters* (Jacobs, 1972) than to spontaneously and informally dramatize such stories afterward? The special vitality given to literature through children connecting it with their lives, adding their bits of humor and ways of perceiving, is a joyful experience. It will not make for a silent library or classroom. The room will abound with rollicking laughter, good for the souls of children, teachers, librarians, and schools.

Almost any folktale or tightly paced, action-packed picture story book can be dramatized with children acting, pantomiming, or improvising. Almost any folktale can be modified in acting, giving another version which children might delight in creating. Puppetry can effectively be used with younger children and by older children for younger children. Reader's theater is still another way of dramatizing, through reading dialogue and narrative parts in stories with several characters. In each of these ways of dramatizing, the literature is given zest, vitality, and personalization as children take ownership of it, read it, share it, and delight in making it their own.

BOOKTALKS

Booktalks are an important strategy for involving young people in literature. Booktalks can be a means of sharing a greater number and wider variety of books than either reading aloud of whole books or storytelling. Essentially, booktalks are teasers, attempts to entice and motivate interest. In booktalks, the teacher/librarian gives a brief summary, telling just enough to whet appetite in reading the book, yet not so much as to give the resolution of the plot away. The interested child listeners then feel they must read the book to find out what happens next. Often one or two tantalizing passages are read aloud to enhance interest.

Booktalks can center around a single theme and include a variety of fiction and/or nonfiction books on that theme. Such themes as sibling rivalry, growing-up problems, divorce, death, animals, fantasy, and mystery are all possibilities. Basically any potential theme for a story hour could be a theme for a booktalk session, except that a larger number and variety of books could be shared. One booktalk session could be on the new books that have come into the library, books which spark interest because of both their content and their newness!

Booktalks can be motivators for all ages. Even picture story books could be sources for booktalks. However, booktalks are most effective for intermediate and upper grade students who need broadening of their acquaintance with a wide variety of books. Booktalks can be very important for reluctant readers, tying in with their interests and readability, motivating them to *want* to read, showing many books they *can* read that can offer both success and enjoyment for them.

By introducing a wide variety of books and exploring books around certain themes, booktalks are a very important means of meeting and extending interests. We must always take children where they are and then help lead them to explore, in the interest of their continued growth. Booktalks can create new interests, whet appetites, and introduce new sights and sounds, new places, new faces, new shoes to step into, and new vistas to view, taste, and ponder.

In her useful resource book, *Books Kids Will Sit Still For* (1984, p.10), Freeman writes of the importance of diversity both in ways of sharing and in the content of the sharing. She advocates, "Vary the fare, alternating from booktalking to reading single chapters and entire books of all genres. Even the best books get monotonous if you stick to just one type. Try some historical, some hysterical, a pinch of sci-fi, a sip of fantasy, a soupçon of mystery, and an adventure or two. Stretch your students and yourself as well."

SYNTACTIC PATTERN LITERATURE

All literature has syntax, but when the structure has repeated patterns of language, it is of special value for young children and reluctant readers. In order to feel success and gain greater language fluency, the reluctant reader and the young reader must be able to understand the flow of language and meanings, and anticipate the basic structure and content. When children can easily recognize and predict the repeated pattern of language and of meanings, then they know they can succeed. They can feel free to enjoy and participate because they are not threatened. They want to try, and will then do so both individually and in groups. The language flow becomes their own.

Syntactic pattern literature need not be artificial, but can be found in the vitality and enjoyment of real literature that has repeated phrases, repeated sequences, cumulative phrases, and predictable sequences of action. It is found in many nursery stories and folktales, and many simple stories, poems, chants, and songs. In the old nursery tales, children love to participate in the tellings or readings whenever repeated phrases and patterns occur. In "The Gingerbread Man," children join in the cumulative passages as the gingerbread man runs away from the old woman, the old man, and many others, to the repeated refrain of "Run, run, as fast as you can, you can't catch me, I'm the Gingerbread Man."

In the utterly delightful story, "La Hormiguita," retold by Hayes (1982), children join in with laughter and enthusiasm as the little ant calls on many creatures and forces in cumulative Spanish phrases to create the action needed to release his foot from the snow, ending with "Nieve, suelta mi patita pa que vaya a mi casita!" The repeated cumulative sequences and exaggerated telling make the story of "La Hormiguita" irresistible for Hispanic children.

Other charming nursery/folktales with repeated syntax of much appeal include "The Little Red Hen," "The Three Bears," "The Three Pigs," "Chicken Little," and "The Enormous Turnip." Yet even more sophisticated folktales abound in repeated sequences and phrases, as in the tantalizing verses in *Strega Nona* (de Paola, 1975), and the humorous, cumulative sequence of names in *The Riddle of the Drum* (Aardema, 1979).

For young children, many enticing picture story books have simple, repeated language patterns with predictable phrases, structures, and content. In *Just Like Daddy* (Asch, 1981) a little bear reveres his father and does everything just like daddy until a surprise ending reinforces the role of mom. *The Chick and The Duckling* (Ginsburg, 1972) charmingly shows a chick wanting to copy a duck even to the point of almost drowning as he uses the repeated phrase of "Me too" until the duck decides to go into the water again. By such opportunities for successful participation, young children are drawn naturally to reading.

POETRY AND CHANTS

Poetry sings. The imagery and sound of poetry; the predictability of rhythm and rhyme; the effective use of repetition of phrase, sound, and idea all provide means for children to feel successful and take delight in language, literature, and sharing. Many of a child's first experiences with poetry are through nursery rhymes with strong rhythm and rhyme, zest and humor, brief story-type sequences, and repeated phrases. Books of rhymes and chants can include *Brown Bear, Brown Bear* (Martin, 1967), *Comic Adventures of Old Mother Hubbard and Her Dog* (de Paola, 1981), and *Mother Goose's Nursery Rhymes* (Atkinson, 1984). In Spanish are the rhymes of *Canciones Tontas* (Bayley, 1982), the chants of Schon's *Doña Blanca* (1983), and the repeated verse patterns of *No Me Asusto a Mi* (Goss & Harste, 1984).

Who can resist Shel Silverstein's poem, "Boa Constrictor" (in *Where the Sidewalk Ends*, 1974)? Enticingly repulsive, the boa constrictor works its way up the body. Children delight in the suspense and fun of dramatization and the success and group spirit they enjoy in orally participating in the shared simulated fear evoked by:

"Oh no, it's nibbling my toe.
Oh gee, it's up to my knee.
Oh my, it's up to my thigh..."

Poetry sharing can lead to participation of all the children in unison with the adult leader. Sometimes choral reading where children read alternating verses can be an enjoyable means of reading and sharing poems together. Strong sources are *The Random House Book of Poetry* (Prelutsky, 1983), *Where the Sidewalk Ends* (Silverstein, 1974), *The Light in the Attic* (Silverstein, 1981), *The Poetry Troupe* (Wilner, 1977), *Honey, I Love, and Other Love Poems* (Greenfield, 1978), and some chants from *Apples on a Stick* (Michels & White, 1983), and many others. When poetry is shared in a context of fun, *all* children can enjoy it.

SONG

Song is a very strong, positive, and universal way of bringing people together in a community of shared response. All peoples have song as part of their culture. All children respond to song. Song is a form of literature with added dimensions of melody and rhythm. Songs inherently have repetition of syntax, predictability in flow of language and idea, and the structure provided by repeated choruses and related verses.

Many books have been published that combine song lyrics with attractive illustrations. These books can naturally and easily promote successful reading for young children and reluctant readers, as well as being enjoyable for all readers. When acquainted with the song first by singing it or hearing it sung, and participating using charts or big books to read the lyrics easily and naturally, the child feels immediate success and ease in predictability while reading and singing the book.

Humorous cumulative sequences are found in *There Was An Old Lady Who Swallowed a Fly* (Adams, 1975) and *Cat Goes Fiddle-e-Fee* (Galdone, 1985). Repeated syntax in logical progressive sequence combined with fun are found in *Hush Little Baby* (Zemach, 1976), *The Thirteen Days of Halloween* (Greene, 1983), and *Over in the Meadow* (Keats, 1971). *Pio, Pio* (Fernandez, 1983), with its zesty rhythm, rhyme, and humor, invites Spanish reading and singing. The collection of songs in the *Silly Song Book* (Nelson, 1981) is an excellent resource with many songs that have predictable language patterns combined with humor, vitality, and natural delight for children. Songs are a form of literature to which children respond naturally and enthusiastically.

MAKING THE RIGHT MATCH

We can do much to motivate children in groups and make literature exciting for them. Yet it must be realized that one of the most important things a librarian and teacher can do is to help children make the "right match" in their individual choices of books for recreational reading. The right match means a book that a particular child can truly enjoy at that time, a book that can matter to that child in some way. It means knowing children's interests generally, but also knowing an individual child's interests in particular. The right match means helping a child find a book that will be of keen enjoyment to read, or will meet a need.

Factors of readability are a consideration in making the right match. It is important that a child feel success in reading. Most choices for recreational reading should not be at a child's frustration level, but rather at a level where the reading flows easily with reasonable effort, and where neither the vocabulary nor the comprehension becomes an obstacle course.

It must be realized, however, that sometimes a child is drawn very strongly to a book because it answers a special interest or need for that child. If a child expresses strong interest or desire for a particular book, even if the teacher or librarian thinks it is too difficult or too easy, the child should be allowed to check out that book. It is very frustrating for a child to have his or her choice of book vetoed by a teacher. Extra effort will be given to reading even parts of a difficult book when there is high interest. Picture story books, though short, may have a rich vocabulary. Even simple books may fill a personal need.

The guidance of an adult knowing and caring about the interests and needs of a child can matter very much. It is always gratifying to help a child find exactly the kind of book he or she is looking for. When one finds a book that brings a smile and thanks from the child, that is what is meant by the "right match."

ENTICING DISPLAYS

Everyone needs stimuli. The classroom and the library must be alive with stimulation to involve children in reading literature. Something is needed to catch the eye, to surprise, attract, entice. One important means of providing such a stimulus is the use of displays: pictorial displays or displays of real objects, suggesting literature or surrounded by literature.

Bulletin boards can be set up with attractive use of book jackets, commercial posters, student-made posters, or pictures centering around a theme of special interest. If a striking bulletin board is set up at the time of Cinco de Mayo, reflecting Hispanic culture and supplemented by a table display of artifacts from Mexico and surrounded by such rich folklore sources as *The Day It Snowed Tortillas* (Hayes, 1982), *Tales the People Tell in Mexico* (Lyons, 1972), *Tales from Hispanic Lands* (Green, 1979), and *Stories That Must Not Die* (Sauvageau, 1984), those books will rapidly disappear from the table.

Materials made by students are especially valuable for display, so that children see that their contributions are valued. In sharing items inspired by craft books, such as paper airplanes, objects made from toothpicks and popsicle sticks, piñatas, and origami, children show they are taking ownership of the ideas in the books and applying them to their own lives. A display of student-made objects and the books that motivated them will be sure to extend interests and awareness and create eagerness by other children to try to do the same or similar activities.

RESOURCE SPEAKERS

Each individual needs something new and different to motivate awareness and promote growth. Other people can provide us with different ideas, understandings, and vicarious experiences. In the use of human resources, we can draw from awareness and appreciation of our own culture and extend awareness and understanding of others.

The librarian and teacher can draw from a wealth of human resources. Many persons in the neighborhood and community can be surprisingly strong sources. Many have special skills, interests, and experiences, and come from rich cultural traditions. We can broaden interests of young people in our classrooms and libraries when we tap the resources of the community.

In sharing careers; in sharing Hispanic traditions, arts, and skills; in promoting multicultural awareness; in extending appreciation of the arts, history, and science; we can draw from the gifts of sharing that can so easily be tapped if only we take time to seek them out. And always, there should be tie-in with books and literature. Before the speaker comes and after the speaker leaves, related books should be accessible to answer and extend the young person's awakened interest, involving the child in reading literature.

CREATING A POSITIVE CLIMATE

From the moment a child walks into a library or classroom, that child senses both a physical climate and an emotional and intellectual climate of response and interaction. That climate is not to be taken lightly. It is one of the crucial factors in building attitudes of association with books, reading, learning, libraries, and schools.

In his acclaimed book, *A Place Called School* (1984, pp. 242–243) Goodlad writes of the impact of the "flat, neutral emotional ambience" of most of the classes studied, and the emphasis on textbooks and workbooks rather than literature.

> Boredom is a disease of epidemic proportions....Why are our schools not places of joy?...One can see how the circumstances of schooling inhibit movement, small group work, and even overt expressions of joy, anger and other feelings. It is far more difficult to understand the relative paucity of vicarious experiences designed to connect students in some more passionate and compassionate way with the wholeness of human existence and especially with such existential qualities as hope, courage and love of humankind. These qualities are portrayed particularly through the humanities and especially through literature—myths and fairy tales, novels, drama and poetry.

As librarians and teachers, we recognize the many factors in a school or school system over which we have no control. Yet there are significant factors over which we *do* have control: the climate for learning and sharing that we create; the experiences, real and vicarious, that we provide; the activities we plan that can involve children and deal with the whole child rather than the "segmented child" decried by Goodlad; and the degree of intellectual stimulation and emotional fullness we evoke and allow.

The library must have an attractive, comfortable, inviting physical environment with a wide variety of books and materials and access to those materials. The library should be a warm, positive, welcoming place providing genuine service and intellectual stimulation. Of utmost importance, the librarian and teacher must genuinely care about young people and books and find joy in helping to bring the two together. Time must be provided for recreational reading of individual choice. Time must be created for frequent oral sharing of literature, expanding children's vicarious experiences and involving them in the riches of literature.

Perhaps in essence, the librarian and teacher must have an extra spark of energy, caring, interest, and willingness to give. Then libraries, classrooms, and schools need not be, in Goodlad's phrase, places of "emotional flatness." Rather, in the sharing of literature in ways that can bring it to life, libraries, literature, and schools can become avenues of vitality reflecting the full range of emotional response evoked by life itself, with joy, sorrow, laughter, excitement, conflict, struggle, and growth. In so doing, the librarian/teacher who models and creates the climate for sharing, can be a knowledgeable, nurturing, vibrant, and memorable force for involving children in literature.

REFERENCES

Professional Books

Baker, Augusta, & Ellin Green. (1977). *Storytelling: Art and technique*. New York: Bowker.

Bauer, Carolyn Feller. (1977). *Handbook for storytellers*. Chicago: American Library Association.

Carroll, Frances Laverne, & Mary Meacham. (1984). *Exciting, funny, scary, short, different and sad books kids like about animals, science, sports, families, songs and other things*. Chicago: American Library Association.

Cottrell, June. (1975). *Teaching with creative dramatics*. Skokie, IL: National Textbook Co.

DeRegniers, Beatrice Schenk. (1969). *Poems children will sit still for*. New York: Citation Press.

Elleman, Barbara. (Ed.) (1984). *Children's books of international interest*. Chicago: American Library Association (International Relations Committee).

Freeman, Judy. (1984). *Books kids will sit still for*. Hagerstown, MD: Alleyside Press.

Goodlad, John. (1984). *A place called school: Prospects for the future*. New York: McGraw-Hill.

Let's Read Together Revision Committee. (1981). *Let's read together. Books for family enjoyment*. Chicago: American Library Association.

Schon, Isabel. (1978). *Books in Spanish for children and young adults: An annotated guide*. Metuchen, NJ: Scarecrow Press.

Schon, Isabel. (1980). *A Hispanic heritage: A guide to juvenile books about Hispanic people and cultures*. Metuchen, NJ: Scarecrow Press.

Stewig, John, & Sam Sebasta. (1978). *Using literature in the elementary classroom*. Urbana, IL: National Council of Teachers of English.

Sullivan, Harry S. (1947). *Conceptions of modern psychiatry*. Washington, DC: William Allanson White Psychiatric Foundation.

Trelease, Jim. (1985). *The read-aloud handbook*. New York: Penguin.

Outstanding Picture Story Books

Aardema, Verna. (1979). *The riddle of the drum*. New York: Four Winds.

Allard, Harry. (1977). *Miss Nelson is missing*. New York: Houghton-Mifflin.

Allard, Harry. (1981). *The Stupids die*. New York: Houghton-Mifflin.

Bang, Mollie. (1985). *The paper crane*. New York: Greenwillow.

Bang, Mollie. (1976). *Wiley and the hairy man*. New York: Macmillan.

Brenner, Barbara. (1977). *Little one-inch*. New York: Coward, McCann & Geoghegan.

Carle, Eric. (1981). *The honeybee and the robber*. New York: Philomel.

de Paola, Tomie. (1975). *Strega Nona*. Englewood Cliffs, NJ: Prentice-Hall.

Gackenback, Dick. (1983). *Binky gets a car*. New York: Clarion.

Goble, Paul. (1978). *The girl who loved wild horses.* Scarsdale, NY: Bradbury.

Keats, Ezra Jack. (1963). *A snowy day.* New York: Viking.

Koshland, Ellen. (1970). *The magic lollipop.* New York: Knopf.

Lionni, Leo. (1966). *Frederick.* New York: Pantheon.

Lionni, Leo. (1960). *Inch by inch.* New York: Obolensky.

Lionni, Leo. (1963). *Swimmy.* New York: Pantheon.

Marshall, Edward. (1980). *Space case.* New York: Dial.

Mayer, Marianna. (1982). *The unicorn and the lake.* New York: Dial

Mayer, Mercer. (1968). *There's a nightmare in my closet.* New York: Dial.

Mosel, Arlene. (1968). *Tikki tikki tembo.* New York: Holt, Rinehart, & Winston.

Peck, Robert. (1976). *Hamilton.* Boston: Little, Brown.

Peet, Bill. (1967). *Buford, the little bighorn.* New York: Houghton-Mifflin.

Poluskin, Maria. (1978). *Mother, mother, I want another.* New York: Crown.

Sendak, Maurice. (1963). *Where the wild things are.* New York: Harper & Row.

Shulevitz, Uri. (1978). *The treasure.* New York: Farrar, Straus & Giroux.

Slobodkina, Esphyr. (1947). *Caps for sale.* New York: Scholastic.

Steig, William. (1969). *Sylvester and the magic pebble.* New York: Simon & Schuster.

Stone, A. Harris. (1967). *The last free bird.* Englewood Cliffs, NJ: Prentice-Hall.

Thaler, Mike. (1982). *Owly.* New York: Harper & Row.

Turkle, Brinton. (1981). *Do not open.* New York: Elsevier-Dutton.

Van Allsburg, Chris. (1981). *Jumanji.* Boston: Houghton-Mifflin.

Van Allsburg, Chris. (1984). *Mysteries of Harris A. Burdick.* Boston: Houghton-Mifflin.

Van Allsburg, Chris. (1985). *Polar express.* Boston: Houghton-Mifflin.

Viorst, Judith. (1972). *Alexander and the terrible horrible no good very bad day.* New York: Atheneum.

Watson, Pauline. (1978). *Wriggles and the little wishing pig.* New York: Clarion.

Folktale Collections

Arbuthnot, May Hill, et al. (1976). *The Arbuthnot anthology of children's literature.* Glenview, IL: Scott Foresman. (Currently published as *Scott Foresman anthology of children's literature,* 1984, edited by Zena Sutherland & Myra Livingston.)

Berends, Polly. (Adaptor) (1970). *Jack Kent's book of nursery tales.* New York: Random House.

Chase, Richard. (1948). "Soap, Soap, Soap" in *Grandfather tales.* Boston: Houghton-Mifflin.

Green, Lila. (1979). *Tales from Hispanic lands.* Morristown, NJ: Silver Burdett.

Haviland, Virginia. (1972). *The fairy tale treasury.* New York: Coward, McCan & Geoghegan.

Hayes, Joe. (1982). "La Hormiguita" and "The Prince" in *The day it snowed tortillas.* Santa Fe, NM: Mariposa.

Jacobs, Joseph. (1972). *Master of all masters.* New York: Grosset & Dunlap. (Also in *English folk & fairy tales,* n.d., New York: Putnam.)

Leach, Maria. (1959). *The thing at the foot of the bed.* New York: Philomel.

Leach, Maria. (1974). *Whistle in the graveyard.* New York: Viking.

Lyons, Grant. (1972). "The Giant and the Rabbit" in *Tales the people tell in Mexico.* New York: Julian Messner.

Mayer, Marianna. (1983). *My first book of nursery tales.* New York: Random House.

Sauvageau, Juan. (1984). *Stories that must not die.* Austin, TX: Oasis Press.

Schwartz, Alvin. (1981). *Scary stories to tell in the dark.* New York: Harper & Row.

Fiction Books for Read Aloud or Booktalks

Ames, Mildred. (1975). *Is there life on a plastic planet?* New York: Dutton.

Blume, Judy. (1980). *Super fudge.* New York: Dutton.

Blume, Judy. (1972). *Tales of a fourth grade nothing.* New York: Dutton.

Byars, Betsy. (1977). *The pinballs.* New York: Harper & Row.

Cleary, Beverly. (1983). *Dear Mr. Henshaw.* New York: Pantheon.

Cleary, Beverly. (1968). *Ramona the pest.* New York: Morrow.

Conford, Ellen. (1975). *Dear Lovey Hart, I'm desperate.* Boston: Little, Brown.

Coville, Bruce. (1982). *The monster's ring.* New York: Pantheon.

Dahl, Roald. (1961). *James and the giant peach.* New York: Knopf.

Erickson, Russell. (1974). *A toad for Tuesday.* New York: Lothrop, Lee, & Shepard.

Gardiner, John. (1980). *Stone fox.* New York: Crowell.

Howe, Deborah. (1979). *Bunnicula.* New York: Atheneum.

Lewis, C.S. (1968). *The lion, the witch and the wardrobe.* New York: Macmillan.

Machlachlan, Patricia. (1985). *Sarah, plain and tall.* New York: Harper & Row.

Miles, Miska. (1971). *Annie and the old one.* Boston: Little, Brown.

O'Brien, Robert. (1971). *Mrs. Frisbee and the rats of NIMH.* New York: Atheneum.

Patersen, Katherine. (1977). *Bridge to Terabithia.* New York: Thomas Y. Crowell.

Patersen, Katherine. (1978). *The great Gilly Hopkins.* New York: Harper & Row.

Pfeffer, Susan. (1981). *What do you do when your mouth won't open?* New York: Delacorte.

Rawls, Wilson. (1974). *Where the red fern grows.* New York: Doubleday.

Roberts, Willo. (1977). *Don't hurt Laurie.* New York: Atheneum.

Rockwell, Thomas. (1973). *How to eat fried worms.* New York: Franklin Watts.

Rodgers, Mary. (1972). *Freaky Friday.* New York: Harper & Row.

Sachar, Louis. (1978). *Sideways stories of Wayside School.* Chicago: Follett.

Shyer, Marlene. (1978). *Welcome home, Jellybean.* New York: Charles Scribner's

Smith, Doris Buchanan. (1973). *A taste of blackberries.* New York: Thomas Y. Crowell.

Wersba, Barbara. (1982). *The crystal child.* New York: Harper & Row.

White, E.B. (1952). *Charlotte's web.* New York: Harper & Row.

Predictable Syntactic Pattern Literature

Asch, Frank. (1981). *Just like daddy.* Englewood Cliffs, NJ: Prentice-Hall.

Barrett, Judi. (1970). *Animals should definitely not wear clothing.* New York: Atheneum.

Brown, Margaret. (1977). *Goodnight moon.* New York: Harper & Row.

Brown, Ruth. (1981). *A dark, dark tale.* New York: Dial.

Burningham, John. (1970). *Mr. Gumpy's outing.* New York: Holt, Rinehart & Winston.

Carle, Eric. (1971). *The very hungry caterpillar.* New York: Thomas Y. Crowell.

Charlip, Remi. (1964). *Fortunately.* New York: Parents Magazine Press.

de Paola, Tomie. (Illus.) (1981). *The comic adventures of Old Mother Hubbard and her dog.* New York: Harcourt Brace Jovanovich.

Gag, Wanda. (1928). *Millions of cats.* New York: Coward, McCann & Geoghegan.

Ginsburg, Mirra. (1972). *The chick and the duckling.* New York: Macmillan.

Goss, Janet, & Jerome Harste. (1984). *No me asusto a mi!* Worthington, OH: School Book Fairs.

Martin, Bill, Jr. (1967). *Brown bear, brown bear, what do you see?* New York: Holt, Rinehart & Winston.

Shaw, Charles. (1947). *It looked like spilt milk.* New York: Harper & Row.

Silverstein, Shel. (1964). *Giraffe and a half.* New York: Harper & Row.

Poetry, Rhymes, and Chants

Atkinson, Allen. (Illus.) (1984). *Mother Goose's nursery rhymes.* New York: Knopf.

Bayley, Nicola. (1982). *Canciones tontas.* Barcelona, Spain: Editorial Lumen.

Gerez, Toni de. (1981). *Mi cancion es un pedazo de jade: Poemas de Mexico antiguo.* México: Editorial Novaro.

Greenfield, Eloise. (1978). *Honey, I love, and other love poems.* New York: Thomas Y. Crowell.

Hague, Michael. (Illus./Selector) (1984). *Mother Goose.* New York: Holt, Rinehart & Winston.

Michels, Barbara, & Bettye White. (1983). *Apples on a stick: The folklore of black children.* New York: Coward, McCann & Geoghegan.

Pomerantz, Charlotte. (1980). *The tamarindo puppy and other poems.* New York: Greenwillow.

Prelutsky, Jack. (Ed.) (1983). *The Random House book of poetry.* New York: Random House.

Prelutsky, Jack. (1977). *The snopp on the sidewalk.* New York: Greenwillow.

Schon, Isabel. (1983). *Doña Blanca and other Hispanic nursery rhymes and games.* Minneapolis, MN: T.S. Denison.

Silverstein, Shel. (1981). *The light in the attic.* New York: Harper & Row.

Silverstein, Shel. (1974). *Where the sidewalk ends.* New York: Harper & Row.

Wilner, Isabel. (1977). *The poetry troupe: Anthology of poems to read aloud.* New York: Charles Scribner's.

Songs

Adams, Pam. (1975). *There was an old lady who swallowed a fly.* New York: Grossett & Dunlop.

Adams, Pam. (1975). *This old man.* New York: Grossett & Dunlap.

Fernandez, Laura. (1983). *Pio, pio: Cantos y rondas infantiles.* México: Editorial Trillas.

Galdone, Paul. (Adaptor) (1985). *Cat goes fiddle-e-fee.* New York: Clarion.

Greene, Carol. (1983). *The thirteen days of Halloween.* Chicago: Children's Press.

Keats, Ezra Jack. (1971). *Over in the meadow.* New York: Harper & Row.

Keller, Charles. (1976). *Glory, glory how peculiar.* Englewood Cliffs, NJ: Prentice-Hall.

Langstaff, John. (1974). *Oh, a hunting we will go.* New York: Atheneum.

Mack, Stanley. (1974). *Ten bears in my bed: A goodnight countdown.* New York: Pantheon.

Nelson, Esther. (1981). *The silly song-book.* New York: Sterling.

Peck, Merle. (1985). *Mary wore her red dress and Henry wore his green sneakers.* New York: Clarion.

Readers Digest. *Reader's Digest children's songbook.* New York: Random House.

Zemach, Margot. (Illus.) (1976). *Hush little baby.* New York: E.P. Dutton.

The Language of Literature

Adela Artola Allen

One of the important roles of a children's librarian is to help young readers become aware of the variety of genres and stylistic devices found in literature. In discussing literature with children, one may therefore often use a good deal of literary terminology. This may be on a simple level as when acquainting young children with categories of literature such as myths and mysteries. It may also be the more sophisticated kind of discussion one could have with older readers about such matters as imagery or point of view. For the librarian with a basic, but less than fluent command of Spanish, such discussions can be enhanced by a knowledge of appropriate Spanish equivalents for literary terminology. The school librarian may also wish to share such terminology with classroom teachers for use in their literary programs.

The bilingual vocabulary list provided here is intended to fill such a need. It is divided into four major categories. "Literary Genres" includes general terminology, as well as words referring specifically to types and elements of fiction, drama, and poetry. "Narrative Elements" includes terms that refer to elements of plot, character, and setting. "Rhetorical Terms" are especially valuable for discussion of style. Finally, "Parts of a Book" provides some necessary terminology for helping readers find information in books.

The reader will notice that the English and Spanish versions of the terms listed below are, for the most part, similar; that is, the language of literature in English and Spanish is largely based on cognates, words that have a common Latin or Green origin. Knowledge of how root words pass from one language to another coupled with knowledge of how different prefixes and suffixes transfer will help in remembering such terms as introduction/*introducción* and simile/*símil*. It is important to be aware of those terms that do not have cognate translations; for instance, the appropriate term for a character in a book is not *caracter* but *personaje*. (*Caracter* is more often used to mean "personality.") Other terms such as "end" (of a story) have no Spanish cognate at all; the translation of "end" is *fin*.

LIST OF TERMINOLOGY

Literary Genres

General
autobiography—autobiografía
biography—biografía
epic—épica
epigram—epigrama
essay—ensayo
fable—fábula
joke—chiste
journal—revista
legend—leyenda
literature—literatura
myth—mito
parable—parábola
parody—parodia
prose—prosa
pun—equívoco, chiste, juego de
    vocablos
riddle—adivinanza, enigma
satire—sátira
style—estilo

Fiction
detective novel—novela
    detectivesca
fairy tale—cuento de hadas
fantasy—fantasia
mystery novel—novela de
    misterio
novel—novela
realistic novel—novela realista
science fiction—ciencia-ficción
short story—cuento corto
spy novel—novela de espias
story—historia
tale—cuento
tall tale—cuento exagerado

Drama
act—acto
comedy—comedia
farce—farsa

melodrama—melodrama
mime—mímica
pantomime—pantomima
scene—escena
slapstick—comedia grotesca
theater—teatro
tragedy—tragedia

Poetry
foot—pie
haiku—haiku
limerick—lira o quintilla jocosa
lyric—lírica
meter—metro
refráin—refrán
rhyme—rima
rhythm—ritmo
sonnet—soneto
stanza—estanza
verse—verso

Narrative Elements

beginning—principio
character—personaje
chorus—coro
climax—climax
conflict—conflicto
dialogue—diálogo
ending—fin
episode—episodio
first-person—primera persona
flashback—atavismo, reversión
    (cine+escena retrospectiva)
fool—bufón
hero—héroe
heroine—heroina
monologue—monólogo
motivation—motivación
narrator—narrador
plot—argumento
point of view—punto de vista

prologue—prólogo
setting—escena, fondo
suspense—suspenso
theme—tema
third-person—tercera persona
unity—unidad

Rhetorical Terms
abstract—abstracto
ambiguous—ambiguo
concrete—concreto
connotation—connotación
denotation—denotación
dialect—dialecto
idiom—expresión idiomática
image—imagen
irony—ironía

metaphor—metáfora
parallelism—paralelismo
sarcasm—sarcasmo
simile—símil
slang—vulgarismo, jerga
symbol—símbolo

Parts of a Book
acknowledgements—reconocimientos
appendix—apéndice
foreward—prólogo
index—índice
introduction—introducción
preface—prefacio
table of contents—tabla de contenido

Terminology for Librarians with Limited Spanish Fluency

Adela Artola Allen
Sarah Barchas

The most important aspect of a library program is communication; communication of ideas and information; communication of genuine respect for the patron and his or her background, heritage, interests, and individuality; and communication of enthusiasm for people and materials, conveying an invitation of genuine help and service. When Hispanic children are involved, such communication might be most feasible and effective when the librarian is bilingual. However, even librarians with limited Spanish skills can effectively serve the Hispanic child, particularly if they have a strong commitment to doing so.

Following is a list of requests, instructions, and general library management expressions, given both in English and Spanish, that can be of help for those librarians of limited Spanish skills who seek to broaden their ability to communicate in the Hispanic child's dominant language. These questions, instructions, and expressions may be categorized in terms of basic usage. They include greetings, finding the right match, general procedures, care of books and materials, self-concept, talk with parents, guiding reading, encouraging cooperation and responsibility, guiding motivation, guiding library skills, and guiding cultural understanding. The list is intended especially for librarians who have rudimentary skills in Spanish and wish to expand their library-related vocabulary.

A. GREETINGS / SALUDOS

1. Welcome to the library. / bienvenido(s) a la biblioteca.
2. Good morning, boys and girls. / Buenos días niños y niñas.
3. Good afternoon. / Buenas tardes.
4. It is good to see you again in the library. / Qué gusto de verlos (verlas) de nuevo en la biblioteca.
5. Can I help you find what you are looking for? / ¿Puedo ayudarte a localizar lo que buscas?

6. Please let me know if I can help you in any way.

Por favor avísame si en algo te puedo ayudar.

7. We have many interesting things in the library.

Tenemos muchas cosas interesantes en la biblioteca.

8. I would like to introduce you to our library clerk who can also help you.

Quiero presentarte con nuestro(a) ayudante que también te puede ayudar.

9. I hope you will come back soon.

Ojalá que vuelvas pronto.

B. WHEN THE BOOK AND THE READER MEET

CUANDO EL LIBRO Y EL LECTOR SE ENCUENTRAN

1. Can I help you find a book...a magazine...a newspaper...a filmstrip...a picture...a film...a record...a computer disk...a videocassette...a cassette tape?

¿Puedo ayudarte a encontrar una revista...un periódico...una filmina...una ilustración...una película...un disco...un cassette una cinta magnetofónica...un videocassette...un disco de computadora?

2. What kind of books do you like?

¿Qué clase de libros te gustan?

3. Do you want a book in English or in Spanish?

¿Quiéres un libro en inglés o en español?

4. Do you want a book about animals...dinosaurs?

¿Quiéres un libro sobre los animales...los dinosaurios?

5. Do you want a true book or a fantasy book?

¿Quiéres un libro sobre lo que es real o fantástico?

6. Do you want a funny book...a sad book...a scary book...an exciting book?

¿Quiéres un libro chistoso...triste...de terror...emocionante?

7. Do you want a mystery...an adventure book...a biography?

¿Quiéres un libro de misterio...de aventuras...una biografía?

8. Do you want a fairy tale? Which one?

¿Quiéres un cuento de hadas? ¿Cuál?

9. Do you want a joke book...a riddle book...a cookbook...a book about sports...a book about drawing...a book about science?

¿Quiéres un libro de chistes...de adivinanzas...cocina...sobre los deportes...de dibujo...sobre la ciencia?

10. What book have you read before that you like?

¿Qué libro has leído que te gusta?

11. Is this book too hard for you? Is it too easy?

¿Está demasiado difícil para ti este libro? ¿Demasiado fácil?

12. Good, this book is for you. I'm glad you like it.

Bien, este libro es para ti. Me alegro que te guste.

C. PROCEDURES

1. Do you know how to check out a book?
2. All books in the library have a card. Write your name on the card and your classroom number.
3. Bring the book and card to the front desk.
4. We will stamp the book and card and keep the card.
5. You can borrow the book for one week...for two weeks.
6. Please use a shelf marker when you pull a book from the shelf.
7. Do you know how to reserve a book?
8. Do you know where to return your books when you bring them back?
9. Please put it in the book drop (slot...the hole).
10. Please bring your books back on time (when they are due).
11. If you want a book that is not here today, we can save it for you when it's returned.
12. If you want a book we do not have in the library, please write the title on the suggestion list and we will try to order it.

REGLAMENTACION

¿Sabes cómo sacar un libro?

Todos los libros en la biblioteca tienen una tarjeta. Pon tu nombre en la tarjeta y el número de tu salón de clase.

Trae el libro y la tarjeta al mostrador.

Le pondremos el sello al libro y a la tarjeta y nos quedaremos con la tarjeta.

Puedes sacar el libro por una semana...dos semanas.

Por favor pon un marcador en el estante cuando saques un libro.

¿Sabes cómo se pone un libro en reserva?

¿Sabes en dónde hay que dejar los libros cuando los devuelvas?

Por favor ponlo en el buzón de libros.

Por favor devuelve tus libros a tiempo (cuando se venzan).

Si quieres un libro que no está aquí hoy, podemos guardártelo cuando lo devuelvan.

Si quieres un libro que no tenemos en la biblioteca, por favor copia el título en la lista de sugerencias y trataremos de pedirlo.

D. CARE OF BOOKS

1. Do you know how to take care of books?
2. How can you take good care of a book?
3. Should you write on it?
4. Should you tear it?

EL CUIDADO DE LOS LIBROS

¿Sabes cómo se cuidan los libros?

¿Cómo se cuida un libro?

¿Debemos escribir en él?

¿Debemos romperlo?

5. Should you let little baby brothers or sisters play with it?

¿Debemos dejar al bebé y a los hermanitos que juegen con él?

6. Should you eat while you are reading a book? Why not?

¿Debemos comer mientras leemos un libro? ¿Por qué no?

7. How should you turn the pages?

¿Cómo se le da vuelta a las páginas?

8. Please turn the pages by the corners, slowly and carefully.

Por favor dale vuelta a la página por las esquinas, despacio y cuidadosamente.

9. Should you look at the book with dirty hands?

¿Debemos hojear un libro con las manos sucias?

10. Do you have a safe place where you can keep your books?

¿Tienes un lugar seguro donde puedes guardar tus libros?

11. What happens if you lose the book?

¿Qué pasa si pierdes el libro?

12. You will have to pay for it.

Tendrás que pagarlo.

13. Please be careful with this book. It is very expensive.

Ten mucho cuidado con este libro. Es muy caro.

E. SELF-CONCEPT

EL AUTOCONCEPTO

1. How well you read!

¡Qué bien lees!

2. What a pretty picture you drew!

¡Qué bonito dibujo pintaste!

3. What a good story you wrote!

¡Qué cuento tan bueno escribiste!

4. Thank you for sharing your book (picture, story, model, etc.) with the library.

Gracias por compartir tu libro (cuento, modelo, etc.) con la biblioteca.

5. You are an excellent reader (author, artist, singer, etc.)

Eres un lector (autor, artista, cantante, etc.) excelente!

6. You can be proud of your good work.

Puedes estar orgulloso de tu buen trabajo.

7. You can be proud of reading so many books.

Puedes estar orgulloso de haber leído tantos libros.

8. I am glad you came to the library today.

Me alegra que veniste a la biblioteca hoy.

9. Keep up the good work!

¡Sigue trabajando bien!

10. I like the way these children are using the library.

Me gusta cómo estos niños usan la biblioteca.

11. How well you think!

¡Qué bien piensas!

12. You showed us you understood the story well.

Nos mostraste que entendiste el cuento muy bien.

F. TALK WITH PARENTS

CONVERSACIONES CON LOS PADRES

1. Thank you for visiting the library.
   Gracias por su visita a la biblioteca.
2. Thank you for paying for the book your child lost.
   Gracias por pagar por el libro que su hijo(a) perdió.
3. You are welcome to check out books to read for your child.
   Si gusta, puede sacar libros para leerle a su niño(a).
4. It is good to read to your child every day.
   Es ventajoso leerle a su niño(a) todos los días.
5. If you take time to read aloud to your child often, your child will learn to love reading.
   Si le dedica tiempo todos los días para leerle en voz alta a su hijo(a), aprenderá a apreciar la lectura.
6. It is good that you take so much interest in helping your child learn.
   Qué gusto ver el interés que tiene usted en ayudar a su niño(a) a aprender.
7. You can be proud of your child.
   Puede estar orgulloso de su niño(a).
8. Thank you for helping your child learn to use the library materials responsibly.
   Le agredecemos su ayuda en enseñar a su niño(a) a usar los materiales de la biblioteca con cuidado.
9. Would you like to be a volunteer parent helper in our library?
   ¿Le gustaría formar parte del grupo de padres voluntarios que nos ayudan en la biblioteca?
10. Thank you for all your help.
    Gracias por toda su ayuda.

G. GUIDING READING

LA LECTURA GUIADA

1. Is this story true or is it make-believe?
   ¿Este cuento es real or fantástico?
2. What do you think will happen next?
   ¿Qué pasará después?
3. Every good story has a well developed beginning, a middle, and an end.
   Todos los cuentos buenos tienen un principio, una parte central y un fin bien desarollados.
4. How do you think this story will end?
   ¿Cómo acabará este cuento?
5. Did you like the ending? If you liked it, why? If you didn't like it, why not?
   ¿Te gustó el final? Si te gustó, ¿por qué? Si no te gustó, por qué no?
6. Which character did you like best? Why?
   ¿Cuál personaje te gustó más? ¿Por qué?
7. How would you change the story if you could?
   Si pudieras, ¿cómo cambiarías el cuento?

8. Which book did you like the best?

¿Cuál libro te gustó más?

9. How did this story make you feel?

¿Qué sentiste cuando leías este cuento?

10. What will you remember most about this story?

¿Qué es lo que más recordarás de este cuento?

11. Would you like to read more books written by the same author?

¿Te gustaría leer más libros escritos por el mismo autor?

12. How do you think the author got the idea to write this book?

¿Cómo se le ocurriría este libro al autor?

H. HOW TO ENCOURAGE COOPERATION AND RESPONSIBILITY OF STUDENTS

COMO INSPIRAR LA COOPERACION Y RESPONSABILIDAD DE LOS ALUMNOS

1. I expect everyone to be a good helper in the library.

Espero que todos ustedes sean buenos ayudantes en la biblioteca.

2. Can you show your new friend how to check out a book?

¿Puedes enseñarle a tu amigo nuevo cómo sacar un libro?

3. Can you help put the materials away?

¿Puedes ayudar a guardar los materiales?

4. Can you help put the chairs in their place?

¿Puedes ayudar a poner las sillas en su lugar?

5. Will you help me pick up the papers from the floor?

¿Me ayudas a levantar los papeles del piso?

6. Boys and girls, please listen carefully.

Niños y niñas, escuchen atentamente por favor.

7. Please, let's have only one child talk at a time.

Por favor, que hable un niño a la vez, nada más.

8. Please raise your hand before speaking.

Por favor levanten la mano antes de hablar.

9. Is everybody ready?

¿Están listos?

10. Wait one moment. We're not done yet.

Un momento. Todavía no acabamos.

11. Now you can check out your books.

Ahora pueden sacar sus libros.

12. If you brought your book back, you can check out another one.

Si devolvieron su libro, pueden sacar otro.

13. Did you bring your books back?

¿Devolviste tus libros?

14. I'm sorry. You cannot check out another book until you bring your book back.

Lo siento. No puedes sacar otro libro hasta que devuelvas el que tienes.

15. You have an overdue library book.

Tienes un libro de la biblioteca que está retrasado.

16. Did you find your overdue book? Good, I'm glad you found it.

¿Encontraste tu libro retrasado? Bien, me alegro que lo hayas encontrado.

17. If you cannot find it, you will have to pay for it.

Si no lo puedes encontrar tendrás que pagarlo.

18. Please be sure to put away the materials carefully when you finish using them.

Por favor guarda los materiales con cuidado cuando termines de usarlos.

19. Please rewind the filmstrip. Then roll it carefully, touching it only on the edges, and put it back in the can.

Por favor desenrolla la filmina. Luego, enróllala con cuidado, tocando únicamente las orillas, y ponla en la latita de nuevo.

20. Please be sure to turn off the audiovisual equipment when you are done.

Por favor apaga los aparatos audiovisuales cuando termines.

21. Thank you for your help. We appreciate the leadership you have shown in the library.

Agradecemos tu ayuda y apreciamos la iniciativa que has mostrado en la biblioteca.

I. IDEAS FOR MOTIVATING STUDENTS

IDEAS PARA MOTIVAR A LOS ALUMNOS

1. We have many interesting things to share today.

Hoy tenemos mucho que compartir.

2. I have a very special story to read to you.

Tengo un cuento muy especial que leerles.

3. I have a surprise for you.

Les tengo una sorpresa.

4. Here are some brand new books all ready for you to check out.

Aquí están unos libros nuevecitos listos para que los saquen ustedes.

5. We will have a special speaker today.

Hoy tenemos una visita muy especial que va a hablar con nosotros.

6. We will have a book fair where you can buy books.

Vamos a tener una Feria del Libro donde pueden comprar libros.

7. We will have a young author's writing festival where you can see all the books the children have written.

Vamos a festejar a los autores juveniles y ustedes podrán ver todos los libros que los niños han escrito.

8. We will give certificates to honor the children who have read many books, who have had perfect attendance, and who have had special achievement in their school work.

Vamos a dar diplomas de honor a los niños que han leído muchos libros, a los que tienen asistencia perfecta, y a los que se han distinguido en su trabajo escolar.

9. How lucky you are to find such a special book!

¡Qué suerte tienes de encontrar un libro tan especial!

10. I hope you will enjoy your book. I think it will be just right for you.

Espero que te agrade tu libro. Creo que será muy apropriado para ti.

J. GUIDING LIBRARY SKILLS

DIRECCION DE DESTREZAS PARA EL USO DE LA BIBLIOTECA

1. Do you know how to use the card catalog?

¿Sabes usar el catálogo fichero?

2. It is divided in three sections: a) the subject catalog, b) the author catalog, and c) the title catalog.

Se divide en tres secciones. a) El catálogo diccionario (o de materias) b) el catálogo de autores (o onomástico) y c) el catálogo de títulos.

3. The subject catalog tells what the book is about.

El catálogo de materias nos dice de qué se trata el libro.

4. If you know the title of a book but you don't know who wrote it, look in the title catalog.

Si sabes el título de un libro pero no sabes quién lo escribió búscalo en el catálogo de títulos.

5. If you want to know what other books we have by the same author, look in the author catalog.

Si quieres saber qué otros libros tenemos escritos por el mismo autor, búscalo en el catálogo de autores.

6. The card catalog is like a key to unlock all the secrets of what is in the library.

El catálogo es como una llave que abre todos los secretos de lo que hay en la biblioteca.

7. You must know how to look for information in alphabetical order.

Tienes que saber cómo se busca la información orden alfabético.

8. The guide cards can help you.

Los ficheros de guía te pueden ayudar.

9. You must know how to spell the words you are looking for.

Tienes que saber cómo se escriben las palabras que buscas.

10. Do you see the number or letters on the left-hand corner of the card?

¿Ves el número o las letras en la esquina de la ficha?

11. That will tell you where to find the book.

Esto te dirá dónde buscar el libro.

12. I will be glad to help you.

Con gusto te ayudo.

13. Do you think you can find it yourself?

¿Crees que puedes encontrarlo tu solo?

14. Let me know if I can help you.

Dime si te puedo ayudar.

15. Do you know how to use the encyclopedia...the table of contents...the atlas...the dictionary?

Sabes usar la enciclopedia...el índice (alfabético)...la tabla de contenido (índice general)...el atlas...el diccionario?

16. I congratulate you for knowing how to use the card catalog.

Te felicito porque sabes usar el fichero.

17. Good for you. You found it all by yourself.

¡Estupendo! Lo encontraste tú solito!

18. Maybe you can teach one of your classmates.

Tal vez puedas enseñarle a uno de tus compañeros.

K. GUIDING CULTURAL UNDERSTANDING

GUIA PARA EL DESAROLLO DE LA COMPRENSION CULTURAL

1. Is this an authentic representation of these people?

¿Es esto(a) una representación auténtica de este grupo cultural?

2. If you were one of these people, how would you feel about this book?

Si tu pertenecieras a esta cultura, ¿qué opinión tendrías de este libro?

3. Would this book make you feel proud of being a member of this group? Why? Why not?

Al leer este libro, ¿estarías orgulloso de ser parte de este grupo? ¿Por qué? ¿Por qué no?

4. Did you learn something new about this group of people by reading this story? What did you learn?

¿Aprendiste algo nuevo sobre este grupo cultural al leer esta historia? ¿Qué aprendiste?

5. Is this idea a fact or an opinion?

¿Es esta idea un hecho o una opinión?

6. How would you change this story to make it more true?

¿Cómo cambiarías este cuento para hacerlo mas auténtico?

7. What contributions have these people made?

¿Qué contribuciones ha hecho este grupo?

8. How are the characters in this story like all other people?

¿En qué se parecen los personajes de este cuento a los demás?

9. How are they different from other people?

¿En qué se diferencian a los demás?

10. Which character would you want for a friend? Why?

¿A quién de los personajes te gustaría tener de amigo? ¿Por qué?

11. What will you remember most about this story?

¿De qué te acordarás más en este cuento?

English-Spanish Library-Related Vocabulary

Francisco Avalos

See the appendix to this chapter, which immediately follows, for the Dewey Classification Table in Spanish.

A

ABC—Abecedario
Abbreviation—Abreviatura, abreviación
Accent mark—Acento
Access point—Punto de entrada; punto de acceso; punto de partida
Activities—Actividades
Added entry—Asiento adicional; entrada adicional
Added title page—Asiento adicional de título
Administration—Administración
Adult department—Sección de adultos
Adventure books—Libros de aventuras
Aesop's fables—Fábulas de Esopo
Alphabet books—Abecedarios
Alphabetical order—Orden alfabético
Alternative title—Título complementario; subtítulo
Analytical entry—Asiento analítico
Animal stories—Cuentos de animales; historias de animales
Annotated bibliography—Bibliografía anotada
Annual—Anual
Anonymous work—Obra anónima
Anthology—Antología
Appendix—Apéndice
Arithmetic—Aritmética
Art—Arte
Art object—Objeto de arte
Article—Artículo (article in journal, newspaper, etc.)
Artist—Artista
Atlas—Atlas

Audience—Público
Audiovisual aids—Medios audiovisuales
Author—Autor
Author catalog—Catálogo onomástico; índice onomástico
Author entry—Asiento de autor
Autobiography—Autobiografía

B

Ballad—Balada; canción
Beginning readers—Libros para empezar a leer; libros para
　principiantes
Bible—Biblia
Bibliography—Bibliografía
Bilingual—Bilingüe
Binding—Encuadernación
Biography—Biografía
Book—Libro
Book cover—Portada
Book display—Exhibición de libros; exhibición
Book drop—Buzón de libros
Book jacket—Cubierta
Book review—Reseña de un libro
Book selection—Selección de libros
Booklet—Libreto; folleto
Bookmobile—Biblioteca ambulante
Books for the teenager—Libros para el adolescente
Books in Spanish—Libros en español
Bookshelves—Estantes de libros
Branch library—Biblioteca filial; biblioteca sucursal

C

Calendar—Calendario
Call number—Número clasificador; número identificador; clave de
　registro; clave de fichero
Card catalog—Fichero
Cartoon—Caricatura
Cassette tape—Cartucho de 'cassette'; cassette; cinta magnetofónica
Catalog card—Ficha bibliográfica
Cataloging—Catalogación
Central, main library—Biblioteca principal
Chapter—Capítulo
Check-in desk—Estación de retorno; mostrador de entregas
Check-out desk—Estación de préstamo; mostrador de préstamo
Child development—Desarrollo de la niñez; desarrollo infantil
Children's department—Sección de niños; sección infantil
Children's literature—Literatura para niños; literatura infantil
Choral readings—Lectura coral

Circulating material—Material circulante
Classification schedule—Cédula de clasificación; código de clasificación
Closed entry—Asiento cerrado
Collection—Colección
Comedy—Comedia
Composer—Compositor
Compound surname—Nombre compuesto; apellido compuesto
Computer—Computadora
Computer terminal—Terminal de computadora
Concept books—Libros de concepto
Conference—Conferencia; junta
Copy—Copia; ejemplar
Copyright—Derecho de autor
Copyright date—Fecha de registro de la propiedad
Corporate entry—Asiento corporativo
Cross-reference—Referencia cruzada
Counting books—Libros para aprender a contar
Couplet—Copla
Cutter system—Tablas de Cutter

D
Dewey decimal system—Clasificación decimal
Dialogue—Diálogo
Dictionary—Diccionario
Dog stories—Cuentos de perros
Drama—Drama
Due date—Fecha de retorno; fecha de devolución; fecha de vencimiento

E
Easy-to-read books—Libros fáciles de leer; libros de lectura fácil
Edition—Edición
Editor—Editor; corrector
Editorial—Editorial
Encyclopedia—Enciclopedia
Entry—Asiento; entrada
Epic poetry—Poesía épica
Errata—Fe de erratas
Ethnic collection—Colección étnica
Exhibit; exhibition—Exhibición; presentación

F
Fables—Fábulas
Facsimile—Facsímil
Fairy—Hada
Fairy tale (fairy story)—Cuento de hadas
Fantasy—Fantasía

Fiction—Ficción
Film—Película
Film projector—Aparato de proyección de películas; proyector
Filmstrip—Transparencias; filmina
Fines—Multas
First name—Nombre de pila
Flash cards—Fichero de conceptos; fichero temático
Folklore—Folklore
Folktales—Cuentos populares; cuentos del folklore
Footnotes—Notas al pie de la página; notas de pie de página

G
Games—Juegos; pasatiempos
Geography—Geografía
Glossary—Glosario
Government—Gobierno
Guide to children's literature—Guía para localizar literatura infantil
Guidewords—Palabras guías

H
Heading—Encabezamiento; encabezado
History—Historia
Holding—Posesiones
Holiday—Día festivo
Horse stories—Historias sobre caballos
Humanities—Humanidades
Humorous stories—Cuentos humorísticos; historietas chistosas; chistes
Hymn—Himno

I
Illustration—Ilustración; dibujo; grabado
Index—Indice; índice analítico
Informational book—Libro de informes; libros de instrucción
Initial—Inicial
Introduction—Introducción
Item—Artículo

J
Jobber—Intermediario

K
Keyword (use for catchword)—Palabra clave

L
LC—Biblioteca del Congreso
Language—Idioma; lenguaje
Last name—Apellido
Legend—Leyenda

Letter—Letra (letter or alphabet); carta (correspondence)
Librarian—Bibliotecario; bibliotecaria
Library—Biblioteca
Library card—Credencial de biblioteca
Library clerk or Library aide—Ayudante del bibliotecario(a)
Library of Congress—Biblioteca del Congreso
Limerick—Quintilla humorística
List of books—Lista de libros
List of words—Vocabulario; lista de palabras
Literary form—Forma literaria
Literature—Literatura; obras literarias
Loan period—Período de préstamo

M
Magazine (use for periodicals)—Revista
Magazines for children—Revista para niños
Main entry—Asiento principal
Manual—Manual
Map—Mapa
Mathematics—Matemáticas
Micro (-fiche, -form, -film)—Microficha, microfilm
Monograph—Monografía
Monthly—Mensual
Motion picture—Película
Music—Música
Mysteries—Obras de misterio
Mythology—Mitología
Myths—Mitos

N
Name—Nombre
Name authority file—Asiento de identidad; archivo de autoridades
News room—Hemeroteca
Newspaper—Periódico
Newspaper article—Artículo de periódico
Nickname—Apodo; sobrenombre
Nonfiction literature—Literatura realista
Number—Número

O
Ode—Oda
Office—Oficina
Old—Viejo
On order—Ordenado
Open entry—Asiento abierto
Open stacks—Anaquel abierto
Oral—Oral

Out of print—Agotado
Overdue—Vencido; retrasado

P

Page—Página
Pamphlet—Folleto
Paper—Papel; periódico (newspaper)
Paperback—Libro de bolsillo
Paragraph—Párrafo
Paraphrase—Paráfrasis
Parody—Parodia
Pen name—Sobrenombre
Performance—Función; actuación; papel
Periodical—Publicación periódica
Periodical index—Indice de publicaciones periódicas
Photograph—Fotografía; foto
Photography—Fotografía
Phrase—Frase
Picture—Pintura; retrato
Picture book—Libro de retratos; libro con estampas
Play—Obra teatral
Plot—Argumento de drama
Poem—Poema
Poet—Poeta
Poetry—Poesía
Point of view—Punto de vista
Posters—Carteles
Preschool—Preescolar
Prologue—Prólogo
Prose—Prosa
Pseudonym name—Seudónino
Public catalog—Catálogo público; índice onomástico
Publisher—Casa editorial
Punctuation—Puntuación; signos de puntuación
Puppets/show—Función de títeres

Q
Question—Pregunta

R
Radio—Radio
Range (stacks)—Anaquel
Read—Leer
Reading—Acto de leer; lectura; recital poético; lectura en alta voz
Reading room—Sala de lectura
Recording—Grabación
Records (and record player)—Discos (music); datos (note)

Reference desk—Mostrador de información; mesa de información
Remedial books—Libros remediales; libros de recapacitación
Renewal of loan period—Renovación de préstamo
Report—Informe (written report); reportar (to report)
Reprint—Reimpresión; nueva tirada
Research—Investigación; estudio
Revision—Revisión
Rhyme—Rima
Role playing—Hacer un papel
Running title—Título corriente; título abreviado

S
Science—Ciencia
Science fiction—Ciencia ficción
Sears list of subject headings—Indice temático Sears
See—Véase
See also—Véase también; ver también
Sequel—Continuación
Series entry—Asiento de serie
Shared responsibility—Corresponsabilidad; responsabilidad compartida
Shelf list—Catálogo oficial
Short story—Historia corta; cuento corto
Size—Tamaño
Slide projector—Proyector; proyector de diapositivas
Slides—Diapositiva
Social studies—Ciencias sociales
Song—Canción
Sonnet—Soneto
Sound—Sonido; ruido (noise)
Source of information—Fuente de información
Special events—Eventos especiales; acontecimiento especial
Spelling—Ortografía
Sport stories—Historia de deportes
Stack—Estante, anaquel
Staff—Personal de oficina
Stanza—Estancia
Statement of responsibility—Manifestación de responsabilidad; declaración de responsabilidad
Story time (or hour)—Hora del cuento
Storytelling time—Hora del cuento
Student—Estudiante
Subject added entry—Asiento de materia
Subject catalog—Catálogo diccionario; catálogo de materias
Subject headings—Encabezamiento adicional de materia; encabezado de tema
Subscription—Subscripción
Suggested reading—Lectura recomendada

Summary—Sumario; resumen
Supplement—Suplemento

T

Table of contents—Indice general; tabla de contenido
Teacher—Maestro; maestra
Telephone—Teléfono
Telephone directory—Guía telefónica; directorio telefónico
Television—Televisión
Text—Texto
Textbook—Libro de texto; libro escolar
Theme—Tema
Thesis—Tesis
Title—Título
Title added entry—Asiento adicional de título
Title catalog—Catálogo de títulos; fichero de títulos
Title entry—Asiento de título
Title page—Hoja titular; primera página
Title proper—Título propio
Title variation—Variante del título
Toys—Juguetes
Tragedy—Tragedia
Transcript—Transcripción
Translated books—Libros traducidos
Translation—Traducción
Typewriter—Máquina de escribir

U

Uniform title—Título uniforme

V

Verse—Verso
Vertical file—Archivo de información; archivador
Video—Video
Volume—Volumen; tomo
Volunteers—Voluntarios; voluntarias

W

Water fountain—Fuente de agua; bebedero
Watercolor—Acuarela
We close at...—Cerramos a las...
We open at...—Abrimos a las...
Week—Semana
Word—Palabra
Word game—Juego de formación de palabras
Wordless books—Libros sin lectura; historias ilustradas
Writer—Escritor; autor
Written for children—Escrito para niños

Y
Year—Año
Yearbook—Anuario
Young adult—Joven

Appendix
Dewey Classification Table in Spanish

000–OBRAS EN GENERAL
    010–Bibliografías
    020–Biblioteconomía
    030–Enciclopedia,
        Almanaques
    070–Periódicos

100–FILOSOFIA
    130–El Cuerpo y La Mente
        Ocultismo
    140–Sistemas Filosóficos
    150–Sicología
    160–Lógica
    170–Sistemas Eticos
    180–Filósofos Antiguos
        Yoga
    190–Filósofos Modernos

200–RELIGION
    210–Teología Natural
    220–Biblias
    230–Teología
    240–Devoción
    260–Organización
    290–Religiones No
        Cristianas

300–SOCIOLOGIA
    310–Estadísticas
    320–Ciencias Políticas
    330–Economía Política

    340–Leyes, Códigos
    350–Administración
        Instituciones
    360–Organización
    370–Educación
    380–Comercio-Comunica-
        ción
    390–Costumbres, trajes
        Folklore

400–FILOLOGIA
    410–Lingüística
    420–Libros para Aprender
        Inglés
    430–Libros para Aprender
        Alemán
    440–Libros para Aprender
        Francés
    450–Libros para Aprender
        Italiano
    460–Diccionarios Bilingües
        Español-Inglés
    470–Libros para Aprender
        Latín
    480–Libros para Aprender
        Griego
    490–Lenguas Menores

500–CIENCIAS NATURALES
    510–Matemáticas
    520–Astronomía

530–Física
540–Química
550–Geología
560–Paleontología
570–Biología
580–Botánica
590–Zoología

600–ARTES UTILES
610–Medicina
620–Ingeniería, Mecánica
de autos
630–Agricultura
640–Economía Doméstica,
Libros de Cocina
650–Comunicación de
Negocios-Mecanografía
taquigrafía
690–Construcción,
carpintería

700–BELLAS ARTES
710–Jardinería
720–Arquitectura
730–Escultura
740–Dibujo
750–Pintura

760–Grabación
770–Fotografía
780–Música
790–Diversiones

800–LITERATURA
860–Literatura Clásica
863–Novelas Modernas
867–Humor, Sátira, Verso
Picaresca
868–Obras selectas y
Collecciones de Obras
completas

900–HISTORIA
910–Geografía y Viajes
930–Historia Antigua
940–Historia Europea
950–Historia Asiática
960–Historia Africana
970–Historia de América
del Norte
972–Historia de México
980–Historia de América
del Sur
990–Historia de Oceanía y
los Polos

Part III

Books, Nonprint Materials, Software, and Resources

The Best Children's Books in English about Hispanics

Isabel Schon

This annotated bibliography of the best children's books in English about Hispanic people and culture includes fiction as well as nonfiction titles. These books will please and enlighten young readers and, at the same time, provide them with an honest and accurate portrayal of Hispanic culture and people in the United States and abroad. Unfortunately, some of these titles are now out of print and others contain information that was true only up to the 1970s (or earlier). It is hoped that this selection will encourage authors, publishers, and librarians to continue their search for books that present Hispanics in an objective and sensitive manner. For the convenience of the selector, I have arranged these books by grade level—Kindergarten through Third Grade, Third through Sixth Grades, and Sixth Grade and Above.

KINDERGARTEN THROUGH THIRD GRADE

Aardema, Verna. (1979). *The riddle of the drum: A tale from Tizapan, Mexico.* Translated and retold by the author. Illustrated by Tony Chen. New York: Four Winds Press. [28 p.]. Grades K–2.
This is a charming Mexican tale about a prince who gains the hand of a princess by solving the riddle of the drum with the aid of his magic friends: Corrin Corran, the runner; Tirin Tiran, the archer; Soplin, Soplan, the blower; Oyin, Oyan, the hearer; and Comin, Coman, the eater. The lively text is entertaining and will delight children with its simple rhymes and riddles. The illustrations are also amusing and gay, even though some of them depict too many stereotyped Mexican people, such as men with big mustaches and sombreros.

Balet, Jan. (1969). *The fence.* New York: Delacorte Press. [28 p.]. Grades K–2.
An amusing comparison of the life, homes, and attitudes of very rich and very poor families in Mexico. It shows the rich family with its servants and luxuries, and the poor family smelling the food from the rich family's kitchen. The beautiful and colorful illustrations add a very real Mexican flavor to the market scenes, the homes, and the judge's office.

Barry, Robert. (1971). *Ramon and the pirate gull.* New York: McGraw-Hill. [36 p.]. Grades K–3.
Ramon, a young boy who lives in Ponce in Puerto Rico, was very surprised when he saw a bright red gull. His mother wouldn't believe him; neither would his friend Miguel nor anyone else until they saw a picture in the post office with a sign saying that "If you have seen a red sea gull, you must report it to the Marine Research Station in San Juan." So, Ramon took the rare sea gull to San Juan in an exciting taxi ride in a "publico." Amusing line drawings complement the story about Ramon and the rare gull.

Belpre, Pura. (1978). *The rainbow-colored horse.* Illustrated by Antonio Martorell. New York: Frederick Warne. [38 p.]. Grades K–3.
A delightfully written Puerto Rican folktale about a farmer, his three sons, and a rainbow-colored horse who had been trampling the family's field of maize. Pio, the youngest son, used his ingenuity to surprise the little horse and save the maize field. The little horse agreed to grant Pio three favors for his kindness, which allowed him to win the hand of the great and wealthy Don Nicanor's daughter in marriage. Pio successfully passed Don Nicanor's tests with the help of the rainbow- colored horse. Modernistic woodcut illustrations complement this amusing Puerto Rican folktale.

———. (1969). *Santiago.* Illustrated by Symeon Shimin. New York: Frederick Warne. [31 p.]. Grades 1–4.
Santiago, a young Puerto Rican boy, was eager to show his friends in New York City pictures of his favorite pet hen, Selina. An understanding teacher and a sensitive mother combine their efforts to tell the children happy things about Puerto Rico. A simple story that should evoke in all children an appreciation for the memories of one boy who left his home to come to New York City.

de Paola, Tomie. (1980). *The Lady of Guadalupe.* Illustrated by the author. New York: Holiday House. [48 p.]. Grades K–3.
Striking color illustrations and simply written text tell the story of Mexico's patron saint, the Lady of Guadalupe, who appeared to a poor Mexican Indian, Juan Diego, in 1531. Young readers will be delighted by this recreation of the legend of the beautiful lady who, in the robes of an Aztec princess, asked Juan Diego to tell the bishop in Mexico City to build a church in her honor on the hill where she was standing. This book is also available in a Spanish edition.

Dewey, Ariane. (1981). *The thunder god's son: Peruvian folktale.* Illustrated by the author. New York: Greenwillow Books. [24 p.]. Grades K–2.
Brilliant, colorful illustrations and a simple text tell how young Acuri

was sent down to earth by his father, the thunder god, to learn about the ways of humans. Amidst delightful Peruvian scenes, Acuri is seen overhearing two foxes talking about a selfish, rich husband and wife who will help no one. Acuri's adventures began in a house with a feathered roof where he cured a sick old man. He also saved the rich woman from two huge serpents hovering over the house. Later he was challenged by Rupay, the couple's son, to participate in very difficult contests. Thanks to the magic help of his father, Acuri succeeded in teaching a lesson to Rupay and the rich man and woman. Acuri then gave the wonderful llamas "as a gift to the villagers, so that all could share in the riches their wool would bring." A charming introduction to Peru, its history, and its folklore.

Duff, Maggie. (1980). *The princess and the pumpkin.* Adapted from a Majorcan tale by the author. Pictures by Catherine Stock. New York: Macmillan. [32 p.]. Grades K–2
In the island town of Palma lived a beautiful princess who suddenly became ill and would not laugh. The king decreed that whoever could make the princess laugh would be kept in comfort forever. Many people tried but "not even a glimmer of a smile crossed the sad Princess' face." When an old granny came to town she decided to make the princess laugh. As she walked toward the palace she saw a huge hole, which led to many unusual occurrences. She narrated all of this to the princess who was delighted and wanted to accompany her to see the hole and walk down the ladder. Finally the princess breaks the wicked spell, turning the old woman into a prince, who then asked for the princess in marriage. Amusing, pale-colored line drawings complement this delightful Majorcan tale. Unfortunately, though, very few scenes capture the alluring beauty of the island of Majorca.

Ets, Marie Hall, & Aurora Labastida. (1959). *Nine days to Christmas.* New York: Viking Press. [48 p.]. Grades K–2.
A touching story about a little girl in Mexico City and her preparations for a Posada—a Mexican pre-Christmas celebration. The authors genuinely describe a typical day of a middle-class family in a Mexican city: life with a servant, a Posada, and scenes of a traditional market. The award-winning illustrations are a tribute to Mexico and its people.

Flora, James. (1955). *The fabulous fire work family.* New York: Harcourt, Brace. [32 p.]. Grades K–2.
This book shows a family that for generations has worked together making fireworks for their village. The story describes all the family at work in building a castle, the day of a fiesta with dancers portraying a story of Moors and Christians, the "toritos" (fireworks), and finally the firing of the castle. Because the castle was such a great success, Pepito was very proud to belong to the fabulous fire work family.

Griego, Margot C., Betsey L. Bucks, Sharon S. Gilbert, & Laurel H. Kimball. (1981). *Tortillitas para Mama and other nursery rhymes: Spanish and English.* Illustrated by Barbara Cooney. New York: Holt, Rinehart and Winston. [28 p.]. Preschool–2.
This is a delightful bilingual collection of 13 well-known Hispanic nursery rhymes passed on by each generation of Hispanic children. It

includes old-time favorites such as "La Viejita" ("The Little Old Lady"), "Colita de Rana" ("Little Frog Tail"), "Los Pollitos" ("The Chicks"), and "Arrullo" ("Lullaby"). Barbara Cooney's undeniable artistic abilities add much charm to each nursery rhyme; however, it is indeed regrettable that most of her illustrations depict stereotyped scenes of barefooted peasants in quaint, rural settings. (Illustrators and editors should update their impressions of Hispanic people. Both in the United States and abroad, most Hispanics live in urban settings.) Only two of the illustrations depict Hispanic people with a sincere warmth and understanding; more illustrations like these would have made this book of nursery rhymes a sure winner.

Holguin, Jimenez, Emma Morales Puncel, & Conchita Morales Puncel. (1969). *Para Chiquitines*. Los Angeles, CA: Bowmar Publishing Corp. [76 p.]. Preschool–2.
Outstanding collection of 15 songs, 22 poems, and 21 finger plays in Spanish that have been sung and recited in Spanish-speaking homes for generations, as well as a few original compositions by the authors. Colorful illustrations complement each tune and poem. The book also includes a glossary providing an English translation of every selection. This book is a source of joy to any Spanish-speaking child and to any English-speaking child who wishes to learn Spanish.

Kouzel, Daisy. (1977). *The cuckoo's reward/El premio del cuco*. Illustrated by Earl Thollander. New York: Doubleday. [28 p.]. Grades K–3.
An attractive adaptation of a Mayan legend that tells why the gray cuckoo lost its splendid feathers and beautiful singing voice and why "the cuckoo lays her eggs in the nests of other birds, who raise her children for her." Because the text is in simple English and Spanish, it could appeal to children who speak either language.

Martel, Cruz. (1976). *Yagua days*. Illustrated by Jerry Pinkney. New York: The Dial Press. [34 p.]. Grades K–3.
Adan Riera was born in New York City and had never been to Puerto Rico. His Puerto Rican parents, who owned a bodega in New York City, decided to visit Uncle Ulise's plantation in Puerto Rico. So Adan had many nice experiences with his family in Puerto Rico. He saw the beautiful mountains; he met many members of his big family; he picked tropical fruits from the trees; and he had lots of fun during Yagua Days. Two-tone line drawings show happy scenes of Adan in Puerto Rico.

Politi, Leo. (1963). *The nicest gift*. New York: Scribner Book Company. [24 p.]. Grades K–2.
An outstanding book to show young children the life of the people that came from "Old Mexico," with colorful illustrations of "el barrio." It tells about tamales and how they are cooked and that "churros are made of sweet dough and cooked in a large kettle of boiling oil...they look like pretzels." It mentions attractive aspects of Mexican-American life, such as "el mercado," restaurants, shops, "piñatas," "payasos," and "boleros."

————. (1946). *Pedro, the angel of Olvera Street*. New York: Scribner Book Company. [28 p.]. Grades K–2.
An attractive view of the "puestos" (shops), Mexican food, music, and many festive activities in Olvera Street as preparations for the traditional Mexican Christmas celebrations. The story tells that the pilgrims requested posada (sought shelter) in "your puestos." This is perhaps a misunderstanding of the nature of a posada; they are not commercial affairs but strictly family and social celebrations. This is, nonetheless, an appealing story about a gay Mexican holiday.

Pope, Billy N., & Ramona Ware Emmons. (1968). *Your world: Let's visit Mexico City*. Dallas, TX: Taylor Publishing Company. [30 p.]. Grades K–2.
Two girls from Texas and their mother take a train ride to Mexico City, where they are invited into the home of a local family. The Mexican girls' beautiful clothes, furniture, and home are a welcome contrast to many books that show only poverty in Mexico. Together they visit Mexico City's interesting sites: the Cathedral; Plaza of the Three Cultures; Palace of Fine Arts; attractive statues, streets, parks; the Aztec Stadium; the zoo; the floating gardens; the pyramids; small shops, open markets, and the breaking of a "pinata" [sic]. Attractive, large pictures in color show the beauty of Mexico City. The book ends by stating: "We will remember our trip to Mexico City for a long time. It is the oldest city in North America. Would you like to visit Mexico City?" Perhaps young children will indeed be enticed.

Prieto, Mariana. (1973). *Play it in Spanish*. Illustrated by Regina and Haig Sherkerjian. New York: The John Day Company. [43 p.]. Grades K–2.
A collection of 17 well-known Latin American and Spanish games and nursery songs that will appeal to all children familiar with the Spanish language, especially children who have a Hispanic heritage. It includes music for the songs and words in Spanish with a free English translation.

Sandoval, Ruben. (1977). *Games games games*. Photos by David Strick. New York: Doubleday. [78 p.]. Grades K–6.
As expressed by the authors, the "purpose of this book is to help maintain the continuity between the games of Mexico and the newer ones played in the barrios of California, and thus to help prepare a truly bilingual and bicultural tradition in the United States" (p. 13). The outstanding black-and-white photographs of happy Mexican-American children at play in the barrio can be enjoyed by anyone. A few of the delightful rhymes, amusing tongue twisters, and diverting games that Mexican children have known for several generations are indeed preserved in this handsome book.

Schon, Isabel. (Ed.) (1983). *Doña Blanca and other hispanic nursery rhymes and games*. Minneapolis, MN: T.S. Denison. [41 p.]. Grades K–6.
Eighteen well-known Hispanic nursery rhymes and games are included in this bilingual (Spanish-English) publication. Two-tone illustrations and simple instructions explain to the reader how to play the games. Some of the rhymes and games included are: "Riquirran," "La Cucaracha,"

"Andale Anita," "A la rueda de San Miguel," "A la vibora," "Matarile-Rile-Ro," and others.

Thomas, Dawn C. (1970). *Mira! Mira!* Illustrated by Harold L. James. New York: J. B. Lippincott. [45 p.]. Grades K-3.
Ramon and his family arrived in New York City full of excitement and joy at seeing their relatives, who owned a big car. But Ramon's greatest expectation was that "tomorrow he would see the snow." (p. 24). Mother was very understanding; she promised: "I am going downtown with your Aunt Rosita. I must buy you a suit for the snow. I must buy you boots and a warm cap. And, of course, I will not forget gloves so that you can make snowballs." (p. 26). Ramon had a very good time playing in the snow with all the children, even though he did not have the proper clothes and he got sick. Line drawings of well-dressed children and adults depict happy Puerto Rican families in New York City.

Wahl, Jan. (1981). *The cucumber princess.* Illustrated by Caren Caraway. Owings Mills, MD: Stemmer House Publishers. [34 p.]. Grades 1-3.
Colorful illustrations inspired by pre-Columbian art beautifully complement this story with a contemporary message: The king is not the stronger just because he is a man, and the beautiful tall lady loved him for showing "real weakness." The mysterious lady describes herself as: "I am She Who Makes the Rain Fall. I am She Who Turns the Corn Ripe. I am She Who Gives. Together, TOGETHER, we can both make a powerful kingdom." Even though there is little information in the story about ancient Mexico, readers might notice the references to magnificent palaces, dry land, and powerful kings, which certainly apply to the Aztecs of pre-Columbian Mexico. The love story between the Cucumber Princess and Totoco-Ahpop, the powerful king, and their delightful contest of wills and strength, will amuse young readers with its action and final outcome.

THIRD THROUGH SIXTH GRADES

Ancona, George. (1982). *Bananas: From Manolo to Margie.* New York: Clarion Books. [46 p.]. Grades 3-5.
Impressive color and black-and-white photographs and a simple, direct text describe the process of growing, harvesting, and transporting bananas. Of special interest is the story of Manolo's family, who live on a banana plantation in Honduras that is owned by a large fruit company. Manolo's father works on the plantation and Manolo's mother works as a packer.

Beck, Barbara L. (1966). *The first book of the Aztecs.* Illustrated by Page Cary. New York: Franklin Watts. [67 p.]. Grades 4-6.
Excellent photographs and an easy-to-understand text depict the achievements and daily life of the Aztecs. This book includes Mexico's early civilizations; the forming of the Aztec nation; the Aztecs, people of the sun; education and the social classes; war and religion; the achievements

of the Aztecs; Tenochititlan; and the Spanish conquistadores. The author must be commended for describing the Aztec civilization very simply and yet preserving the authenticity of Aztec history. Many of the outstanding pictures that complement the text were taken from original Aztec codexes. There is, however, one oversight on page 65: Cortes did not speak English; he spoke Spanish.

Belpre, Pura. (1973). *Once in Puerto Rico*. Illustrated by Christine Price. New York: Frederick Warne. [96 p.]. Grades 2–6.

A charming collection of 17 Puerto Rican popular tales and legends that tell of the island's early history, as well as its customs and beliefs. The book includes short and simple tales about Puerto Rico's pre-Columbian Indians, the Spanish conquistadores, the English attack of 1797, and Puerto Rico's animal tales. A joyous introduction to the people and history of Puerto Rico by a superb native storyteller.

Bierhorst, John. (Translator). (1984). *Spirit child: A story of the Nativity*. Illustrated by Barbara Cooney. New York: William Morrow. [32 p.]. Grades 3–6.

The story of the Nativity as told by the Aztecs is exquisitely presented in this beautifully illustrated book. The Aztec culture and the Christian religion are honestly depicted in the carefully translated text and in the stunning pre-Columbian-style illustrations. This is definitely a joyous introduction to the Aztecs, as well as a message of hope through the spirit child.

Brenner, Barbara. (1981). *Mystery of the plumed serpent*. Illustrated by Blanche Sims. New York: Knopf. [78 p.]. Grades 3–6.

This is a captivating mystery story about Mexico, snakes, smuggled treasures, and two twins, Michael and Elena Garcia, that should appeal to all readers. It includes excitement and adventure as the twins try to unravel the mystery of the golden snake. Grandma and Mama Garcia complete the attractive family that is shown living in a Spanish section of New York City. There are positive references to Grandma "reading her Spanish paper" and interesting yet simple explanations about pre-Columbian history and legends. The twins' natural flair for thrills amidst the potential seriousness of a smuggling ring involving a rare pre-Columbian Mexican treasure helps to make this a humorous and entertaining story.

Burland, C.A. (1962). *Inca Peru*. Illustrated by Yvonne Poulton. Philadelphia: Dufour Editions. [93 p.]. Grades 4–8.

This book includes interesting facts about Peru at the time of the Viracocha Inca about A.D. 1450. In a simple and readable text with small black-and-white drawings, young readers learn about the Incas in Peru, including sections on animals, the army, boats, children and school, clothes and jewelry, farming, food and drink, geography, gods and religion, government, homes and houses, medicine, metalwork, music and dance, people and life, pottery, spinning and weaving, stone work, towns, and travel. An example of the book's simple and straightforward approach to Inca life is the following paragraph that tells about the much criticized Inca form of law: "Inca rule might be hard, but it was so wise that people hardly realized that they had lost all their freedom. They were sure of their homes and a piece of land on which to grow their food. If there was a famine the Inca fed them from his stores. If they needed clothing they had a fair share from the town storehouses, to which they had already given some of their own work. Everything was so well organized that ordinary people found nothing to worry about." (p. 86).

Clark, Ann Nolan. (1962). *Paco's miracle.* New York: Farrar, Straus, and Giroux. [32 p.]. Grades 3–6.
This book beautifully describes Spanish formal customs, marriage cere- monies, Christmas celebrations, and clothing through the lives of an old man and a young boy (Paco) who live in seclusion in the mountains of northern New Mexico. An attractive writing style illustrates the theme of kindness to all things.

Colorado, Antonio J. (1978). *The first book of Puerto Rico.* 3d ed. New York: Franklin Watts. [66 p.]. Grades 4–8.
Like the previous edition, this is a faithful introduction to Puerto Rico by a Puerto Rican who loves his country and is eager to describe its beauties. In a very simple manner, the author tells about the island and its people, early history, politics, economics, and cities, as well as other important facts up to 1976. Attractive black-and-white photographs com- plement the easy-to-read text.

Glubok, Shirley. (1966). *The art of ancient Peru.* New York: Harper & Row. [41 p.]. Grades 3–10.
Through the magnificent art of ancient Peru the reader is introduced to the pottery, textiles, jewelry, and architecture of the Chavin, Mochica, Nazca, Tiahuanaco, Chimu, and Inca cultures. Simple explanations and striking photographs should entice young readers to explore the outstand- ing achievements of ancient Peru.

Hall, Lynn. (1981). *Danza!* New York: Charles Scribner's Sons. [129 p.]. Grades 4–8.
A touching story that describes the strong feelings between Paulo, a Puerto Rican boy, and Danza, a magnificent Paso Fino stallion. Paulo's life on a farm in Puerto Rico with his family, his dignified grandfather, Diego Mendez, and a special mare and her stud colt Danza are movingly depicted. The characterization of Paulo as a sensitive boy and young man, and his relationship with Danza, his grandfather, and Major Kessler are sympathetically depicted. The excitement caused by some people's ruthless will to win horse shows adds drama and suspense for the reader throughout the book. The author can be faulted only for commenting that the Borinquen Indians "had played their deadly games" and that "the blood of sacrificial offerings had soaked away to nourish the roots of the flowers." Mentioning the Borinquen Indians adds au- thenticity to a story set in Puerto Rico, but these descriptions are too negative. The following is also completely unnecessary: "Ball game. I should have known. What else would a Puerto Rican be doing on a Saturday afternoon?" (p. 19).

Hancock, Sibyl. (1983). *Esteban and the ghost.* Illustrated by Dirk Zimmer. New York: Dial Books for Young Readers. [32 p.]. Grades 3–5.
Esteban, a merry tinker, had heard a fabulous tale about a haunted castle

near Toledo in Spain. He decided to go to the castle to try for the 1,000 gold reales offered by the owner of the castle to anyone who could drive the ghost away. Esteban's good humor and delightful common sense will charm readers; the black-line drawings with full-color illustrations add a sense of excitement to this ghost tale, without creating undue horror or violence.

Huber, Alex. (1984). *We live in Argentina*. (Living Here Series) New York: The Bookwright Press. [60 p.]. Grades 4–8.
Like other titles in this series, this book includes 26 first person interviews of people from Argentina who describe their lives and occupations and the area of the country in which they live. Outstanding, colorful photographs complement the informative two-page interviews. In contrast to other titles in this series, those from Argentina who were interviewed represent a cross-section of people: truck driver, museum guide, doctor, TV broadcaster, gaucho, lawyer, farmer, etc., making this book a well-balanced introduction to Argentina and its people.

Krumgold, Joseph. (1953). *...and now Miguel*. New York: Crowell Publishers. [245 p.]. Grades 3–8.
A brilliant, human description of a boy and his family who own sheep in the mountains of New Mexico. Miguel's desire to go up the high mountain to spend the whole summer with the men who tend sheep there is touching and revealing. It very successfully describes the family life of Mexican Americans in the Southwest: their customs, backgrounds, and strong religious beliefs. In spite of some assimilation into American society, the families maintain their saints, holidays, food, and some of their language.

McMullen, David. (1977). *Mystery in Peru: The lines of Nazca*. Milwaukee, WI: Raintree Children's Books. [48 p.]. Grades 3–6.
Jim Woodman, a modern day explorer, "is searching for the reason an ancient people [used] to carve lines and pictures in the sun-baked Nazca soil" (pp. 5–6). Black-and-white and color photographs show huge aerial views of designs of monkeys, spiders, condors, and strange spirals carved into the ground at least 2,000 years ago. The author believes that "ancient balloonists...gazed down at these Nazca lines some 2,000 years ago" (p. 47); other theories also try to explain why the ancient lines were drawn. This is an interesting introduction to the study of ancient Peruvian culture.

Mangurian, David. (1979). *Children of the Incas*. New York: Four Winds Press. [73 p.]. Grades 3–6.
In an astonishingly honest manner, Modesto Quispe, a 13-year-old Peruvian boy, narrates the pathetically poor and hopeless existence that he and his family have lived for several generations in Coata, a Peruvian town in the highlands of South America. Mangurian, the author and photographer, has done an excellent job of describing his stay with the family during which he "never had milk or chicken or beef or pork or lamb or green vegetables or any fruit" (p. 8). He describes a town without electricity or water or telephones. Modesto poignantly tells why various members of his family chew coca leaves: "They say coca makes the pain go away. They say coca keeps them from feeling hungry" (p. 53). The dramatic black-and-white photographs complement the text in

conveying to the reader/viewer the deplorable living conditions of the people in Coata. Unfortunately, there are no similarly powerful books in English that might provide balance by describing to young readers the joy, beauty, and happiness also present in Peru.

Markun, Patricia Maloney. (1979). *The Panama Canal*. Revised Edition. New York: Franklin Watts. [66 p.]. Grades 3–6.
This is a well-written revised edition of Markun's *The First Book of the Panama Canal*. It describes the great effort needed to put a ship through the complicated system of gates and locks. It also gives the history of both the political background and the actual work involved in building the canal. In addition, it includes very interesting chapters on the importance of the canal to world trade and the future of the canal. Historical and current black-and-white photographs complement this good introduction to the Panama Canal.

Neurath, Marie. (1966). *They lived like this: The ancient Maya*. Illustrated by John Ellis. New York: Franklin Watts, Inc. [32 p.]. Grades 4–6.
Authentic drawings based on Mayan wall paintings and designs and a simple text describe outstanding aspects of Mayan civilization: pottery, agriculture, gods, cities, religious buildings, pyramids, jewelry, ceremonies, wars, houses, astronomy, calendar, and mathematics.

Palacios, Argentina. (1979). *The knight and the squire*. Illustrated by Ray Cruz. New York: Doubleday. [96 p.]. Grades 3–7.
Young readers should be delighted with this abridged version, with amusing black-and-white drawings, of the adventures of Don Quixote and Sancho, who set out as knights of old to right wrongs and punish evil. The simple, straightforward text includes the following chapters, encompassing the most famous and charming of Cervantes' episodes: A knight in armor, Don Quixote leaves home; The price of meddling; Don Quixote and Sancho Panza have some strange adventures; More strange adventures; Back to La Mancha again; Don Quixote learns he is already famous; On the road again; The knight of the wood; The adventure of the lions; The puppet show; At the duke's palace; The adventure of the wooden horse; Don Quixote advises Sancho; Sancho, governor for life; Danger at the island; Sancho's wisest decision; Knight and squire reunited; The knight of the white moon; and Don Quixote's last illness.

Piggott, Juliet. (1973). *Mexican folk tales*. New York: Crane Russak. [128 p.]. Grades 4–Adult.
An excellent collection of 11 tales, mostly from pre-Columbian Mexico. The introduction to the tales gives a very good account of the swift conquest of Mexico by the Spaniards. It is important to note that several of the tales emphasize the wisdom that pre-Columbian people admired in their leaders: "Jiculi, Prince of the Huichol tribe...was a young man, endowed with wisdom, modesty and practicality beyond his years." (p. 32) The book also includes the well-known story of Tepoztecatl when he cut his way out of Xochicalcatl's stomach: "But all Tepoztecatl had to say about it at the time was: 'I am nearly a man!'"(p. 128).
    The attractive pre-Columbian illustrations and authentic tales offer an authentic introduction to the fascinating culture of Mexico. The book retells very well-known tales as "Popocateptel and Ixtlaccihuatl," popular

animal tales like "The Rabbit and the Two Coyotes," and some explain the world's creation, such as "Story of the Flood," and "The Golden Man and the Finger Men," which explains that "There would be rich men and poor men on the earth...and that they would all fill the heavens with their praises." (p. 56).

Rutland, Jonathan. (1980). *Take a trip to Spain.* New York: Franklin Watts. [32 p.]. Grades 2–4.
The beauty and diversity of Spanish cities and geographical areas are beautifully depicted in 35 color photographs with accompanying text. The simple text describes life in Madrid and Barcelona, historical sites, favorite dishes, architecture, weather, bullfights, traditional costumes and dances, agriculture, and other attractions. This is an excellent introduction to Spain for young readers.

Singer, Jane, & Kurt Singer. (1969). *Folk tales of Mexico.* Minneapolis, MN: T.S. Denison. [110 p.]. Grades 4–10.
An outstanding collection of 10 Mexican folktales from pre-Columbian times through Pancho Villa and the Mexican Revolution; the tales highlight important beliefs of the Mexican people. It includes well-known pre-Columbian legends: Quetzalcoatl, the Plumed Serpent; Ixtlaccihuatl and Popocatepetl; Yallo, the wise fool (a Zapotec legend); and How the Earth was Created (a Mayan legend). From the colonial period come the legends of the China Poblana and the Virgin of Guadalupe. From the nineteenth century comes a legend of Benito Juarez, and from the Twentieth Century, "How Pancho Villa Sold his Soul to El Diablo." This is a marvelous introduction to Mexico and its history through Mexico's fascinating folktales.

Singer, Julia. (1977). *We all come from Puerto Rico.* New York: Atheneum. [71 p.]. Grades 4–6.
Through black-and-white photographs and a brief text, the author describes many kinds of people who live in Puerto Rico today; Grandfather Barcelo's very large finca (farm), where he grows bananas, coffee, oranges, and citron; Grandfather Carlos, who raises Paso Fino horses and has won many trophies; Uncle Tonio, who is a retired mayor of Vieques; Hector's dreams to become a professional baseball player; and Legnaly's dreams to become a prima ballerina.

————. (1976). *We all come from someplace: Children of Puerto Rico.* New York: Atheneum. [88 p.]. Grades 4–6.
Black-and-white photographs and a brief text describe the life of Puerto Rican children from various villages and the city of Mayaguez. Jose and Willy introduce the reader to their island; Jonas tells about the Day of the Three Kings; Raquel describes the Christmas holiday season; Sonia and Jolie tell about their life in Mayaguez; Tanto describes the life in Puerto Real, a fishing village; and Jose and Willy explain about life in Ensenada, where "almost everybody in one way or another is affected by the sugar....Either they grow the sugar or cut sugar or load the cut cane onto trailers, or they work in the mill." (p. 72).

Stein, R. Conrad. (1984). *Mexico.* (Enchantment of the World Series). Chicago: Children's Press. [126 p.]. Grades 4–8.
The amazing variety and contrasts of Mexico's geography, history, economy, culture, government, and people are interestingly described in this well-written introduction to our neighbor to the south. Attractive color photographs capture the beauty and joy of Mexico. In addition, the author needs to be commended for explaining in an honest and straightforward manner the problems of Mexico today, such as Mexico's severe unemployment, poverty, and smog in Mexico City. The only regrettable note, in this otherwise outstanding introductory book, is the large number of misaccented, misspelled, or misused Spanish words.

———. (1982). *The story of the Panama Canal.* Illustrated by Keith Neely. Chicago: Children's Press. [31 p.]. Grades 3–5.
The history of the Panama Canal is presented in a lively story format. It begins with Columbus' cruise along the coast of present-day Panama, continues with the importance of the area in the mid-1800s, and concludes with the vast number of engineering and medical problems that had to be resolved before the engineering miracle of the Panama Canal was finally constructed. Regrettably, the two-tone illustrations do not do justice to the informative text.

de Treviño, Elizabeth Borton. (1965). *I, Juan de Pareja.* New York: Dell Books. [180 p.]. Grades 3–8.
A well-told story that describes the Spanish court during the seventeenth century. Through the life and work of the great Spanish artists Velazquez, the reader meets Murillo, Rubens, King Philip IV, and Pope Innocent X. This Newbery Award winning book offers many historical glimpses of Spanish civilization and customs.

———. (1974). *Juarez, man of law.* New York: Farrar, Straus and Giroux. [150 p.]. Grades 3–8.
A simply-written biography that emphasizes Juarez' great personal attributes and dedication in setting up laws that guaranteed equal rights to all people. Juarez' early life, marriage and exile, the Reform Laws, the Maximilian problem, and the victory of the Republic are interestingly described. It also deals honestly with Mexico's problems of misery and ignorance.

Villacana, Eugenio. (1971). *Viva Morelia.* Philadelphia: Lippincott. [110 p.]. Grades 3–6.
This book genuinely describes the author's feelings as he learns about "being a Mexican." Born in the state of Michoacan, he had a Spanish father and an Indian mother. The illustrations depict middle-class homes, well-dressed children, a bullfight, and trips to several cities of Michoacan (Quiroga, Patzcuaro, Janitzio, Uruapan, and Paricutin), as well as school days and holidays.

Whitney, Alex. (1976). *Voices in the wind.* New York: McKay. [57 p.]. Grades 2–8.
An outstanding collection of legends from six pre-Columbian civilizations. This book is an excellent introduction to the Mayas of Yucatan; the Aztecs of Mexico; the Quiche Mayas of Guatemala; the Chibchas of

Colombia and Panama; the Amerinds of Guyana, Surinam, and Brazil; and the Incas of Ecuador, Bolivia, and Peru.

Wojciechowska, Maia. (1972). *The life and death of a brave bull.* Illustrated by John Groth. New York: Harcourt Brace Jovanovich. [44 p.]. Grades 3–6.
Through beautiful line drawings and a simple text, the author explains the feelings of a brave bull: "Its unending bravery, its pride, one might even say its Spanish haughtiness, were the very qualities expected of the Spanish knights." The book describes a bull's first years in an endless sea of grass, and feelings when "he discovers himself the owner of a wondrous toy—his horns." The bullfighter's feelings about a brave bull are also described: "[He] grew to love him for his courage, for his great mobility, for his immense strength and his endless wish to attack." This is a well-written story that could serve as an excellent introduction to the art of bullfighting.

SIXTH GRADE AND ABOVE

Blackmore, Vivien. (Adaptor) *Why corn is golden: Stories about plants.* Illustrated by Susana Martinez-Ostos. [46 p.].

de Gerez, Toni. (Adaptor) *My song is a piece of jade: Poems of ancient Mexico in English and Spanish.* Illustrated by William Stark. [45 p.].

Hinojosa, Francisco. (Adaptor) *The old lady who ate people: Frightening stories.* Illustrated by Leonel Maciel. [47 p.].

Kurtycz, Marcos, & Ana Garcia Kobeh. (Adaptors) *Tiger and opossums: Animal legends.* Illustrated by the authors. [45 p.].

Each Volume: (Boston: Little, Brown, 1984). Grades 5–10.
The striking color illustrations and beautiful presentations are indeed appropriate in this outstanding series of Mexican legends, poems, and folktales. All text is in English, with the exception of the Toltec poems, *My Song is a Piece of Jade*, which are in both English and Spanish. *Why Corn is Golden* is a collection of six pre-Columbian legends about plants, flowers, and fruits that should appeal to most readers. *My Song is a Piece of Jade* is an excellent introduction to pre-Columbian culture, gods, and literature through Nahuatl poems. *The Old Lady Who Ate People* includes four Mexican legends of spirits and phantoms. Finally, *Tigers and Opossums* is an excellent adaptation of six Mexican legends about animals that will charm readers with their wit and resourcefulness.

Bowen, J. David. (1976). *The land and people of Chile.* New York: J. B. Lippincott. [155 p.]. Grades 7–10.
This is a simple introduction to Chile's geography, history, government, economy, culture, and people, with information up to 1976. It emphasizes the problem of Chile's severe isolation during colonial times as well as Chile's dependence on copper. It briefly mentions the "Chilean election of 1970 [that] was the most important that had taken place in

Latin America in modern times....It was the first time voters had been given a clear opportunity to choose or to reject Marxist socialism in a free election....In 1970 Chile was the first country in the world to elect to the presidency a man dedicated to revolution on Marxist principles. Salvador Allende became the 'comrade president' of Chile" (p. 150). Equally succinct is the statement that on "...September 11, 1973, in a move that many had expected for months, the Chilean army called for Allende's resignation. He refused and swore he would die at his post....The socialist experiment was over" (p. 155).

Bristow, Richard. (1984). *We live in Spain.* (Living Here series). New York: The Bookwright Press, distributed by Franklin Watts. [64 p.]. Grades 6–12.
Through 28 first-person interviews of Spanish people of all ages, interests, occupations, and backgrounds, young readers are exposed to life in modern Spain. In a most personal manner, people relate their problems with the government in Madrid, their lives as flamenco dancers, bullfighters, teachers, members of the civil guard, and many others. The outstanding photographs in color and the honest and well-selected interviews make this an excellent portrait of life in Spain in the 1980s.

Carpenter, Allan. (1970). *Enchantment of Peru.* Chicago: Children's Press. [90 p.]. Grades 5–10.
In a very readable, direct manner, the author describes Peru yesterday and today, up to 1969. Attractive photographs and maps complement the description of Peru's geography, earliest civilizations, people, natural treasures, and the contrasts between the very rich and the very poor. It is an especially good introduction to the Inca Empire. The author emphasizes important achievements of the Incas, such as "The Inca Empire has been called the best working socialistic government in the history of the world" (p. 32). It contrasts the life of the Incas with modern Peru: "The lives of the Sierra Indians, also, have changed little over the centuries. In fact, in many ways, Peru is less advanced than it was during the Inca times. The Inca people cultivated much more of the land, and their people had more to eat, than the Indians do now....Not only did the Inca Empire have more extensive agriculture than present day Peru, but it also had a more extensive highway system. Inca roads reached many places where modern roads still do not go" (pp. 62, 77).

Carpenter, Allan, & Enno R. Haan. (1970). *Enchantment of Venezuela.* Chicago: Children's Press. [94 p.]. Grades 5–10.
This is a good overview of Venezuela up to 1968, with attractive photographs and maps. In a very readable, simple manner, it shows real differences between Venezuela and other countries in Latin America: "Carlos' father is an engineer in the oil industry...[He] gets a big salary from the oil business" (p. 23). "When the oil profits started to come in, the country was able to pay up all of its foreign debts" (p. 45). "Venezuela's oil equals about 6 or 7 percent of the total world oil reserves" (p. 64). "However, about one third of the people throughout the country are still in need of better housing and living conditions" (p. 70). It also includes chapters on Venezuela's history, government, people, and culture.

Clark, Ann Nolan. (1952). *Secret of the Andes*. Illustrated by Jean
Charlot. New York: Viking. [138 p.]. Grades 5–8.
Through the sensitivity of a great author, the reader is introduced to the
marvelous Inca culture. Cusi, an Indian boy, and Chuto, the old Inca
llama herder, still maintain many of the values and traditions of the
Incas: love of music, affection toward llamas, pride in history, and
reverence toward nature and their temples. Two well-known Inca legends
are beautifully interspersed with Cusi's growing up dilemmas.

De Messieres, Nicole. (1981). *Reina the galgo*. New York: Elsevier/
Nelson. [211 p.]) Grades 6–9.
The life of an American family living in Peru is beautifully and honestly
depicted through Colette, the 11-year-old daughter. She describes the
excitement and warmth that followed the family's acquisition of a remarkable greyhound, Reina, who had extraordinary speed and strength
as well as an independent spirit. The book deals with the family's
friends, outings, and joys in Peru, as well as later problems. The loss of
Mr. Livingston's job in Peru and the family's return to the United States,
where Mr. Livingston had a hard time finding a new job, are told amidst
a whole series of exciting adventures with the courageous Reina. The
feelings of a young girl growing up, her attachments to Peru and her
beloved Reina, and her apprehensions about her new life in the United
States are touchingly described in this family/dog novel.

Gemming, Elizabeth. (1980). *Lost city in the clouds: The discovery of
Machu Picchu*. Illustrated by Mike Eagle. New York: Coward,
McCann, and Geoghegan. [82 p.]. Grades 4–8.
The story of Hiram Bingham's astonishing discovery of the "lost city in
the clouds," Machu Picchu, is interestingly told by Gemming. The author
worked from Bingham's own descriptions and recounts with genuine
amazement the spectacular sights and achievements of the Incas.
Through passages of fictional dialogue, the author interjects important
episodes of Inca history, as well as exciting aspects of Bingham's inves-
tigations in Peru in the early 1900s. This book can also serve as an
especially good introduction to the remarkable Inca civilization. Unfortunately, the 13 black-and-white line illustrations do not convey to the
reader/viewer the majestic grandeur of Machu Picchu and its surroundings.

Glubok, Shirley. (1967). *The fall of the Incas*. Illustrated by Gerard
Nook. New York: Macmillan. [114 p.]. Grades 5–10.
The author has abridged and adapted two sixteenth-century documents,
one by the Inca Garcilaso de la Vega and the other by Pedro Pizarro, a
cousin of the well-known conquistador. This story of the rise and fall of
the Inca Empire includes real and imaginary pre-Empire Inca rulers; the
period of the Inca Empire, which began around 1438; an eyewitness
account of the conquest; and commentaries of Inca life, customs, laws,
beliefs, and rules of conduct. The Inca drawings add authenticity to the
narrative. Good readers who would like to increase their understanding
of the Inca civilization will find this book most enlightening.

Griffiths, Helen. (1979). *The last summer: Spain 1936*. Illustrated by
Victor Ambrus. New York: Holiday House. [152 p.]. Grades
6–10.
Sensitively and poignantly, Griffiths tells a story about the tragedy,
horrors, and wanton destruction that occurred in Spain during the summer of 1936. Eduardo, an 11-year-old boy from a wealthy Spanish
family, must stay with his father on the family's country estate, instead
of going to Galicia with his mother. There he learns about Gaviota, a
beautiful mare that once belonged to his amazing aunt. Suddenly, the
war shatters Eduardo's life: his father is killed, his servants are shot, and
he finds himself alone with the horse amidst a cruel senseless war that
kills friends and enemies alike. After experiencing kindness and abuse
from many people, he finally is reunited with his mother, who never
understood the bitterness and grief he endured. This excellent book
touchingly conveys to young readers the tremendous impact that the
Spanish Civil War had on the Spanish people.

Hall, Elvajean. (1972). *The land and people of Argentina*. Revised
Edition. New York: J. B. Lippincott. [155 p.]. Grades 6–10.
This is an interesting introduction to Argentina, its history, and its
people. The author offers simple contrasts to explain differences between
the United States and Argentina. "[In North America] we had settlers; in
South America they had exploiters...the exploiters might have been called
Ferdinand and Columbus, Incorporated....Everything done in the New
World had to meet one test only: would it make money for the Crown?"
(p. 45). The author then continues to explain how this resulted in the
restrictive policy that no trade could be shipped through the port of
Buenos Aires during Spanish colonial times. It describes Argentina's fight
for Independence; Juan Domingo Peron, and his controversial wife, Eva
Duarte; the gauchos; and life in Buenos Aires: "One of the first things a
visitor today notices is the appearance of wealth and luxury....The fash-
ionable shopping streets, Avenida Santa Fe and Calle Florida, can be
compared with Fifth Avenue in New York" (p. 109). "Argentina is the
one South American country in which there is a large middle class" (p.
117).

Hargreaves, Pat. (Ed.) (1980). *The Caribbean and Gulf of Mexico*.
Morristown, NJ: Silver Burdett. [72 p.]. Grades 5–9.
The Caribbean Sea and the Gulf of Mexico are introduced to young
readers through outstanding black-and-white and color photographs, and
important facts about the region. The history of the region, animal and
plant life on and under the surface, and the coral reefs and sea shore are
described, as well as a brief tour of the islands. A glossary, index, and
reading list add to this book's usefulness.

Haverstock, Nathan A., & John P. Hoover. (1974). *Cuba in pictures*.
New York: Sterling Publishing. [63 p.]. Grades 6–12.
This is a very objective and well-written book on Cuba. Black-and-white
photographs add valuable information on the land, history, government,
people, and economy of Cuba. The authors are to be commended for
constantly keeping a balanced perspective on the Castro regime: "The
controversy over the pros and cons of the Castro regime has been
marked with an emotionalism which has obscured the problems of the

Cuban people" (p. 5). The U.S. role in Cuban affairs since 1898 is also objectively presented: "The U.S. military authorities did all of those things that would in their eyes make occupied Cuba conform to the American rather than the Cuban scale of cultural, social and political values. The result was that Cuba became a client state—a protectorate—of the United States" (p. 28). It mentions many of the accomplishments of the Castro government as well as many of the incalculable losses.

Irizarry, Carmen. (1974, 1976). *Spain: The land and its people.* London: Macdonald Educational; Morristown, NJ: Silver Burdett. [59 p.]. Grades 6–12.
This is an outstanding introduction to Spain written by an author who truly knows the country and the people. It briefly describes important aspects of Spanish personality, history, and customs in short two-page chapters. Drawings, maps, charts, and color photographs complement the author's many views of Spain, including discussions of family life, food, faith and ritual, important monarchs, Madrid, tourism, giants of art and thought, and many others. The following are two examples of the author's forthright style: "Contradiction is the hallmark of the Spanish character. The average Spaniard can be generous to a fault, but intolerant like few men on earth. He will take pride in calling himself an individualist while conforming to the standards of a closed society" (p. 50). And, regarding politics in Spain, she states: "Some Spaniards believe their country should adopt a more open, European system, but most Spaniards do not give any thought to politics. They think all forms of government are corrupt, and are content to enjoy the consumer goods and modern conveniences industrialization has brought" (p. 52).

Johnson, William Weber, & the Editors of Time-Life Books. (1972). *Baja California.* Photographs by Jay Meisel. New York: Time-Life Books. [184 p.]. Grades 6–12.
Remarkable color photographs and an enthusiastic narrative present the reader/viewer with a fascinating view of the dry, long, and rocky peninsula of Baja California. The author contrasts Southern California, "one of the world's most densely populated areas" (p. 48) with isolated Baja California, "a region so seemingly dead and sterile [that it] is, in fact, an abundant giver and protector of life" (p. 153). It includes chapters on the peninsula's land forms, canyons, deserts, plants, rocks, islands, animals, and its southern reaches. The author constantly describes Baja California's matchless beauties and the adaptations to nature found there; for example, "While such adaptations are not unique to Baja, many of Baja's plants are themselves unique. In the cactus family alone, 80 of the peninsula's 110 species grow nowhere else on earth" (p. 102).

Larralde, Elsa. (1964). *The land and people of Mexico.* New York: Lippincott. [158 p.]. Grades 6–12.
This is a very good overview of the history of Mexico up to 1964. Unfortunately, many of the statistics reported in this book are now obsolete, such as population figures, exports of natural resources, and facts that are no longer true. The author states that in Mexico City, "a subway is out of question; there is too much water underneath the surface" (p. 122); Mexico City does have a beautiful modern subway. But

this book has excellent chapters on the history of Mexico: sections on ancient tribes, the Conquest, the Colonial Period, Independence, the Texas War, and Porfirio Diaz and the Revolution give young readers good insight into Mexico's troubled history. It also indicts Mexico and the United States for the Texas War: "The events that led to the Texas War are numerous and complex, and it may be said, in all sincerity, that Mexico and the United States are equally to blame for the war, and for fostering the machinations and ambitions that finally caused the outbreak of hostilities" (p. 72).

Lindop, Edmund. (1980). *Cuba.* New York: Franklin Watts. [64 p.]. Grades 5–8.

This objective and well-written introduction to Cuba includes a brief overview of the geography and history of the island, as well as several chapters on Cuba after Castro. In a simple, forthright manner, the author explains controversial aspects of recent U.S.-Cuban history such as the Bay of Pigs and the Missile Crisis of 1962. Excellent descriptions of the Cuban economy and the way of life in communist Cuba emphasize the problems as well as the achievements of Cuba today. For example, the author correctly states that: "Today Cuba has the most extensive educational system in Latin America: from preschool day care units to the island's four universities and many vocational schools, all education is free" (p. 54); he also points out that "literature has suffered more than the other art forms in communist Cuba. Since the government controls all the printing presses, the works of novelists, poets, playwrights, and nonfiction writers must conform to the revolutionary spirit in order to be published" (p. 59). Eight recent color photographs provide additional views of life in Cuba from an unbiased perspective.

McKowan, Robin. (1973). *The image of Puerto Rico: Its history and its people on the island—on the mainland.* New York: McGraw-Hill. [88 p.]. Grades 6–10.

This is an excellent account of the history of Puerto Rico from its discovery by Columbus through reconsideration of its political status in 1968. The author is to be commended for her well-balanced report of Puerto Rico's history, social problems, and political dilemmas. The following is a brief example of the author's direct style in describing Puerto Rico before the American takeover: "Half of the island's budget of 1898 went to upkeep of the church and the navy. Nearly three times as much was spent on the church as on education. Eighty percent of the population were illiterate. The majority of the people were abysmally poor" (p. 64).

Markun, Patricia Maloney. (1983). *Central America and Panama.* New York: Franklin Watts. [86 p.]. Grades 5–8.

This is a revised edition of *The First Book of Central America* published in 1961 and 1973. It is an up-to-date, realistic introduction to the geography, history, economics, and politics of the seven republics—Guatemala, Honduras, El Salvador, Nicaragua, Costa Rica, Panama, and Belize—which form Central America. It includes informative black-and-white photographs of the region, although, unfortunately, most of them show the ever-present poverty of Indian women. The author summarizes her book in a forthright manner: "Every country on the Central American isthmus except Costa Rica has had a history of violence and revolution and unstable governments. Never has the violence been so great, so present in nearly every country as in the late 1970's and early 1980's. Never has the future of Central America looked so bleak" (p. 76).

Meyer, Carolyn, & Charles Gallenkamp. (1985). *The mystery of the ancient Maya.* New York: Atheneum. [159 p.]. Grades 6–12.

Maya achievements in art, architecture, mathematics, astronomy, and writing are interestingly depicted in this simply written book with numerous black-and-white drawings and photographs. In vivid prose, the authors relate the excitement of the early explorers, the magnificence of the Classic Mayas, their bloody sacrifices, their outstanding intellectual achievements, their everyday lives, and their puzzling disappearance. It is unfortunate that none of the illustrations are in color, which would have conveyed much more dramatically the beauty of the original works. Despite this limitation, this is indeed a most readable and informative introduction to the ancient Maya civilization.

Millard, Anne. (1980). *The Incas.* Illustrated by Richard Hook (New York: Warwick Press. [44 p.]. Grades 5–10.

The splendor and achievements of the Inca civilization are magnificently portrayed through excellent color photographs, drawings, and a straightforward text. It describes the life of the ruler and his nobles, the organization of the empire, the Incas' amazing building skills, and the beautiful crafts practiced by the people living in the Andes, as well as many other aspects of Inca civilization. This book is a marvelous introduction to the Inca Empire that "was built in the 15th century and lasted less than a hundred years."

Mohr, Nicholasa. (1977). *In Nueva York.* New York: The Dial Press. [192 p.]. Grades 6–10.

In this collection of eight interrelated short stories, Mohr describes in her deeply moving style the sad, depressing, and difficult life of many people of New York's Lower East Side. The characters evoke sympathy in their apparent hopeless existence: Old Mary, who escapes her dreary reality by sipping beer, is married to Ramon, who spends his wages on drink. Old Mary explains why she never supported or sent for her son in Puerto Rico: "I got to New York all right, but I was only here a short while and had another baby. And no man wants an extra burden, especially one that ain't his. So it went, I had another baby and soon found myself alone again, this time with two small kids" (p. 12–13). Yolanda, a high school dropout, narrates her poignant dependency on drugs. Johnny and Sebastian are involved in a seemingly satisfying homosexual relationship that includes constant arguments and frequent outbursts. And Lali, who just arrived from Puerto Rico, is married to a man one year younger than her father. These true stories are indeed intimate and tragic portraits of many Puerto Ricans.

Moser, Don. (1975). *Central American jungles.* New York: Time-Life Books. [179 p.]. Grades 6–12.

The enchanting wilderness of Central America is marvelously described for the reader through the author's interesting experiences and superb color photographs of excellent Time-Life quality. The luxuriant complexity and abundance of life of the Central American countries (Guatemala, El Salvador, Honduras, Nicaragua, Costa Rica, Panama, and Belize) are depicted in captivating detail. The land, volcanoes, mountains, vegetation, birds, monkeys, coasts, swamps, wild animals, and forests are described. The following is an example of how vividly the author tells about life in the jungle: "I was stunned by the speed and ease with which the ants had killed the scorpion. It had been no contest at all. I felt a little uneasy standing right in the midst of the columns, but Jim assured me that the ants were no danger to humans or other large animals—we could simply move out of range in a few steps....The ants raid human habitation at the edge of the jungle periodically, he said, and when this happens, the people clear out. Such raids are not regarded as unmitigated evils, for the ants clean out cockroaches and other vermin as thoroughly as any exterminator might" (p. 93).

Perry, Roger. (1974). *Patagonia: Windswept land of the south.* New York: Dodd, Mead. [117 p.]. Grades 6–12.
This is an enthusiastic and simply-written description of Patagonia, "the region at the far south of the American continent. It is shared between Argentina and Chile and runs at its tip into the bleak archipelago known as Tierra del Fuego" (p. 11). Interesting black-and-white photographs complement the text that narrates the beauties of the Strait of Magellan, the eastern steppes, fiords and glaciers, and the emerging Patagonia culture, as well as brief historical references to the early peoples and the first explorers. The author's great joy in writing about his travels to this region is evident throughout the book. The following is a short example of his description of the Muñoz Gamero Peninsula: "In the morning the clouds parted and I had my first glimpse of calm sea and nearby slopes were bathed in sunlight. The clouds, even as they cleared, were suffused with soft pastel colors which matched the tranquility of the scene" (p. 18).

Reeves, James. (1962). *Exploits of Don Quixote.* Illustrated by Edward Ardizzone. New York: Henry Z. Walck. [219 p.]. Grades 6–12.
This is a marvelous introduction for young readers to Cervantes' *Don Quixote.* Reeves has maintained Cervantes' good humor by depicting in a fluid, simple writing style Don Quixote's delightful adventures, knightly absurdities as well as Sancho Panza's incessant search for material well-being. Reeves has selected and adapted appealing adventures of Don Quixote, Sancho Panza, Rosinante, and Dulcinea, and successfully conserved Cervantes' enduring human spirit. This Spanish masterpiece of a poor gentleman who tries to relive the heroic days of old by going in search of adventures in the manner of a knight errant of medieval romance should be enjoyed by all lovers of classical literature in the world.

Wilde, Oscar. (1979). *The birthday of the infanta.* Illustrated by Leonard Lubin. New York: Viking. [55 p.]. Grades 5–8.
Through Oscar Wilde's engaging text and Leonard Lubin's detailed illustrations, the reader is exposed to the somber splendor of the Spanish court. The teaching story of a grotesque dwarf who falls in love with the beautiful infanta on her birthday will affect all readers. His tragedy comes when his innocent belief that his love is returned is destroyed

upon seeing his own repulsive reflection in the court's mirror. The formality and wealth of the Spanish court, the Escorial, will be appreciated through the festivities prepared in honor of the infanta, such as a marvelous bullfight with a bull made of wickerwork, as well as the exquisite descriptions of the rooms and halls in the palace.

Recent Noteworthy Children's Books in Spanish

Isabel Schon

Choosing children's books in Spanish with a high potential for reader involvement and interest should be the goal of every selector. The following are recent noteworthy children's books in Spanish published in Spain, the United States, Mexico, and Venezuela. An attempt has been made to include a balance of fiction and nonfiction books, including some titles of permanent value and others of great immediate interest. The overriding concern is to include excellent children's books in Spanish that are readily available through book jobbers in the United States or in Spanish-speaking countries. To that end, I have provided full bibliographic and ordering information for each book reviewed, including ISBN numbers and prices.

For the convenience of the selector, I have arranged these books by grade level—Pre-Kindergarten through Third Grade, Third through Sixth Grades, and Sixth Grade and Above—but the individual child's Spanish reading ability, interest, tastes, and purpose should be the main criteria for determining the true level at which each book is used.

PRE-KINDERGARTEN THROUGH THIRD GRADE

Altamirano, Francisca. (1985). *El Niño y el globo (The boy and the balloon)*. Illustrated by the author. Mexico: Editorial Trillas. [12 p.]. ISBN 968-24-1845-3. $3.50. Grades K–2.
This wordless picture book shows a boy and his big blue balloon in the city, in the sky, in the country, over the ocean, over snowcapped mountains, and on a tree. The striking illustrations will attract children's attention.

Animales. (Animals). 3 vols.

Enséñame cosas. (Show me things). 3 vols.

Mis primeras palabras. (My first words). 3 vols.
Each Volume: Colección Palabras. (Madrid: Susaeta Ediciones, 1984). [12 p.]. ISBN 84-305-1385-X for the series. $3.00. Preschool–1.
This series of nine board books is characterized by simple, clear color illustrations of common animals, things, or words. The selection of objects common to young children makes this series especially useful for preschoolers.

Aprendiendo las figuras. (Learning shapes). (1985). Illustrated by Carlos A. Michelini. Madrid: Edaf. [24 p.]. ISBN 84-7640- 004-7. $10.00. Grades K–2.
See-through, sturdy board pages, spiral binding, colorful illustrations and rhyming text encourage children to touch and become acquainted with the principal shapes that surround them: circles, squares, and triangles. This toy book will withstand lots of touching by eager little hands.

Charles, Donald. *El año de Gato Galano. (Calico Cat's year).* Translated by Alma Flor Ada. ISBN 0-516-33461-1.

———. *Cuenta con Gato Galano. (Count on Calico Cat).* Translated by Lada Kratky. ISBN 0-516-33479-4.

———. *El libro de ejercicios de Gato Galano. (Calico Cat's exercise book).* Translated by Lada Kratky. ISBN 0-516-33457-3.

Each Volume: Illustrated by the author. Calico Cat Storybook Series. (Chicago: Children's Press, 1985). [32 p.]. $8.25. Preschool–2.
Each of these stories includes amusing, colorful illustrations of Calico Cat involved in activities to which young children can readily relate. *El Año de Gato Galano* describes, in a rhymed Spanish text the characteristics of the four seasons. *Cuenta con Gato Galano* is a simple counting book based on Calico Cat's garbage can. *El Libro de Ejercicios de Gato Galano* shows Calico Cat demonstrating various simple exercises to four mice. These books will entertain as well as instruct young Spanish-speaking children.

Delgado, Eduard. *Mientras Tim juega en el campo. (While Tim plays in the country).* ISBN 84-344-0153-3.

———. *Mientras Tim juega en los grandes almacenes. (While Tim plays in the big department stores).* ISBN 84-344-0215-7.

Each Volume: Illustrated by Francesco Rovira. Colección Mientras Tim Juega. (Barcelona, Spain: Editorial Ariel, 1984). [20 p.]. $5.50. Grades 1–3.
Witty, busy, colorful illustrations with a lot of detail are the salient characteristics of this amusing series with simple texts about Tim, a little boy involved in preposterous situations. *Mientras Tim Juega en el Campo* shows Tim and his friends going to the town's market with some of their treasures; the trip results, to everyone's delight, in strange happenings in the town's square. *Mientras Tim Juega en los Grandes Almacenes* tells about Tim's experiences when he volunteers to help others move a big piano in a busy department store, that causes mass

confusion and minor calamities. Ultimately, the piano is placed in a nice, quiet terrace to provide background music for the customers. Other titles in this series are: *Mientras Tim Juega en el Parque de Attracciones (While Tim Plays in the Amusement Park)*, *Mientras Tim Juega en la Playa (While Tim Plays at the Beach)*, *Mientras Tim Juega en el Puerto (While Tim Plays at the Port)*, *Mientras Tim Juega en la Plaza (While Tim Plays in the Plaza)*.

Denou, Violeta. (1984). *Los animales de Teo. (Teo's Animals)*. Barcelona, Spain: Editorial Timun Mas. [10 p.]. ISBN 84-7176-519-5. $4.95. Preschool–2.
Sturdy board pages and bright colorful illustrations are ideal to tell young children about Teo and his animals, which include caterpillars, turtles, a puppy, a parrot, and a fish. This wordless picture book is a charming introduction to animals.

———. (1985). *Es Navidad, Teo. (It's Christmas, Teo)*. Barcelona, Spain: Timun Mas. [10 p.]. ISBN 84-7176-666-3. $4.00. Preschool.
Colorful illustrations on sturdy, cardboard pages show happy scenes related to Christmas. This wordless picture book includes children with Santa Claus, setting up a nativity scene, talking to a wise man, opening gifts, and removing the decorations from the Christmas tree. Hispanic Christmas celebrations are presented simply in this attractive, durable book. Other "Teo" titles are: *Teo Come (Teo Eats)*, *Teo Juega (Teo Plays)*, *Los Animales de Teo (Teo's Animals)*.

———. (1983). *Llueve, Teo. (It is raining, Teo)*. Illustrated by the author. Barcelona, Spain: Editorial Timun Mas. [10 p.]. ISBN 84-7176-520-9. $3.95. Preschool–K.
Delightful color illustrations and sturdy board pages with no text show children what happens when it rains, as well as the special clothes children wear in the rain. The illustrations of children and animals in the rain and under a rainbow are sure to appeal to preschoolers.

Friskey, Margaret. (1984). *Pollito Pequeñito cuenta hasta diez. (Chicken Little count to ten)*. Illustrated by Katherine Evans. Translated by Lada Kratky. Chicago: Children's Press. [30 p.]. ISBN 0-516-33431-X. $8.25. Grades 1–3.
The popular Chicken Little, who sets out to see the world but doesn't know how to drink water, is now available to Spanish-speaking children. Pollito Pequeñito (Chicken Little) learns how ten different animals get a drink, and, at the same time, counts from one to ten.

Greene, Graham. (1985). *La pequeña apisonadora. (The little steamroller)*. Illustrated by Edward Ardizzone. Madrid: Editorial Debate. [46 p.]. ISBN 84-7444-061-0. $7.50. Grades 2–4.
A little steamroller and its operator, Antonio, move fast and stop a gold smuggler at the London airport. The fast pace and powerful illustrations make this story interesting reading for children of all ages.

Hill, Eric. *Spot va a la escuela. (Spot goes to school)*. ISBN 0-399-21223-X.

————. *Spot va a la playa. (Spot goes to the beach).* ISBN 0-399-21259-0.

Each Volume: Color illustrations. Libros de Spot. (New York: G. P. Putnam's Sons, 1984). [22 p.]. $9.95. Preschool–2.

Like previous Spot books, these include simple texts in Spanish, colorful illustrations, and specially designed flaps that children must open to read all of the story. *Spot Va a la Escuela* shows Spot's first day at school: being greeted by his teacher and new friends, singing songs, playing with blocks, showing his bone, playing outdoors, listening to a story, painting pictures, and feeling delighted about his new experiences. *Spot Va a la Playa* shows Spot enjoying a day at the beach with his parents: he gets a new hat, plays ball with his father, builds sand castles, goes fishing, falls into the ocean, finds a new girl friend, and returns home. These are indeed fun books for young readers.

Oxenbury, Helen. *En casa de los abuelos. (At grandparent's house).* ISBN 84-261-2065-2.

————. *Nuestro perro. (Our dog).* ISBN 84-261-2066-0.

————. *La visita. (The visitor).* ISBN 84-261-2067-9.

Each Volume: Translated by Concepción Zendrera. Los Libros del Chiquitín. (Barcelona, Spain: Editorial Juventud, 1984). [18 p.]. $5.00. Grades K–2.

Charming, pastel illustrations and easy-to-read texts describe happy moments in the lives of children. *En Casa de los Abuelos* tells about a little girl's weekly visits to her grandparents' house. Some readers may object to some stereotypical views of older people, such as grandmother knitting and wearing house slippers, and grandfather not being able to crawl out from under a table. This is nonetheless a warm story about a little girl and her grandparents. *Nuestro Perro* shows what happens when a little boy and his mother take their dog out for a walk. *La Visita* describes the day mother had an important visitor at home, with embarrassing consequences.

Parramón, Josep M. *Los abuelos. (Grandparents).* Illustrated by Maria Rius. ISBN 84-342-0526-2.

————. *Los jóvenes. (Young people).* Illustrated by Carme Sole Vendrell. ISBN 84-342-0524-6.

————. *Los niños. (Children).* Illustrated by María Rius. ISBN 84-342-0523-8.

————. *Los padres. (Parents).* Illustrated by Carmen Sole Vendrell. ISBN 84-342-0525-4.

Each Volume: Las Cuatro Edades. (Barcelona, Spain: Parramon Ediciones, 1985). [30 p.]. $6.00. Grades K–2.

The purpose of this series is to teach children about their family and to love all family members. The charming illustrations of middle-class Spanish grandparents, older brothers and sisters, and children and parents in everyday activities, as well as a simple text, make this series a good introduction to the family.

Satchwell, John. *Contamos. (Counting).* ISBN 84-372-3500-6.

————. *Es diferente! (Old one out).* ISBN 84-372-3502-2.

————. *Formas. (Shapes).* ISBN 84-372-3501-4.

————. *Grande y pequeño. (Big and little).* ISBN 84-372-3503-0.

Each Volume: Illustrated by Katy Sleight. Translated by Maria Puncel. Primeras Matemáticas. (Madrid: Ediciones Altea, 1985). [28 p.]. $3.50. Preschool–2.
The purpose of this series is to teach children basic math concepts in an amusing manner. They will enjoy the colorful illustrations of monsters and will learn to count from 1 to 10, to distinguish a different element, to distinguish forms, and to compare opposite situations. Unfortunately, the small size (4 ½" x 6 ½") of these paperback publications detracts from their appeal.

Sendak, Maurice. (1984). *Donde viven los monstruos. (Where the wild things are).* Illustrated by the author. Translated by Agustín Gervas. Madrid: Ediciones Alfaguara. [38 p.]. ISBN 84-204-3022-6. $15.00. Grades K–2.
Sendak's award-winning *Where the Wild Things Are* has been delightfully translated for the Spanish-speaking reader. Young readers will enjoy Max's dream of going where the wild things are, ruling them, sharing their rumpus, and, finally, returning home where someone loves him.

Stinson, Kathy. (1985). *El rojo es el mejor. (Red is best).* Illustrated by Robin Baird Lewis. Translated by Kiki & Clarisa de la Rosa. Caracas, Venezuela: Ediciones Ekaré-Banco del Libro. [28 p.]. ISBN 84-8351-034-0. $6.50. Preschool–2.
Isabella, a little girl, tells why she thinks the color red is best. She can jump higher with her red stockings. She feels like Little Red Riding Hood with her red jacket. She can walk better with her red slippers. Orange juice tastes better in her red glass. And she looks beautiful with her red bows. Engaging three-tone line illustrations show Isabella delighted with the color red. Young children will be charmed by Isabella's reasoning.

THIRD THROUGH SIXTH GRADES

Armellada, Fray Cesareo de. (1985). *El tigre y el cangrejo. (The tiger and the crab).* Illustrated by Laura Liberatore. Adapted by Veronica Uribe. Colección Narraciones Indígenas. Caracas, Venezuela: Ediciones Ekaré-Banco del Libro. [32 p.]. ISBN 84-8351-033-2. $7.00. Grades 2–5.
In a most amusing manner, this tale tells why tigers have very bright eyes and why they must kill to pay their debt to King Zamuro. Striking watercolor illustrations of the tiger and the crab add much zest to this tale.

Blake, Quentin. (1985). *La historia de la rana bailarina. (The story of the dancing frog).* Illustrated by the author. Madrid: Ediciones Altea. [36 p.]. ISBN 84-372-24500-0. $4.50. Grades 3–6.
Gertrudis, a young widow, is confronted with serious problems in her life. Unexpectedly, she finds Jorge, a dancing frog. Jorge travels around the world as a vaudeville success, with Gertrudis as his agent. Sophisticated readers will be moved by Gertrudis' life and by the affecting, though not pretty, illustrations.

Blume, Judy. (1983). *¿Estás allí Dios? Soy yo, Margaret. (Are you there God? It's me, Margaret).* Translated by Alma Flor Ada. Scarsdale, NY: Bradbury Press. [159 p.]. ISBN 0-02-710950-X. $9.95. Grades 4–6.
Margaret, a 12-year-old, is faced with the usual problems of growing up: choosing a religion, wearing a bra, menstruation, and normal family arguments. This is a good translation of *Are You There God? It's Me, Margaret*, with a few typographical errors that do not detract from the lively and amusing story of a girl and her private dialog with her God.

Bravo-Villasante, Carmen. (1984). *El libro de las adivinanzas. (The book of riddles).* Illustrated by Carmen Andrada. Valladolid, Spain: Editorial Miñon. [168 p.]. ISBN 84-355-0697-5. $18.00. Grades 4–10.
More than 600 riddles from the Spanish-speaking world are included in this beautiful publication with outstanding illustrations.

Cárdenas, Magolo. *La zona del silencio. (The silent zone).* Illustrated by the author. ISBN 968-39-0077-1.

Ramirez, Elisa. *Adivinanzas indígenas. (Indigenous riddles).* Illustrated by Maximino Javier. ISBN 968-39-0089-5.

Each Volume: Coleccion Piñata. (México: Editorial Patria, 1984). [31 p.]. $3.00. Grades 1–3.
Like previous titles in this series, young children will delight in the colorful illustrations and simple texts. *La Zona del Silencio* narrates in a rhymed, easy-to-read text, a trip through a desert zone in northern Mexico. *Adivinanzas Indígenas* is a collection of 12 riddles from ancient Mexico. Each riddle is followed by an illustration on the following page that provides the answer. These books are indeed an enchanting introduction to Mexico.

Claret, María. (1983). *La ratita Blasa. (Blasa, the little mouse).* Barcelona, Spain: Editorial Juventud. [28 p.]. ISBN 84-261-1957-3. $5.00. Grades 3–5.
Blasa is a pretty little rat. She lives alone, but one day decides to get married. She meets a duck, but he loves to swim in cold water. She meets a sparrow, but he loves to fly all the time. She meets a lamb, but he loves to jump. She meets a frog, but he loves to stay in the water. And so on, until one day she meets a little gray rat.... Charming, pastel illustrations show Blasa with her many suitors.

Cleary, Beverly. (1983). *Henry Huggins.* Illustrated by Louis Darling. Translated by Argentina Palacios. New York: William Morrow and Co. [159 p.]. ISBN 0-688-02014-3. $10.25. Grades 4–6.
The popular adventures of Henry Huggins and his beloved dog, Ribsy, are now available for Spanish readers in this translation that maintains the flavor and fun of the original. Spanish translations of famous American books are always in demand by eager Spanish readers; this one will be no exception.

———. (1984). *Ramona, la chinche. (Ramona, the pest).* Illustrated by Louis Darling. Translated by Argentina Palacios. New York: William Morrow and Co. [181 p.]. ISBN 0-688-02783-0. $9.50. Grades 4–6.
The delightfully human experiences of Ramona Quimby in kindergarten class are now available for Spanish-speaking readers. Ramona's sad and happy times, as well as the many misunderstandings with her parents, teacher, and friends, have been translated into easy flowing Spanish. It must be noted that the translator has done an especially fine job of describing incidents meaningful to English-speaking children in the United States, such as Halloween parties in school and Ramona's confusion regarding "The Star Spangled Banner" (p. 163), which otherwise could not have been understood by Spanish-speaking children unfamiliar with customs in the United States.

Company, Merce. (1984). *La casa del Gatus. (Gatus' house).* Illustrated by Montserrat Ginesta. Translated by Angelina Gatell. Barcelona, Spain: La Galera, S. A. Editorial. [54 p.]. ISBN 84-246-3815-8. $4.50. Grades 4–7.
Nobody knows the real name of the short, eccentric, smiling old man who everybody in town calls Gatus. He lives alone in a very strange place—under a bridge close to town. Suddenly, an old woman and an old man who also do not have a home of their own ask Gatus if they can share a piece of the bridge. The three old people work together to help each other make a living. The people in town decide to help them, first by giving them odd jobs, and then by fixing up an old house for them. But a terrible storm takes the old people away before they can move to their new home. Two-tone, realistic illustrations add a touching glow to this heartwarming story about delightful old people.

Company, M., & R. Capdevila. *Las tres mellizas, Blancanieves y los siete enanos. (The triplets, Snow White and the seven dwarfs).* ISBN 84-344-0256-4.

———. *Las tres mellizas y Barba Azul. (The triplets and Blue Beard).* ISBN 84-344-0243-2.

———. *Las tres mellizas y Caperucita Roja. (The Triplets and Little Red Riding Hood).* ISBN 84-344-0245-9.

———. *Las tres mellizas y Cenicienta. (The triplets and Cinderella).* ISBN 84-344-0258-0.

Each Volume: Las Tres Mellizas. (Barcelona, Spain: Editorial Ariel, 1985). [32 p.]. $5.00. Grades 3–5.
Purists may demur, but children will rejoice in these modern versions of well-known fairy tales. Witty watercolor illustrations add a contemporary touch to: Snow White, who is now the mother of three princes; Blue Beard's young wife, who gets rid of the evil Blue Beard; Little Red Riding Hood, who constantly overpowers the bad wolf; and Cinderella, who goes to the dance riding a motorcycle. The mischievous triplets—Ana, Elena, and Teresa—are the new characters who assist the heroines in overpowering their enemies.

Company, M., & R. Capdevila. (1985). *Las tres mellizas hacemos negocios. (The triplets go into business)*. Colección Las Tres Mellizas. Barcelona, Spain: Editorial Ariel. [20 p.]. ISBN 84-344-261-0. $6.50. Grades 3–5.
The triplets—Ana, Elena, and Teresa—come up with various ways to make money and enjoy themselves at the same time. Witty watercolor illustrations and a lighthearted text make the triplets' adventures in moneymaking a joy to read.

Corona, Pascuala. *La seda. (Silk)*. Illustrated by the author. ISBN 968-39-0074-7.

Giron, Nicole. *El azúcar. (Sugar)*. Illustrated by Ana Villaseñor. ISBN 968-39-0099-2.

María, Beatriz de, & Campos Castello. *Tres colorantes pre-Hispánicos. (Three pre-Hispanic dyes)*. Illustrated by Pascuala Corona. ISBN 968-39-0100-X.

Molina, Silvia. *El papel. (Paper)*. Illustrated by Felipe Ugalde. ISBN 958-39-0081-X.

Each Volume: Coleccion Piñata, Serie: Las Materias Primas. (México: Editorial Patria, 1985). [31 p.]. $3.00. Grades 3–5.
Like previous titles in this series, these books introduce children to the manual preparation of various products. Colorful illustrations and simple, direct texts tell about the origins and production of silk in China and other countries, about the growing and harvesting of sugar in rural Mexico, about the history and cultivation of three pre-Hispanic dyes in the Mexican state of Oaxaca, and about the manual preparation of paper in rural Mexico.

Gantschen, Ivan. (1985). *El lago de la luna. (Moon lake)*. Translated by Francisco González Aramburo. México: Editorial Trillas. [28 p.]. ISBN 968-24-1680-9. $3.00. Grades 4–6.
An old shepherd and his grandson, Pedro, live alone in the mountains. When the old shepherd dies, Pedro continues happily caring for his sheep. One day one of his sheep wanders off into a huge ravine and into Moon Lake, where Pedro finds precious jewels and a wise fox who teaches him an important secret about Moon Lake. Striking watercolor illustrations add an appropriate mood to the story about a courageous shepherd boy.

Jane, Jordi. *Juanote y las tres bolsas de oro. (Juanote and the three bags of gold).* Illustrated by Joma. Translated by José A. Pastor Cañada. ISBN 84-246-1647-0.

Sennell, Joles. *El mejor novio del mundo. (The best suitor in the world).* Illustrated by Carme Peris. Translated by Jose A. Pastor Cañada. ISBN 84-246-1648-0.

> Each Volume: Cuentos Populares. (Barcelona, Spain: La Galera, 1984). [24 p.]. $5.00. Grades 3–6.
> These are the two newest titles in this series of 47 popular stories with engaging texts and alluring watercolor illustrations. *Juanote y las Tres Bolas de Oro* shows how a poor boy becomes wealthy after visiting other lands and using common sense to solve other people's problems. *El Mejor Novio del Mundo* tells how the papa and mama of the prettiest mouse in the world go in search of a suitor for their daughter. After exploring the situation with the sun, a cloud, the wind, and the Chinese Wall, they decide that the best suitor is their neighbor—a mouse who has been in love with their daughter for a long time. The only regrettable aspect about these stories is the series of questions and review topics at the end of the stories. These "exercises" are sure to detract from the stories' appeal and enjoyment.

Kipling, Rudyard. (1985). *El pequeño elefante. (The elephant's child).* Illustrated by Lorinda Bryan Cauley. Translated by Maria del Carmen Rodríguez Mederos. Madrid: Editorial Debate. [46 p.]. ISBN 84-7444-180-3. $7.50. Grades 2–5.
Delightful translation of R. Kipling's version of the famous folktale about a young curious elephant who insists on knowing what crocodiles eat for dinner. Excellent illustrations of animals in Africa perfectly complement this amusing tale that tells why elephants now have long trunks.

Korschunow, Irina. (1985). *Yaga y el hombrecillo de la flauta. (Yaga and the little man with the flute).* Illustrated by Pablo Echevarría. Translated from the German by Ma. Dolores Romero. Madrid: Ediciones SM. [71 p.]. ISBN 84-348-1551-6. $4.00. Grades 3–5.
When Yaga, the witch, plays the trumpet, mean thoughts prevail in town: children become destructive and adults fight with each other. So everybody is delighted when the little man plays the flute and good things start to happen. This angers Yaga, who prevents the little man from playing his flute. Fortunately, Yaga allows the little man to play his flute again and everyone is happy. Poignant pastel illustrations set the appropriate mood for this story about a mean witch and a kind little man.

Leutscher, Alfred. *Agua. (Water).* Illustrated by Nick Hardcastle. ISBN 84-7525-212-5.

———. *Tierra. (Earth).* Illustrated by John Butler. ISBN 84-7525-209-5.

Lloyd, David. *Aire. (Air).* Illustrated by Peter Visscher. ISBN 84-7525-210-9.

Satchwell, John. *Fuego. (Fire)*. Illustrated by Tom Stimpson. ISBN 84-7525-211-7.

Each Volume: Translated by Juan Manuel Ibeas. Los Elementos. (Madrid: Ediciones Generales Anaya, 1985). [26 p.]. $8.00. Grades 4–7.

The basic elements—fire, air, earth, and water—are presented to young readers through outstanding illustrations and an easy-to-understand text. Each volume introduces one of the elements and explains how it affects our lives.

Rivero Oramas, Rafael. (1985). *El mundo de Tío Conejo. (Uncle Rabbit's world)*. Illustrated by Alicia Ulloa. Caracas, Venezuela: Ediciones Ekaré-Banco del Libro. [111 p.]. ISBN 980-257-007-9. $6.00. Grades 3–6.

An enchanting collection of 16 popular Venezuelan tales that describe the constant misunderstandings among Uncle Rabbit, Uncle Tiger, and other animals. Children will enjoy these clever animal tales full of excitement and adventure, even though the black-and-white line illustrations do not add much to the tales.

Solano Flores, Guillermo. *La calle. (The street)*. Illustrated by Gloria Calderas Lim. ISBN 968-24-1780-5.

———. *El campo. (The countryside)*. Illustrated by Silvia Luz Alvarado. ISBN 968-24-1779-1.

———. *La lluvia. (The rain)*. Illustrated by Gloria Calderas Lim. ISBN 968-24-1777-1.

———. *El mercado. (The market)*. Illustrated by Silvia Luz Alvarado. ISBN 968-24-1781-5.

———. *El viento. (The wind)*. Illustrated by Norma Josefina Patiño Domínguez. ISBN 968-24-1871-2.

Each Volume: Ojos Abiertos. (México: Editorial Trillas, 1986). [16 p.]. $3.00. Grades 2–4.

Young children are introduced to simple concepts through unassuming illustrations in color and easy-to-read texts. *La Calle* describes various activities that take place on city streets. *El Campo* tells about life in the country among trees and animals. *La Lluvia* shows what happens when it rains. *El Mercado* shows a boy going to a market with his mother. *El Viento* describes what happens when there is a lot of wind. Other titles to be included in this series are: *El Periodico (The Newspaper), Mi Propio Museo (My Own Museum), El Teatro (The Theater)*.

Tison, Annette, & Talus Taylor. (1985). *Records de animales. (The big book of animal records)*. Madrid: Ediciones Montena. [93 p.]. ISBN 84-7515-652-5. $17.00. Grades 3–6.

The world of zoology is amusingly presented to children through colorful illustrations and amazing facts and figures about the largest, the smallest, the fastest, the slowest, the strangest, the oldest, and the most unusual animals. Purists may disagree, but this is definitely an interesting manner to introduce children to the study of various forms of life.

Varley, Susan. (1985). *Gracias, Tejón. (Badger's parting gifts)*. Illustrated by by the author. Translated by Juan R. Azaola. Madrid: Ediciones Altea. [26 p.]. ISBN 84-372-6601-7. $11.50. Grades 2–5.
Children of all ages will be moved by this poignant story with touching pastel illustrations about a kind old badger who used his wisdom to help his many friends. Upon his death, his loving friends find comfort in their memories of a true and giving friend. This is definitely an honest and moving story about death and the sadness of grieving.

Wilde, Oscar. (1985). *El gigante egoísta. (The selfish giant)*. Illustrated by Lisbeth Zwerger. Translated by Juan R. Azaola. Madrid: Ediciones Altea. [24 p.]. ISBN 84-372-6602-5. $11.50. Grades 4–8.
Accurate translation of the melancholy story about the selfish giant who becomes kindhearted and finally allows poor children to play in his beautiful, private garden. Exquisite pastel illustrations perfectly complement the solemn text.

SIXTH GRADE AND ABOVE

Aiken, Joan. (1985). *Mendelson y las ratas. (Mice and Mendelson)*. Illustrated by Julia Díaz. Translated by Alvaro Forque. Madrid: Ediciones SM. [101 p.]. ISBN 84-348-1547-8. $5.50. Grades 5–7.
The adventures of Mendelson, an elderly pony who loves music and the moon, and who loves his midnight park as well as his mouse friends, are told in a lighthearted manner. Children will delight in Mendelson's struggles to keep his piano, get rid of the hiccups, and learn to fly. Simple black-and-white illustrations perfectly complement these amusing adventures.

Asimov, Isaac. 1. *¿Cómo descubrimos el espacio? (Outer space)*. [55 p.]. ISBN 84-272-5461-X.

———. 2. *¿Cómo descubrimos la energía nuclear? (Nuclear Power)*. [52 p.]. ISBN 84-272-5462-8.

———. 3. *¿Cómo descubrimos los orígenes del hombre? (Our human roots)*. [52 p.]. ISBN 84-272-5463-6.

———. 4. *¿Cómo descubrimos los números? (Numbers)*. [52 p.]. ISBN 84-272-5464-4.

———. 5. *¿Cómo descubrimos el átomo? (Atoms)*. [52 p.]. ISBN 84-272-5465-4.

———. 6. *¿Cómo descubrimos el petróleo? (Petroleum)*. [52 p.]. ISBN 84-272-5466-3.

———. 7. *¿Cómo descubrimos agujeros negros? (Black holes)*. [52 p.]. ISBN 84-272-5467-9.

———. 8. *¿Cómo descubrimos los cometas? (Comets).* [44 p.]. ISBN 84-272-5468-7.

Each Volume: Translated by Diorki. Cólección ¿Cómo Descubrimos...? (Barcelona, Spain: Editorial Molino, 1984). $5.50. Grades 5–8.
These titles, originally written by Isaac Asimov in 1977, are, fortunately, now available to young Spanish-speaking readers. Each book presents the history as well as the process of development of specific scientific topics, such as astronomical phenomena, energy, mathematics, and human evolution. Unfortunately, the black-and-white drawings and charts are much too simple and do not add much excitement to Asimov's informative text.

Baum, L. Frank. (1985). *El maravilloso mago de Oz. (The wonderful wizard of Oz).* Adapted by Rafael Díaz Santander. Illustrated by Carlos Gallego. Madrid: Ediciones Auriga. [151 p.]. ISBN 84-7281-184-0. $7.00. Grades 6–8.
The fantastic story of Dorothy, who, with her companions the Scarecrow, Tin Woodman, and Cowardly Lion, goes on a magical journey to request special favors from the Wizard of Oz, is delightfully translated for Spanish readers. Unfortunately, the black-and-white line illustrations lack the excitement of Baum's fantasy.

Blume, Judy. (1983). *La ballena. (Blubber).* Translated by Alma Flor Ada. Scarsdale, NY: Bradbury Press, distributed by Macmillan. [172 p.]. ISBN 0-02-710-940-2. $5.00. Grades 5–7.
Jill, a thin fifth-grader, joins the rest of her class in tormenting Linda, an overweight girl. Later, she finds out that she, too, can become the target of scorn and abuse from the other children. An accurate translation of *Blubber.*

Doyle, Sir Arthur Conan. (1985). *Aventuras de Sherlock Holmes. (Sherlock Holmes' Adventures).* Adapted by R. Diza & M. Martín. Madrid: Ediciones Auriga. [141 p.]. ISBN 84-7281-192-1. $7.00. Grades 6–10.
An excellent adaptation of six mysteries by the great Arthur Conan Doyle that will certainly intrigue and entertain young readers. The brief introduction to the author and his work should be of interest to newcomers to this genre.

Goscinny, Rene. *Los amiguitos del pequeño Nicolás. (Little Nicholas' friends).* [119 p.]. ISBN 84-204-4092-2.

———. *El pequeño Nicolás. (Little Nicolas).* [139 p.]. ISBN 84-204-4090-6.

———. *Los recreos del pequeño Nicolás. (Little Nicolas' amusements).* [115 p.]. ISBN 84-204-4091-4.

———. *Las vacaciones del pequeño Nicolás. (Little Nicolas' vacations).* [150 p.]. ISBN 84-204-4093-0.

Each Volume: Illustrated by Sempe. Translated by Esther Benitez. El pequeño Nicolás. (Madrid: Ediciones Alfaguara, 1985). $6.50. Grades 5–7.

This series, originally published in France in 1960, tells about little Nicolas' adventures at home, at school, with his friends, and on vacation. Some children may not relate to the European ambience of these stories—all boys' school, soccer, life in Paris in the 1960s—but the amusing experiences of little Nicolas are indeed fresh and spontaneous. There is an appealing honesty to each adventure; for example, the day Nicolas and his friend Alcestes learn how to smoke a cigar, with disastrous consequences. The witty black-and-white line illustrations add much merriment to Nicolas' adventures.

Guillén, Jorge. (1984). *Jorge Guillén para niños. (Jorge Guillen for children)*. Edited by Antonio A. Gómez Yebra. Illustrated by John Rosenfeldt. Madrid: Ediciones de la Torre. [125 p.]. ISBN 84-85866-66-5. $7.00. Grades 6–12.

The poems that Jorge Guillen dedicated to his children, grandchildren, and great-grandchildren serve as an introduction for young readers to this great Spanish poet who died in 1984. The informative introduction to his life and work is indeed worthwhile reading; unfortunately, the blurred black-and-white illustrations are, at best, bland decorations.

Hawkes, Nigel. *Ordenadores—¿Cómo trabajan? (Computers, how they work)*. ISBN 84-267-0580-4.

———. *Robots y ordenadores. (Robots and computers)*. ISBN 84-267-0579-0.

Irvine, Mat. *Satélites y ordenadores. (Satellites and computers)*. ISBN 84-267-0578-2.

McKie, Robin. *Láseres. (Lasers)*. ISBN 84-267-0575-8.

Young, Frank. *Radio y radar. (Radio and radar)*. ISBN 84-267-0576-6.

Each Volume: Translated from the English by Luis Ibañez Morlan. La Revolución Electrónica. (Barcelona, Spain: Marcombo, 1985). [29 p.]. $10.00. Grades 5–9.

This excellent introduction to the world of electronics contains outstanding photographs, diagrams, and illustrations. A simple text explains basic facts about computers and how they work, robots in the working world, satellites and communication, how lasers are built and used, and why radio and radar technologies are two of the most important aspects of the electronic revolution. Also in this series: *TV y Video (TV and video)*.

Histoira de los inventos. (History of inventions). (1984). Madrid: Salvat Editores. [260 p.]. ISBN 84-345-4197-1. $28.00. Grades 6–10.

This book contains striking photographs and drawings in color and black-and-white, as well as an informative text describing the origins, technological evolution, and applications of more than 120 inventions ranging from handmade tools to artificial satellites. The excitement of new inventions is indeed conveyed in this book that highlights scientific achievements.

Kurtz, Carmen. (1984). *Oscar y la extraña luz. (Oscar and the strange light)*. Illustrated by Odile Kurz. Barcelona, Spain: Editorial Juventud. [175 p.]. ISBN 84-261-2045-8. $6.50. Grades 6–9.
Oscar, a 12-year-old boy, and Rafael Roca, a wealthy Spanish industrialist, are kidnapped by a gang of incompetents. In their escape, Oscar and Mr. Roca are aided by a beautiful and pregnant young woman, two young women who excel in judo, a brave older woman who does not mind jumping out of windows, and other kind people who go out of their way to make sure that the victims return home safely. The greatest hero is a laser that is constantly on the lookout for Oscar and that allows him to perform incredible feats when all else fails. At the end, the kidnappers are forgiven and everybody lives happily ever after. This is a fast-paced adventure story with a few strange occurrences: a woman gives birth assisted by the heroes, and the laser is never a convincing force.

Massa, Renato. (1985). *India. (India)*. (Enciclopedia de la Naturaleza). Madrid: Editorial Debate. [126 p.]. ISBN 84-7444-188-9. $23.00. Grades 8–12.
Excellent photographs in color, as well as drawings, maps, and charts and an informative text, describe the flora, fauna, geography, and ecology of the Indian subcontinent. This series, sponsored by the World Wildlife Fund, includes 24 volumes organized by geographical areas of the world.

Olaizola, Jose Luis. (1985). *Bibiana y su mundo. (Bibiana and her world)*. Madrid: Ediciones SM. [134 p.]. ISBN 84-348-1613-X. $5.50. Grades 6–10.
Bibiana, an 11-year-old girl, dearly loves her father who is an alcoholic and who refuses to work. Her neighbors and teachers feel sorry for her because of her father's apparent neglect and because her mother died when Bibiana was born. Perhaps some of the incidents in Bibiana's life will seem too farfetched to young readers, but Bibiana emerges as an adorable, warm, and strong girl who survives her father's abuses and manages to create her own happiness. If all alcoholic fathers were as loving and, ultimately, as concerned about their children's happiness as Bibiana's father, the results would be many more confident, self-assured, happy children like Bibiana.

Uribe, Verónica. (Ed.) (1984). *Cuentos de espantos y aparecidos, Vol. III. (Tales about ghosts and specters)*. Illustrated by Marcela Valdeavellano and others. Caracas, Venezuela: Ediciones Ekaré-Banco del Libro. [93 p.]. ISBN Unavailable. $5.50. Grades 5–10.
The mystery of death and the fear of the unknown combined with European traditions of witches and ghosts and the pre-Columbian and African traditions of spirits appear in these 11 tales and legends about ghosts and specters from Guatemala, Brazil, Mexico, Ecuador, the Dominican Republic, Colombia, Argentina, Puerto Rico, Peru, Venezuela, and Nicaragua. The fast pace, brevity, and excitement of these tales should appeal to all readers.

Bibliography of Bilingual Nonprint Materials

Nita Norman

RECORDS AND CASSETTES

El Abecedario. Record.
A new, musical method of learning to read and write the letters of the alphabet.

Alerta Sings: Children's Songs in Spanish and English from Latin America, the Caribbean and the U.S.A. Record.
The rich voice of Argentine folk singer Suni Paz makes this recording of songs for children a delight. Alerta is a program developed at Teachers College, Columbia University, which stresses the values of biculturalism and bilingualism. The songs and singing games provided here come from many sources and enrich us all.

Canciones Infantiles Interpretadas por Olga y Tony (Olga and Tony Sing Children's Songs). Record.
Charming numbers about snails, crocodiles, ducks, wizards, Mickey Mouse, and scorpions, and the birthday song.

Canciones para el Recreo (Children's Songs for Listening). Record.
Suni Paz ingratiates herself to children, singing songs from all over Latin America. Incomparable are her renditions of "La Gatita Carlota" and "Cuando estoy triste." In these, as in all the songs on this record, she envelops us in her charm and sweeps us up in sound.

Children's Songs and Games from Ecuador, Mexico, and Puerto Rico. Record.
Another fine collection of children's songs, recorded on location. While clapping patterns, animal imitations, and dance steps take on regional and ethnic characteristics, the Spanish origin of these songs is unmistakable, demonstrating the persistence of the Spanish legacy in the New World.

Cosas de Niños (Assorted Numbers for Children). Cassette.
A delightful, comical collection of children's and popular songs, such as "Baila con el Hula Hoop" and "Queridos Reyes Magos," a song sung in Spanish to the melody of the American song, "Santa Claus is Coming to Town."

Latin American Children's Game Songs. Record.
An unusual collection of songs recorded in Mexico and Puerto Rico, and sung by children from the villages and towns of those places. The Mexican songs are often Spanish in origin; the Puerto Rican songs are frequently mixed with English and show an affinity with African music. This fine recording is a fascinating cultural document.

Los Grandes Exitos de Cri-Cri (Cri-Cri's Greatest Hits). Cassettes.
Who is Cri-Cri? A legendary cricket who sings such perennial favorites as "On the Road to School," "The Parade of the Letters," and "The Cowboy Mouse." Cri-Cri recordings are hard to find, and this cassette explains why. We loved it!

Los Grandes Exitos de Rondas Infantiles (The Best Rounds for Children). Cassette.
Favorite songs and rounds of Spanish-speaking children are also games; they are fun just to listen to! Our favorites include "La vibora del mar," "Naranja dulce," and "El patio de mi casa."

16mm FILMS

Key to Symbols

p = primary   s = senior
i = intermediate   ya = young adult
j = junior   a = adult

Big Red Barn. Aims. 11 minutes, color, p.
Farm scenes depict the beauty of rural life. Margaret Wise Brown's "The Big Red Barn" supplies the inspiration for this film, which encourages the writing of original stories as well as reading.

Chick, Chick, Chick. Churchill. 12½ minutes, color, nonverbal, p-i.
About chickens and the intense drama of an old-fashion barnyard. Great fun. For creative expression, language skills, sensory awareness, and many other uses.

Clever Hiki Ichi. Coronet. 12 minutes, color, p.
A feudal lord needs a champion to save his realm by weighing a giant with staves and lifting a huge stone. The little boy Hiki Ichi solves all problems with a bit of applied science and personal pluck in this delightful animated tale of medieval Japan.

Cow. Churchill. 11 minutes, nonverbal, color, p.
A beauty-filled exploration of cows on a peaceful day in the pasture; the texture of noses, the shapes of bodies, grinding of jaws, swishing of tails. Natural sounds, without narration.

Cuckoo Clock that Wouldn't Cuckoo. Coronet. color, p-i.
This is a delightful story of a silent little cuckoo bird in the royal cuckoo clock, and of how Hans Ticktock, master clockmaker, broke the spell of her silence and helped her to cuckoo happily once more. Colorful in its picturesque old world setting. The film is designed to arouse children's interest in reading and oral expression.

Curious George Rides a Bike. WES. 10 minutes, color, p.
From the book by H.A. Rey. The madcap escapes of a little monkey enlivened by a musical score tailored to the mood of each scene. Iconographic.

Feeling Left Out. Aims. 13½ minutes, color, p-i-j.
This film is designed to help children of divorcing parents through the emotional adjustments of resettlement.

Feliz Navidad. Disney. 4 minutes, color, p-i-j.
Donald Duck's friends, Jose and Panchico, show him the Mexican Christmas celebration of Las Posadas, the traditional candlelight search for shelter that ends with parties, piñatas, gifts, and fireworks.

Ferdinand the Bull. Disney. 8 minutes, color, p-i-j.
The delightful tale of a peace-loving bull who would rather smell the flowers than fight.

Frog Princess. Coronet. 6 minutes, color, p-i.
The quaint fairyland setting of this film in animation will excite children. The prince shoots an arrow into the air and the one who returns it will be his bride. A frog, who is a princess under the spell of a wicked magician, finds the arrow, and the prince then encounters many dangers as he frees her from the enchantment.

The Giving Tree. Churchill. 10 minutes, color, i-ya-a.
Adapted from Shel Silverstein's book. Unselfishly, a tree offers itself to a boy for climbing, shade, and pleasure. As the boys grows, he wants different things from the tree. Adulthood takes him away, but old age brings their relationship full circle.

Golden Fish. LCA. 20 minutes, color, nonverbal, p-a.
Charming, wordless film that describes a young boy's affection for a fish that he wins at the carnival, and what happens when a cat threatens it. Produced by Jacques Cousteau.

Great Piggybank Raid. Coronet. 12 minutes, color, p-i.
Our forest town friends try to raise enough money to buy red and gold uniforms for their band concert. When they come up $2 short, Coslo takes it from his sister Taffy's piggybank. What happens next provides a lesson in honesty and mutual trust.

How the Elephant Got His Trunk. LCA. 7 minutes, color, p.
A young elephant learns the price of curiosity and reaps its rewards in this animated version out of Rudyard Kipling's *Just So* stories. When the stub-nosed elephant asks the crocodile what it ate for dinner, the croco-

dile replies by clamping the elephant's nose in its teeth and stretching it completely out of shape. The baby elephant is surprised to discover that a long trunk can be useful in many ways.

How the Whale Got His Throat. LCA. 7 minutes, color, p.

This animated film, adapted from the *Just So* stories of Rudyard Kipling, tells about the whale who ate all the fish in the sea and then consumed a sailor on a raft. When the sailor escaped from the whale's mouth, he lodged his raft in the whale's throat where it acted like a huge sieve so that even today the whale can eat only small fish.

I'm Feeling Alone. Churchill. 8 minutes, color, p.

I'm Feeling Happy. Churchill. 9 minutes, color, p.

I'm Feeling Sad. Churchill. 10 minutes, color, p.

I'm Feeling Scared. Churchill. 9 minutes, color, p.

I'm Mad at Me. Churchill. 9 minutes, color, p.

I'm Mad at You. Churchill. 8 minutes, color, p.

Each film is introduced by a song "Everybody Has Feelings" and a delightful animated sequence of children and faces. Each film also is played to songs, and is a series of evocative vignettes illustrating situations in which children are angry, sad, lonely, happy, or frightened. The film experiences help children talk about and understand their own feelings.

Itzu Guari y el Niño. PHO. 12 minutes, i-ya.

Filmed in the Mexican state of Michoacan, this film is a modern fairy tale, filled with beauty, adventure, and a little boy's joy in the world around him. It is also a tribute to the beauty and variety of nature's greatest resource, water.

Little Rooster Who Made the Sun Rise. Coronet. 10½ minutes, color, p.

The well-known fable with a moral is retold in this colorful animated cartoon. Children will be delighted by the animals of the farmyard and by the little rooster who discovers that his crowing does not really make the sun rise, but who acquires an even better pride in doing his job of waking his farmyard friends.

Littlest Angel. Coronet. 14 minutes, color, p-i-j-s.

To the gates of heaven came a small and very lonely angel who, though he tried very hard, just couldn't seem to behave like an angel. But when the Understanding Angel listened to his feelings of homesickness and granted his wish for the one thing that would make him happy, the cherub's conduct and appearance became beyond reproach. And when the Christ Child was born, it was the Littlest Angel's gift that was chosen by God to shine as the Star of Bethlehem.

Magic Well. Coronet. 14 minutes, color, p-i.

When Gretchen slips and falls into a well, she finds herself in an enchanted fairyland where she has several adventures, and, because of her kindness, earns a wonderful reward from Mother Hollie. Later, her selfish stepsister makes the same journey with very different results.

Mermaid Princess. Coronet. 13½ minutes, color, p-i.
A mermaid from the magic undersea world rescues a drowning prince
and falls in love with him. To win his heart she is made human by the
sea witch, but when the prince marries a princess, the unhappy mermaid
returns to the sea and is transformed into a beautiful circle of light in the
sky.

Musicians in the Woods. Coronet. 13½ minutes, color, p.
Animated puppets enact the Grimms' fairy tale about the forsaken
animals who set out to make their way in the world. The adventures in
which the donkey, dog, cat, and rooster outwit a band of thieves and
gain a fortune are told here in a colorful and amusing fashion.

Rapunzel. Coronet. 10 minutes, color, p-i.
"Rapunzel, Rapunzel, let down your hair." This classic tale is retold in
animation of exquisite texture and beauty enhanced by haunting original
music. As the story is spun of the child, isolated in a tower by an
enchantress, the borders of the scenes abound with symbolic forms
reflecting each turn of the plot. When a prince blinded by thorns
wanders the world and comes at last upon Rapunzel, her tears restore his
sight and they live happily ever after.

Red Balloon. Films Incorporated. 23 minutes, color, nonverbal, p-
i-j-s.
A boy "befriends" a balloon, and suddenly the balloon has a life of its
own and follows the boy everywhere. The two enjoy a wonderful friendship on the streets of Montmartre.

Roundabout. Churchill. 19 minutes, color, nonverbal, p-i.
A dramatic fantasy to set young minds prowling. A story about a young
boy's experience with an old man who owns a magic toy merry-go-round
(roundabout) and what happens when it is stolen by the boy's friends.
This film is about responsibility and consideration for others, but also
sparks the imagination.

Rumpelstiltskin. Coronet. 11½ minutes, color, p-i.
A miller falsely boasts to a king that his lovely daughter can spin straw
into gold. When the greedy king puts her to the test, a mysterious little
man appears and offers to do the magical job for a price—her first born
child when she marries the king. Later on, the girl saves her child by
guessing Rumpelstiltskin's name.

Shoemaker and the Elves. Coronet. 13 minutes, color, p.
The story of the elves who slip into the shoemaker's shop and make
shoes for him is retold with animated puppets. This charming film,
based on a Grimm fairy tale, tells what happens when the shoemaker
and his wife leave new clothes, food, and sweets for the elves one night.

Tom Thumb in King Arthur's Court. Coronet. 19½ minutes, color, p-i.
In a bright and colorful style this animated film traces the career of the
fabled hero. From his birth in the heart of a rose to the day when he is
made a knight of the Round Table. Tom's adventures will amuse and
entertain while teaching us that valor is not a matter of size, but of
spirit.

SOUND FILMSTRIPS

Andy and the Lion. (1967). Weston Woods. 42 frames, color, p-i.
James Dougherty's adaptation of the Androcles legend. Andy helps a distressed lion and is repaid when the lion helps him become a hero.

Angus and the Cat. (1962). Weston Woods. 34 frames, color, p-i.
The story of a curious little dog named Angus, who after an encounter with a couple of ducks became less curious.

Arrow to the Sun. (1974). Weston Woods. 33 frames, color, i-j-s.
An ancient Pueblo Indian tale about a boy who searches for his true identity.

Bilingual Beginner Book Filmstrip Set 1 and 2. Random House. 8 filmstrips, color, p-i.
Set 1 contains "Mr. Brown Can Moo, Can You" (Seuss), "Bears on Wheels" (Berenstain), "Are You My Mother?" (Eastman), and "The King, the Mice and the Cheese" (Gurney). Set 2 includes "Great Day for Us" (Seuss), "He Bear, She Bear" (Berenstain), "Put Me in the Zoo" (Lopshire), and "Go Dog, Go!" (Eastman).

The Camel Who Took a Walk. (1959). Weston Woods. 46 frames, color, p-i.
Dramatizes the suspense of danger awaiting an unsuspecting camel.

Charlie Needs a Cloak. (1977). Weston Woods. 32 frames, color, p-i.
Children learn how wool from a sheep becomes a coat for someone to wear.

Charlotte's Web, (1979). Films, Inc.. 34 frames, color, p-i.
E.B. White's story of the humor, pathos, and reality of life's cycle centering around Wilbur the pig, Charlotte the spider, and a little girl.

Chicano History of the Southwest. Bilingual Educational Services. 8 filmstrips, color, i-j-s.
Contributions of Mexican Americans to the history of the Southwest are depicted in the following films: 1. "Mother of God"; 2. "Dispossessed Ranch"; 3. "Joaquin: Hero or Outlaw"; 4. "Migrant Worker"; 5. "Mestizo"; 6. "Vaquero"; 7. "Pachuco-Zoot Suiter and Vato Loco"; and 8. "A Chicano from Aztlan."

Christmas Songs in Spanish—A Series. (1963). Society for Visual Education. 15 minutes, color, j-s.
Presents traditional Christmas carols sung in Spanish

Curious George Rides a Bike. (1960). Weston Woods. 58 frames, color, p-i.
Tells of the adventures of a monkey who makes mischief a habit.

The Elves and the Shoemaker. (1965). Society for Visual Education. 42 frames, color, p-i.
From the Brothers Grimm fairy tale about the poor shoemaker who is helped by little elves to make his shoes and befriends them in return.

The Five Chinese Brothers. (1960). Weston Woods. 56 frames, color, p-i.
Tells the story of how five identical-looking Chinese brothers outwit the townspeople and save themselves from tragic death.

Five Families. (1972). Scholastic Magazine. 5 filmstrips, color, p-i-j.
Shows a variety of families and cultures in the United States. The five filmstrips include: 1. "The Yangs, from San Francisco's Chinatown"; 2. "The Pullins, a Black Family from New York City"; 3. "The Bahes, a Navajo Family from the Navajo Reservation"; 4. "The Andrades, a Mexican Family from Phoenix, Arizona"; and 5. "The Del Molinos, a Traveling Circus Family."

The Four Musicians. (1971). Society for Visual Education. 11minutes, color.
Four animals who are too old to work make their way in the world.

Make Way for Ducklings. (1968). Weston Woods. 43 frames, color, p-i.
A family of ducks takes up residence in Boston's public garden.

The Old Woman and Her Pig. (1962). Weston Woods. 52 frames, color, p-i.
Relates the predicament of the little old woman and her stubbornly disobedient pig.

Peter's Chair. (1966). Weston Woods. 32 frames, color, p-i.
Peter runs away because of his jealousy of the new baby.

The Snowy Day. (1966). Weston Woods. 22 frames, color, p-i.
Expresses the delight of a young boy romping in the snow.

Stone Soup. (1957). Weston Woods. 42 frames, color, p-i.
An old French folktale about a clever trick used by three soldiers who request food and lodging from a selfish group of peasants.

The Story about Ping. (1972). Weston Woods. 41 frames, color, p-i.
A poor little Chinese duck narrowly escapes many dangers and manages to return home safely.

The Three Robbers. (1966). Weston Woods. 20 frames, color, p-i.
Tells the story of three fierce robbers who took an orphan girl prisoner. She changed their views of life and showed them a new use for the goods they had stolen.

Computer Software for Spanish-Speaking Students: A Selected and Annotated Bibliography

F. Lance Hoopes

Computer software is supplied on floppy disks. Because they consist of thin plastic coated with a magnetic recording medium, these disks are extremely susceptible to damage by untrained users. Static electricity, a magnet, heat, a speck of dust, or a myriad of other small problems can completely destroy the usefulness of a computer disk. Because of this fragility, public libraries are not now typically providing software as a service to the general public.

School libraries are, however, beginning to purchase computer programs for distribution to teachers and students. This chapter will be devoted, in the main, to educational software that is available to assist teachers and students in the schools. The following list is not intended as suggested literature for public libraries at this time.

The bulk of the software being published is educational in nature, and most of the educational software designed for the Hispanic population is published under the apparent assumption that Spanish-speaking people want, more than anything, to learn English. The past several years have seen a tremendous increase in the availability of computerware devoted to English as a second language (ESL), specifically for Spanish-speaking learners. Very little available software is written in Spanish, has instructions in Spanish, and is completely usable by non-English speakers.

Because of the nature of the software, almost all of it will require a teacher/helper to get the Spanish-speaking user started. For this reason, the annotations presented will, in most cases, refer to use by teachers. It is the author's belief that computers and computer software are most appropriately used in classrooms for educational purposes; the choice of items presented here is based on that belief.

Three types of software are listed herein. (1) Bilingual software is designed to teach specific concepts to Spanish speakers. It usually consists of instructions in English followed by lessons and/or games in Spanish, or lessons and/or games in English with Spanish prompts and reinforcement. (2) Useful nonbilingual software is in English, but consists of games or lessons that can be entered by the teacher. In those cases, lessons in Spanish can be entered by the teacher for use by Spanish-speaking students. (3) "Authoring" and word processing programs are also included in the following bibliography. Authoring programs allow teachers to design their own lessons for use later by Spanish-speaking students. The word processing programs listed are all programs that allow the use of special marks inherent in the Spanish language. Programs are listed alphabetically by title within each system.

The bibliography that follows is by no means a complete list of available software. It is, however, a list of previewed and selected software that is readily available and useful for Spanish speakers. For further research on course ware in other languages, refer to *Guide to Microcomputer Courseware for Bilingual Education* (1985). This guide is available from: National Clearinghouse for Bilingual Education, 1555 Wilson Boulevard, Suite 605, Rosslyn, VA 22209. A list of addresses and phone numbers for major software publishers can be found in the appendix to this chapter.

The following is a key to the entries. It follows, at least in format, the style of entries used by most computer review media, and it closely resembles the entries used in the above guide.

Key to Entries

TI	*Title of software program.*
PB	Publisher—All addresses are listed in the appendix at the end of the chapter.
HW	Hardware (types of computers) on which program will run.
PE	Special peripherals needed to use program.
LN	Language program is written in Spanish or English.
GL	Grade level of program.
PR	Price of software program for computers listed.

BILINGUAL SOFTWARE

TI	*Alicia, A Bilingual Reader*
PB	George Earl
HW	Apple II+, IIe, IIc
PE	None

LN   Spanish/English
GL   Grades 4–8 (or above with low reading levels)
PR $29.95

> **Comments**: In this program, students study a translation of "Alice in Wonderland" and respond using a word-by-word test method. A paragraph from the story is displayed on the screen using a special screen alphabet that is much more attractive than typical computer type. The paragraph may be displayed in either Spanish or English (user's choice). After reading the paragraph the student is given words to translate from Spanish to English or vice versa. Accents or tildes are used and are automatic when the student types in the words.

TI   *Anagramas Hispanoamericanos*
PB   Gessler Educational Software
HW   Apple II+, IIe, IIc
PE   Color monitor helpful but not required
LN   Spanish/English
GL   Grades 7–12
PR $29.95

> **Comments**: Teaches geography in lesson and game formats. When students unscramble anagrams of countries or capitals the location appears on a screen map (in color if you use a color monitor). This program can be helpful in teaching names, locations, and capitals of South America, Central America, Mexico, and the Caribbean.
>
> Student management files for use by the teacher keep track of who has used the program, how many times they tried it, and the final score for each student.

TI   *Bilingual Education: History and English*
PB   Schoolhouse Software
HW   Apple II+, IIe, IIc
PE   Printer (optional)
LN   Spanish/English
GL   Grades 4–8 (or above with low reading levels)
PR $110.00 each level (has seven levels)

> **Comments**: Each level contains two program disks with review and explanatory material to be tested. Tests are done in a game format. Level 1 drills interrogative and present perfect tense; Level 2, irregular past tense and interrogatives; Level 3, irregular past tense and plurals; Level 4, homonyms and vowels (long and short); Level 5, durative tense and possessive adjectives; Level 6, capitalization and contractions; and Level 7, presidents and history/culture skills.

TI   *CALL (Computer Aided Language Learning)*
PB   BIPACS
HW   Apple II+, IIe, IIc
PE   Two disk drives and Superduper talker (required); color monitor, printer, and light pen (all optional)
LN   Spanish/English/French
GL   Grades 4–12
PR $25.00 each

Comments: Color graphics and digitized voice enhance this package that focuses on the structure of the language it is in. The program presents ten humorous dialogs and students participate in a role- playing manner, eventually playing all roles. Structures included are: perfect progressive, present, future, past, mass-count nouns, comparatives, present progressive, and past progressive.

The computer maintains a record of students' scores which the teacher can use to check on progress. If a printer is connected, the teacher has access to a score printout at any time.

TI   *Cities of the U.S.*
PB   BIPACS
HW   Apple II+, IIe, IIc
PE   Light pen
LN   Spanish/English
GL   Grades 4–8
PR $49.00

Comments: This program can be used to teach students the names and locations of U.S. cities or to drill on the spellings of the cities. Students key in the names of cities and watch them appear on the computer screen map of the U.S.

TI   *Developing Language Skills—ESL*
PB   Intellectual Software
HW   Apple II+, IIe, IIc
PE   Color monitor (optional)
LN   Spanish/English
GL   Grades 3-7
PR $795.00 (25 disks)

Comments: The programs are in a game format in which the user chooses to identify a picture by pointing at a word or to identify a word by pointing at a picture. The word or picture is chosen from three that appear on the screen by using the computer's arrow keys to move an on-screen arrow.

Many categories are included in both Spanish and English.

Each disk is in one language or the other; languages are not mixed on the same disk.

English categories are: vehicles, games, animals, colors and numbers, outside, clothing, food, things we like to do, furniture, what are they doing?, and inside. The same categories are provided in Spanish.

TI *Fahrenheit and Centigrade*
PB BIPACS
HW Apple II+, IIe, IIc; IBM PC, PC Jr.
PE None
LN Spanish
GL All levels
PR $49.00

Comments: Instruction is given by the program in converting to centigrade from fahrenheit and vice versa, and in estimating from one system to the other. Help is always available during the game that follows. In the game, students are shown two thermometers on the screen and asked to convert or estimate from one scale to the other.

TI *Third Grade Reading Comprehension—ESL*
    Fourth Grade Reading Comprehension—ESL
PB Intellectual Software
HW Apple II+, IIe, IIc; IBM PC, PC Jr.
PE None
LN English/Spanish
GL Any level with fourth-grade reading capability
PR $65.00

Comments: The program presents short paragraphs in English, then asks questions below the paragraph (also in English). The questions are designed to test comprehension of the paragraph read.

A correct response to the question will receive a positive comment in Spanish ("Bueno" and "Correcto" appear to be the only ones used).

An incorrect response to the question causes the appropriate section of the text to be highlighted to show the student what she/he missed in reading the text. This seems to be a very positive approach to teachihg reading comprehension.

TI *Grammar Mastery—Series A, B, and C*
PB Regents ALA Company
HW Apple II, II+, IIe, IIc
PE None

LN   English
GL   Beginning to intermediate ESL
PR   See Comments

Comments: These three series focus on areas of persistent difficulty in acquiring English as a second language. They may be integrated with or used as a supplement for any curriculum or program of study.

Series A deals with basic verb tenses, nouns and pronouns, yes/no and "wh" words, prepositions, adjectives, and adverbs.

Series B covers present perfect, quantity, comparatives and superlatives, and relative clauses.

Series C deals with past perfect, passive voice, noun clauses, and infinitives and gerunds.

Six lesson diskettes and one start up diskette cost $195.00 for each series. An optional teacher management diskette is available to record scores for all students at a cost of $95.00. The teacher diskette can be used to put custom information into the program as well. The same teacher diskette will work for all series.

TI   *Learn to Tell Time*
PB   BIPACS
HW   Apple II+, IIe, IIc
PE   None
LN   English/Spanish/French
GL   Grades 1–8
PR $49.00

Comments: This program can be used to teach the students to tell time or to drill them on previously learned material. The students can make the choice themselves when they begin the program or the teacher can place them at the correct point in the program.

TI   *The Lectura Series*
PB   BINET International
HW   Apple; IBM PC
HW   None
LN   Spanish
GL   Grade 1–8
PR $250.00

Comments: These lessons run the gamut from decoding and beginning Spanish reading to practice in reading comprehension and skills in math, science, social studies, and career education. They are designed to supplement other courses of study and to help students learn all areas of the curriculum in their native language while learning to read and speak English.

The programs use no accents, tildes, or inverted punctuation marks in the presentation of the Spanish language.

Students are given information and then asked to respond to questions in which they have to guess what words the author had in mind.

All responses are made by filling in blanks. The blanks always have the exact number of spaces required for the answer. Hence, for a yes/no answer there will be two spaces if the answer is "no" and three spaces if it is "yes." It is not therefore necessary to know the answer to get the question correct.

Some grammatical errors occur in the presentation of the material. "La 'C' tiene el sonido de la 'K' cuando se usa antes de *las vocales* 'A', 'O', y 'U'" is one example. (Emphasis mine)

TI	*Numbers*
PB	BIPACS
HW	Apple II, II+, IIe, IIc
PE	None
LN	Spanish/English/French
GL	All levels for ESL, primary grades to teach numbers to native speakers
PR	$49.00

Comments: Students are given number words in the language they are learning and must key in the proper numerals. This program can teach numbers in ESL classes at any age, and could be used to teach native speakers in the primary grades.

TI	*Reading and Thinking—ESL*
PB	Intellectual Software
HW	Apple II, II+, IIe, IIc; IBM PC, IBM PC Jr.
PE	None
LN	English/Spanish
GL	All ages with third- to fifth-grade reading level
PR	$54.95

Comments: Short, one-paragraph stories in English are followed by questions that require the student to draw inferences about the story. An example follows: "It was late evening and the man was sitting quietly by the fire. He got up and went over to the door. Then he went back to his chair and began reading."

Question: Why did he go over to the door? Answer: To turn on the light.

Question: Was it winter or summer? Answer: Winter. An incorrect response elicits a sentence in Spanish explaining why the answer was wrong.

TI   *Says to Read Words—ESL*
PB   Intellectual Software
HW   Apple II, II+, IIe, IIc
PE   None
LN   English/Spanish
GL   Beginning English reading at any age
PR $59.95

> **Comments**: The program is designed to supplement beginning programs in English reading. The instructions on the disk are in English, but the questions are in Spanish. The program asks for the student's name, then uses the name in all interactions while running.
>
> Two disks are included in the program. Disk One deals with word shapes, beginnings, endings, consonants, and vowels. Disk Two covers long vowels, vowel rules, reading vowels, long words, and endings.

TI   *Spanish-English ESL Vocabulary Games*
PB   Intellectual Software
HW   Apple II+, IIe, IIc
PE   None
LN   Spanish/English
GL   Grades 4–8 (or higher with low reading level or for ESL)
PR $39.95

> **Comments**: Contains seven word games for two players or for one or two players. The two-player games may be played by one person by using the same name for both. The seven games are: "Dictionary" (a translation game), "Hangman" (user's choice of Spanish or English), "Scrambled Eggs" (unscramble words in either language), "Spelling Bee" (Spanish or English), "Superguess" (guess a word from a word list when given one letter), and "Tic-Tac-Toe" (translation or fill in missing letters). A teacher utility makes it possible for the teacher to easily add his/her word lists to any of the programs.

TI   *Spanish Hangman*
PB   George Earl
HW   Apple II, II+, IIe, IIc; TRS-80 model I, model III, model 4
PE   None
LN   Spanish/English
GL   All levels
PR $39.95

> **Comments**: The game we all know by this title is used in conjunction with the high resolution graphics screen. The special alphabet used makes a more readable and attractive screen. The program

uses 1,600 words and 450 sentences for the games. There is no provision for teacher modification to add words.

TI	*Spanish Language Math Practice*
PB	MECC
HW	Apple II, II+, IIe, IIc
PE	None
LN	Spanish
GL	Grades 2–8 (or above with low math skills)
PR	$39.00

Comments: This is a Spanish-language version of MECC's "Elementary Volume 1: Mathematics" program. It contains 11 easy-to-use math games for elementary and junior high school math levels. All instructions and on-screen comments are in Spanish. Program types include: making change, rounding numbers, locate "Hurquito" using graph coordinates, and drills in the four arithmetical operations (user selects difficulty). The program comes with a teacher's manual in English with Spanish worksheets.

TI	*The Transitional English Reading Software Series*
PB	BINET International
HW	Apple II, II+, IIe, IIc; IBM PC, PC Jr.; Commodore 64 & 128
PE	None
LN	English
GL	Grades 4–8
PR	$200.00

Comments: Contains lessons in English in many areas of reading difficulty including syllabication, comprehension, vocabulary, phonics, and sentence building.

Information is given in English, then questions are asked in English. Answers to questions are always blanks to fill in and the number of spaces always corresponds to the answer. For yes/no answers the "yes" blank is three spaces wide and the "no" blank has two spaces, thus giving away the answer.

TI	*Vocabulary Mastery: Series A and B*
PB	Regents/ALA Company
HW	Apple II, II+, IIe, IIc
PE	None
LN	English
GL	Beginning ESL at any age
PR	$175.00 each series; optional teacher management disk, $95.00

Comments: The program presents the first 1,000 words of English for ESL students. It is designed to promote mastery and not just recognition. Each series consists of five lesson disks and a start-up disk.

The teacher management disk allows the teacher to monitor and record student scores on a separate disk as well as customize the exercises for the students.

QUALITY ENGLISH PROGRAMS EASILY ADAPTABLE FOR SPANISH SPEAKERS

TI *Math Blaster*
PB Davidson & Associates
HW Apple II+, IIe, IIc; IBM PC, PC Jr.
PE None
LN English
GL Grades 4–8
PR $49.95

Comments: Although this program has no Spanish language in it, it could be quite useful since it deals mainly with numbers and math facts. After the teacher gets it into game mode, the Hispanic student could take it from there.

The program is in an arcade game style to drill and practice math facts. Teachers can develop their own data files for an unlimited number of problems. The students can learn while playing a challenging game.

TI *Spellicopter*
PB Designware
HW Apple II+, IIe, IIc
PE Joy stick (optional)
LN English
GL Grades 3–8
PR $39.95

Comments: Although the program and instructions are in English, the teacher can make up all components of the games in Spanish. No accents or tildes are available in the writing of the components, however.

The game involves reading a sentence with one word left out, then flying a helicopter through a maze to pick up letters from a scrambled version of the missing word. Letters are to be picked in the correct order to properly spell the word.

With the teacher utility it is easy to supply your own set of words and sentences for the program to use.

TI   *Tic Tac Show*
PB   Computer Advanced Ideas
HW   Apple II+, IIe, IIc
PE   None
LN   English
GL   All levels
PR $39.95

Comments: The program and opening instructions are in English, but teachers can use their own questions in any language (without accents or other marks). Students play a game based on the T.V. show "Tic Tac Dough" in which they answer questions to get X's and O's on a tic tac toe grid.

A built-in authoring program makes it as easy as typing to create questions for any subject area. This is one of the best programs of its kind this author has seen.

WORD PROCESSING AND AUTHORING PROGRAMS IN, OR ADAPTABLE TO, SPANISH

TI   *El Asistente del Instructor*
PB   MECC
HW   Apple II+, IIe, IIc
PE   Printer (optional)
LN   Spanish
GL   All levels (for use by teachers)
PR $39.00

Comments: This is an easy-to-use program to allow teachers to make reviews and quizzes for their students to use on the computer. It is appropriate for any subject area and level. No knowledge of programming is required to use it.

TI   *Bank Street Writer*
PB   Broderbund Software
HW   All major computers
PE   Printer
LN   English/Spanish/French/German
GL   All levels
PR $69.95

Comments: This is an easy-to-learn word processing program for students or teachers. The program can be put into a special mode for any foreign language. In Spanish it allows for accents, tildes, and inverted punctuation marks. Special Spanish characters do not look right on the screen, but will come out properly when printed on a compatible printer.

TI	*Crossword Magic*
PB	Mindscape, Inc.
HW	Apple II+, IIe, IIc
PE	Printer (optional)
LN	English
GL	All levels
PR	$49.95

Comments: This program allows the user to create crossword puzzles. Teachers or students can use the program to create and save crossword puzzles to be played at the computer or printed out for classroom use. Unlike earlier crossword puzzle programs, this one makes puzzles that look and play just like the real thing.

The program is very easy to use and almost entirely self-explanatory. Words and clues can be entered in any language, although no accents, tildes, or other specialized marks are available. The final result is a very professional looking puzzle with clues for across and down words along with an answer facsimile printed on a separate page.

TI	*Express Trainer*
PB	BIPACS
HW	Apple II+, IIe, IIc
PE	Superduper talker (required); color monitor, printer, light pen, (all optional)
LN	Multilingual
GL	All levels
PR	$250.00

Comments: This program allows teachers to create their own computer course ware. It is an extremely versatile program allowing digitized voice, accents and tildes, color graphics, and music.

The program is not the easiest to learn of the authoring systems, but it is definitely the most versatile and probably worth the time to learn. With it, you can create computer programs yourself with no programming knowledge. You type in plain language and the computer converts your instructions to commands it can use.

TI *Select Bilingual*
PB Summa Technologies
HW IBM PC, XT
PE Dot matrix printer
LN Spanish/English
GL All levels
PR $395.00

> **Comments**: This is an excellent word processing program that allows switching from Spanish to English with ease and uses all accents, tildes, and inverted punctuation in Spanish. The user can type and print in either language or use both languages in one document.

Appendix
List of Software Publishers

BINET Bilingual Software
5407 Rocking Horse
Oceanside, CA 92056
(619) 941-5911

BIPACS (Bilingual Publications
   and Computer Services)
33 Walnut Street
Long Beach, NY 11561
(212) 685-3459

Broderbund Software
17 Paul Drive
San Rafael, CA 94903
(415) 479-1170

COMpress
PO Box 102
Wentworth, NH 03282
(603) 764-5225

Computer-Advanced Ideas
1442A Walnut Street, Suite 341
Berkeley, CA 94709
(415) 526-9100

Davidson & Associates
6069 Groveoak Place, #12
Rancho Palos Verdes, CA
   90274
(231) 378-7826

Fireside Computing, Inc.
5843 Montgomery Road
Elkridge, MD 21227
(301) 736-4165

George Earl
1302 South Gen. McMullan
San Antonio, TX 78237
(512) 434-3681

Gessler Educational Software
900 Broadway
New York, NY 10003
(212) 673-3113

Intellectual Software
798 North Avenue
Bridgeport, CT 06606
(203) 335-0908

MECC (Minnesota Educational
    Computer Consortium)
2520 Broadway Drive
St. Paul, MN 55113
(612) 376-1105

Micro Lab Learning Center
2310 Skokie Valley Road
Highland Park, IL 60035
(312) 433-7550

Mindscape, Inc.
3444 Dundee Road
Northbrook, IL 60062
(312) 480-7667

Phoenix Performance Systems,
    Inc.
324 South Main Street
Stillwater, MN 55082
(612) 430-2980

Regents/ALA Company
2 Park Avenue
New York, NY 10016
(212) 839-2780/2781

Schoolhouse Software
290 Brighton Road
Elk Grove, IL 60007
(312) 526-5027

Summa Technologies, Inc.
PO Box 2046
Beaverton, OR 97006
(503) 644-3212

Bibliography of Resources about Hispanic Culture for Librarians

Maria Segura

The intent of this bibliography is to list materials that will enable the librarian or teacher to better understand and serve Hispanic children's unique needs. First and foremost, the adult who works with Hispanic children must never lose awareness of the fact that Hispanic children are children: they are curious, imaginative, playful, hopeful, and active humans in development. Hispanics are unique in having the benefits and, if any, the drawbacks, of having an additional culture with sets of values, lifestyles and families, responsibilities, beliefs, and legends unlike those of the "typical" American family. They may participate in unique festivals and ceremonies, and enjoy different music, dances, and foods. They need to be proud of their uniqueness, and to see that their customs are respected by others. Those who serve Hispanics must, of course, avoid prejudgments and negative expectations, as well as the other extreme, which sometimes takes the form of a patronizing, gushing adoration for all things "ethnic." Respect is the end for which we must strive, and understanding leads to respect.

Listed first, then, among the sources below are several works on library services to Hispanics; included are fairly recent and/or older works. Works were selected either because of their currency or because they had something unique to offer. In addition, they had to be in English for use by the typical American librarian or teacher. To have selected only those items currently in print would have been impossible in many cases, since few English-language materials are available for some subjects. Among the materials on services to the Spanish speaking are some ERIC documents. These have the ED number given at the end of the bibliographic citation. They will presumably be available at any federal depository library.

Next are listed sources that devote a substantial amount of their content to reviews of children's books and media. Though not all of these will have articles or reviews specific to Hispanic needs in every issue, all of them will feature articles or reviews at least occasionally. As noted in the annotation under *Children's Book Review Index*, hundreds of periodicals, may, on occasion, review children's books.

The section labelled "Sources for Background" lists books that focus on either the history or the civilization of Hispanic groups, whether in their own countries or in the United States. Because the three largest Hispanic groups in the United States are of Mexican, Puerto Rican, and Cuban origin, these three groups were chosen as a focus. Recent media attention has been directed to various Central American and Colombian groups in the United States, but book materials on these disparate groups are not widely distributed. Mexico is more "written about" than any other Latin country, perhaps because of its proximity to the United States, or its size, or its huge "exile" population, or its uniquely romantic past, or, most probably, for all of these reasons.

The section labelled "Art and Antiquities" is once again overwhelmingly dominated by Mexico, mostly because of the unavailability of books on other individual countries or on Latin America as a whole. It is difficult, too, to find English-language adult books on Puerto Rican or Cuban folklore, or even on the folklore of Latin America as a whole. Though the focus is generally on adult books, children's books on handicrafts were selected; they seem more appropriate for use in teaching units for children in the crafts they feature. Results are more satisfactory in libraries or classrooms when children's craft books are used.

With regard to food and cookbooks, a glance at the *Subject Guide to Books in Print* will immediately convey that Mexican cookbooks far outnumber those dedicated to the cuisines of Puerto Rico and Cuba, let alone Colombia, Chile, or the Central American countries. Consequently, any available books that dealt with Latin America as a whole were selected.

Finally, an appendix to this chapter contains a list of addresses of important publishers and distributors of Spanish-language and Hispanic-oriented materials, whether in the United States, Spain, or a Latin American country.

SOURCES OF INFORMATION ON LIBRARY SERVICES TO HISPANICS

Buttlar, Lois, & Lubomyr R. Wynar. (1977). *Building ethnic collections: An annotated guide for school media centers and public libraries.* Littleton, CO: Libraries Unlimited.
Deals with over 44 ethnic groups ranging from Basques through East Indians. Intended for collectors of ethnic materials for all ages. Content includes bibliographies, encyclopedic types of sources, dictionaries, handbooks, curriculum materials, and fictional and audiovisual materials, as well as sources for statistics about the individual groups. Directory of producers and distributors, and indexes of authors, titles, and audiovisual materials.

Cabello-Argandona, Roberto, & Roberto Peter Haro. (1977). *System analysis of library and information services to the Spanish speaking community of the United States.* Los Angeles: Chicano Studies Center. ED 143368.
Academic discussion of theory and previous works on library services to Hispanics.

Dale, Doris Cruger. (1985). *Bilingual books in Spanish and English for children.* Littleton, CO: Libraries Unlimited.
Current and thorough. Discusses publishers, dealers, bibliographies. Continues with an annotated bibliography, decade by decade, from 1940 to the mid-1980s. Summary and conclusions paragraph about Spanish and bilingual materials. Various indexes, among them: subject index, title and series index, and name index.

Davila, Daniel. (1976). *Library service for the Spanish-speaking user: Source guide for librarians.* Bronx, NY: New York Metropolitan Reference and Research Library Agency. ED 135400.
Lists bibliographies and materials published from 1950 to 1975 "reflecting character, history and psychology of Spanish-speaking groups." Resource list for New York metropolitan area: TV programs, bookstores, schools offering courses of interest to Hispanics, and a model for a library skills guide in Spanish, with English translation provided.

Duran, Daniel Flores. (1979). *Latino materials: A multimedia guide for children and young adults.* (Selection Guide Series, Vol. 1). New York: Neal-Schuman.
Introductory essays on Latino library services and literature; followed by annotated list of general resources (book and film) divided by elementary and secondary grade levels. Separate sections for Mexican-American resources and Puerto Rican resources. Provides glossary, list of distributors, subject index, and author/title index.

Hawkins, John N. (1975). *Teacher's resource handbook for Latin American studies: An annotated bibliography of curriculum materials, preschool through grade 12.* (UCLA Latin American Center Reference Series, Vol. 6). Los Angeles, CA: UCLA Latin American Center Publications.

Divides materials by grade, country or group of countries, and type: multimedia, filmstrips and slides, posters and pictures, films, records, tapes, and books. Lists publishers and distributors. Useful as checklist for materials already in place.

Jordan, Lois B. (1973). *Mexican Americans: Resources to build cultural understanding.* Littleton, CO: Libraries Unlimited.
Long, annotated lists of printed materials on various aspects of Mexico's history; Mexican Americans in the United States; Mexican and Mexican-American arts, drama, theater, music, dance, and literature, as well as biography and fiction. Continues with lists of audiovisual materials and other media of various types; then lists noted Mexican-American personalities, Mexican-American organizations, periodicals and newspapers; as well as reference works, author, title, and subject indexes.

Josey, E. J., & Marva L. de Loach. (Eds.) (1983). *Ethnic collections in libraries.* New York: Neal-Schuman.
Compilation of essays discussing importance of ethnic materials collection, problem areas, criteria for evaluation, nonprint ethnic resources, and government documents. Describes specific Puerto Rican and Chicano collections, and discusses the history of services to the Spanish speaking. Chapters on Caribbean peoples and many other ethnic groups as well. Section dedicated to archives, programming, federal policy, and linkages to professional ethnic associations. Bibliographies follow chapters. Index.

Litsinger, Dolores Escobar. (1973). *The challenge of teaching Mexican American students.* New York: American Book Company.
Explores Chicano history; contrasts cultural values; examines social problems and teacher attitudes. Offers strategies and lesson plans to meet particular challenges. Discusses importance of language. Bibliographies and index.

Meier, Matt S. (Compiler). (1984). *Bibliography of Mexican American History.* Westport, CT: Greenwood Press.
Thorough bibliography of 500 pages proceeding from general works to and through historical periods, listing books, theses, and periodicals. Continues with chapters on labor, immigration, and the border region; civil rights; and culture. Some annotations. Lists bibliographies and guides to the study of Mexican-American history. Names principal research collections, archives, and libraries. Lists journals. Author and subject indexes.

Moyer, Dorothy Clausen. (1976). *The growth and development of children's books about Mexico and Mexican Americans.* Ann Arbor, MI: University Microfilms.
Doctoral dissertation. Author addresses the increased American interest in Mexico and the growth in publications about it. Author makes observations about the past treatment of Mexico in books versus present treatment, and concludes that there is improvement in understanding and portrayal of Mexico, but that more is needed. Lengthy text discusses developments, citing specific works to demonstrate points. Various appendices are comprised of such items as books and journals on children's

literature, and long bibliographies listing and rating juvenile works of fiction and nonfiction for various age levels. Thorough.

Peterson, Anita R. (1977). *Library service to the Spanish speaking.* Inglewood, CA: Inglewood Public Library.
Discusses goals and objectives in library services to Hispanics (administration and organization). Provides activities leading to achievement of goals and objectives. Discusses types of collections and policies as well as programs. Provides sample job descriptions, flyers and brochures, as well as written measures of evaluation. Acknowledgement lists sources for more materials on library services for Hispanics.

Reilly, Robert P. (1977). *A selected and annotated bibliography of bicultural classroom materials for Mexican American studies.* San Francisco, CA: R & E Research Associates.
Introductory matters are followed by annotated bibliography of bicultural materials in art, drama, history, literature, music, and social studies. Lists of teacher resources.

Schon, Isabel. (1978). *A bicultural heritage: Themes for the exploration of Mexican and Mexican American culture in books for children and adolescents.* Metuchen, NJ: Scarecrow Press.
Divides material by grade level groupings. Within those groupings, lists desired outcome of activities with the materials listed. Provides lists of recommended and unrecommended books. Evaluative comments on both of these types delineate both appropriate, positive aspects of their content, and negative, innappropriate aspects. Use of this technique gives specific insights into culture and its perception. Reveals unconscious errors in books portraying Mexico and Mexicans. Proposes follow-up activities and discussion topics. Author and title indexes.

———. (1978). *Books in Spanish for children and young adults: An annotated guide/Libros infantiles y juveniles en Español: Una guia anotada.* Metuchen, NJ: Scarecrow Press.
English and Spanish.· Divided by Spanish-speaking country, and with each country by type, for example: fiction, legend, poetry, and song. Each book is assigned a grade level, annotated, evaluated, and rated. Lists bookdealers in Spanish-speaking countries as well as those in the United States. Author, title, and subject indexes.

———. (1983). *Books in Spanish for children and young adults: An annotated guide, Series II/Libros infantiles y juveniles en Español: Una guía anotada, Series No. II.* Metuchen, NJ: Scarecrow Press.
This second book in a series of three does more of what Schon did in the first book of the series. Books listed here were in print as of October, 1982.

———. (1985). *Books in Spanish for children and young adults: An annotated guide, Series III/Libros infantiles y juveniles en Español: Una guia anotada, Series No. III.* Metuchen, NJ: Scarecrow Press.
Schon continues this third book in the series with the same insight and thoroughness shown in the first two, listed above.

————. (1980). *A Hispanic heritage: A guide to juvenile books about Hispanic people and cultures.* Metuchen, NJ: Scarecrow Press.
Written as "an aid for librarians and teachers who are interested in exposing students to the cultures of Hispanic people." Arranged into chapters that explore specific countries and cultures. Recommends critical reading of all materials, and gives reasons. Lengthy annotations, often with quotes from the source being annotated, convey the essence of the books and help readers to discern what is desirable and what is not, as well as why. Author, title, and subject indexes.

United States Task Force on Library and Information Services to Cultural Minorities. (1983). *Report of the task force on library and information services to cultural minorities.* Washington, DC: National Commission on Libraries and Information Science. SuDocs No. Y3: 61/2 61/4.
Issues 42 recommendations, based on findings, for improving library services to minorities. These include continuing assessment of service, recruitment of library personnel, purchase of better materials, and improvement in financing. Footnotes, charts, and sample self-evaluation questionnaires. No index.

Urzua, Roberto, Martha P. Cotera, & Emma Gonzalez Stump. (1978). *Library services to Mexican Americans: Policies, practices, and prospects.* Las Cruces, NM: ERIC Clearinghouse on Rural Education and Small Schools. ED 151110.
Introduces historical background of specialized library service and its inherent problems. Also discusses efforts made by librarians and educators to solve the problems. Provides some practical suggestions and checklists to check results. Lists of relevant periodicals. Book's age and focus on all library services limit its usefulness for children's collections.

SOURCES FOR REVIEWS OF SPECIFIC MATERIALS

Booklist, including Reference Books Bulletin. Chicago: American Library Association.
Twice monthly September through June and monthly in July and August. Though mostly adult in focus, this source regularly reviews children's books and, often, books in Spanish. Occasional articles on aspects of library services to minorities.

Bulletin of the Center for Children's Books. Chicago: The University of Chicago Graduate Library School.
Annotates and rates children's books.

Children's book review index: Master cumulation 1965-1984. (1985). Detroit, MI: Gale Research.
Five volumes index reviews appearing in hundreds of periodicals. Access available by author and title.

Horn Book Magazine. Boston: Horn Book.
Published six times yearly. Reviews children's books; occasionally will feature articles on Spanish-language books.

Interracial books for children. New York: Council on Interracial Books for Children.
Features articles and reviews written from the viewpoint of promoting cultural understanding and the abolition of racism.

Lector. Berkeley, CA: Hispanex.
Bimonthly, self-labelled as "The review journal of Spanish language and bilingual materials from Latin America and the United States for readers everywhere." Regular features include listings of new books and reviews of children's books by grade level groupings and type, as well as features on Chicano titles in print. Indexes its own reviews.

School Library Journal. New York: R. R. Bowker.
Published monthly except June and July. Regularly features a division labelled "Books in Spanish." Regularly reviews children's books, audio-visual materials, and computer software, as well as professional literature. Occasional articles on services to the Spanish speaking.

Wilson Library Bulletin.
Although this source deals with various types of books, it reviews children's books and software in regular features.

SOURCES FOR BACKGROUND

Cuba

Boswell, Thomas D., & James R. Curtis. (1983). *The Cuban-American experience: Culture, images and perspectives.* Totowa, NJ: Rowman and Allanheld.
Broad scholarly study of Cubans in the United States. Gives history of revolution, and of Cuban migration to the United States. Provides demographic profiles; discusses language and religion; mentions Mariel boatlifts. Explores artistic expression and cuisine. Deals with Cuban family acculturation and assimilation. Notes and index.

Harvard encyclopedia of American ethnic groups. (1980). Cambridge, MA: Belknap Press of Harvard University.
Indispensable source gives information on many aspects of ethnic groups in the United States. Encompasses history, geographic distribution, economics, marriage patterns, religion, education, and political orientation of many Hispanic groups in the United States. Bibliographies end the individual articles.

Llanes, Jose. *Cuban Americans: Masters of survival.* (1982) Cambridge, MA: Abt Books.
Cuban exiles, emigrating at various times and numbering 187, tell the poignant stories of their old and new lives, providing deeper understanding of their plight. Bibliography. No index.

MacCorkle, Lyn. (Compiler). (1984). *Cubans in the United States: A bibliography for research in the social and behavior sciences, 1960-1983.* (Bibliographies and Indexes in Sociology, Vol. 1), Westport, CT: Greenwood Press.
Discusses bibliography; business, labor, and economics; education and language; public policy and administration; psychology and health; politics; sociology, demographics, and anthropology. Extensive, though coding used to describe types is confusing and time-consuming. Index.

Matthews, Herbert L. (1975). *Revolution in Cuba: A new look at Castro's Cuba by America's foremost authority.* New York: Charles Scribner's Sons.
Attempt at objective history of the Cuban Revolution. Focus is on the leaders who carried it out. Index.

Mexico

Brenner, Anita. (1971). *The wind that swept Mexico: The history of the Mexican Revolution of 1910–1942.* The Texas Pan American Series. Austin, TX: The University of Texas Press.
Reprinted in 1984, this book is definitive on the great Mexican Revolution, written by a woman raised in Mexico. Among the 184 black-and-white photographs are many that are striking and remarkable. Chronology, list of sources, and index.

Coe, Michael D. (1980). *The Maya.* Revised and Enlarged Edition. (*Ancient People and Places,* Vol. 96). New York: Thames and Hudson.
Well illustrated history of the Maya; useful particularly in art projects for its colored illustrations and black-and-white photographs. Index.

Harvard encyclopedia of American ethnic groups. (1980). Cambridge, MA: Belknap Press of Harvard University.
Special section dedicated to Mexican Americans in this indispensable source. Encompasses history, geographic distribution, economics, marriage patterns, religion, education, and political orientation. Bibliography at end of section.

Mayo, Samuel H. (1978). *A history of Mexico from pre-Columbia to present.* Englewood Cliffs, NJ: Prentice-Hall.
History of Mexico from pre-Columbian times to present. Incorporates facts about culture, religion, education, and economic outlook. For those wishing historical background. One map. No other illustrations. Bibliographies and index.

Simpson, Lesley Byrd. (1941). *Many Mexicos.* Berkeley, CA: The University of California Press.
Often reprinted and revised work gives the reader a notion of the vast mosaic of Mexico's geography and peoples. Balanced history of Mexico from the time of the Conquest to the time following the Revolution. Glossary. Index.

Puerto Rico

Cooper, Paulette. (Ed.) (1972). *Growing up Puerto Rican.* New York: Arbor House.
In each chapter, a different individual tells his or her story. Though the anecdotes give some insight into the loneliness and despair of the people telling them, the book tends to cast a negative and hopeless picture. No index.

Fitzpatrick, Joseph P. (1971). *Puerto Rican Americans: The meaning of migration to the mainland.* (Ethnic Groups in American Life Series). Englewood Cliffs, NJ: Prentice-Hall.
Factual, objective treatment of Puerto Rican Americans. Discusses migration, culture, economics, family life and structure, color, religion, and problems unique to immigrants. Information about social services. Index.

Harvard encyclopedia of American ethnic groups. (1980). Cambridge, MA: Belknap Press of Harvard University.
See listing under "Cuba."

Mapp, Edward. (Ed.) (1974). *Puerto Rican perspectives.* Metuchen, NJ: Scarecrow Press.
Various Puerto Ricans' views on a range of subjects: education, arts, community leaders, ordinary people. Good cross-section of people to introduce readers to Puerto Rican Americans. Brief biographical sketches of contributors. Index.

Parry, J.H., & P.M. Sherlock. (1971). *A short history of the West Indies.* 3d ed. Macmillan African and Caribbean Histories Series. London: Macmillan.
Gives general history of the West Indies with much space devoted to Cuba, some to Puerto Rico. This adult book lacks the pro-American polemics shown in many children's books on the subject. Gives suggestions for further reading. Bibliography. Index.

Steiner, Stan. (1974). *The islands: The worlds of the Puerto Ricans.* New York: Harper and Row.
Steiner describes Puerto Rico and its people in colorful, emotive language and images, emphasizing topics of human interest. Uses descriptions of people's lives to convey his message. Useful for background. Black-and-white photographs. Index.

Wagenheim, Kal, & Olga Jimenez de Wagenheim. (Eds.) (1973). *The Puerto Ricans: A documentary history.* New York: Praeger.
Selected documents and explanatory inserts give 500 years of Puerto Rican history, with emphasis on recent history. Useful for background. Notes, index.

ART AND ANTIQUITIES

Cervantes, Maria Antonieta. (1978). *Treasures of ancient Mexico from the National Anthropological Museum.* New York: Crescent Books.
Ninety-four pages of colored photographs and text display objects from Mexico's best museum. Depicts a variety of sculpted pieces as well as photos of codexes and dioramas. Sparse index.

Chase, Gilbert. (1970). *Contemporary art in Latin America: Painting, graphic art, sculpture, architecture.* New York: The Free Press.
Brings together some difficult-to-find information. Largely text. Begins with Mexico; continues with the Caribbean and Central America. Does not cover Puerto Rico. Twenty-four reproductions in black-and-white. Bibliography and index.

National Museum of Anthropology, Mexico City. (1970). Great Museums of the World. New York: Newsweek.
Heavily illustrated with color photographs, mostly of sculptures and ceramics. Each item depicted is given a brief description. Bibliography. No index.

Spinden, Herbert J. (1975). *A study of Maya art, its subject matter and historical development.* New York: Dover.
Anthropological study. Reproduces Maya art in black-and-white line drawings, which could be used as a source for art projects. Otherwise is detailed, academic work with many tables of finds and chronologies. Lengthy bibliography and index.

Westheim, Paul, et al. (1972). *Prehispanic Mexican art.* A Giniger Book. New York: G.P. Putnam's Sons.
Large book, heavily illustrated with both black-and-white and color photographs. Ample text gives background. Covers different periods in sculpture, ceramics, architecture, painting, and featherwork. Chronological table. Index of illustrations and bibliography. No index to text.

CULTURE, CUSTOMS, FOLKLORE, AND HOLIDAYS

Aiken, Riley. (1980). *Mexican folktales from the borderland.* Dallas, TX: Southern Methodist University Press.
Folktales from Mexican states bordering Texas. Brief stories, reflecting traditional folk motifs, but with a Tex-Mex flavor. Entertaining, despite

stilted, "quaint" language often used by writers trying to emulate Hispanic speech. For older children and young adults.

Campos, Anthony John. (1977). *Mexican folk tales*. Tucson, AZ: The University of Arizona Press.
Short, illustrated book readable by children in or above sixth grade. Relates tales of the devil, the saints, and humans versus beasts. Probably best enjoyed read aloud to fourth graders and older.

Comins, Jeremy. (1974). *Latin American crafts and their cultural backgrounds*. New York: Lothrop, Lee and Shepard.
Shows how to make such articles as foil relief masks and pendants, laminated cardboard "sculptures," wax carvings, papier-mache sculptures, incised wood designs, imitation *molas*, wool pictures, needlepoint, and jewelry, among others. All these objects either imitate native crafts from throughout Latin America or use Latin American motifs, or both. Several added pages show motif patterns. Bibliography, glossary, and index.

Cordry, Donald. (1980). *Mexican masks*. Austin, TX: University of Texas Press.
Richly illustrated both in color and black-and-white. Scholarly discussion of the functions of masks in general and the specific festival or ritual functions of Mexican masks. Descriptions of the masks pictured. Long text is followed by maps, a survey of mask-makers from different parts of Mexico, a bibliography, and an index.

Fowler, Virginie. (1981). *Folk arts around the world and how to make them*. Englewood Cliffs, NJ: Prentice-Hall.
Juvenile book gives instruction for making Puerto Rican sunburst tiles and Spanish tiles, as well as Mexican lanterns and piggy banks. Lists sources for supplies. Index.

Garza-Lubeck, Maria, & Ana Maria Salinas. (1977). *Mexican celebrations*. Austin, TX: University of Texas Institute of Latin American Studies.
Teaching units give background of various Mexican feasts, along with recipes, activities, and songs.

Milne, Jean. (1965). *Fiesta time in Latin America*. Los Angeles, CA: The Ward Ritchie Press.
Follows monthly calendar format. With each month discusses ways selected religious and national holidays are celebrated in their countries. Brief lists of days follow for selected countries. Unfortunately, it excludes both Cuba and Puerto Rico.

Pettit, Florence H. (1976). *Christmas all around the house: Traditional decorations you can make*. New York: Crowell.
This juvenile book dedicates 2 of its 14 chapters to making Mexican crafts (piñatas and tin ornaments). Other chapters show how to make Mexican straw stars and Peruvian *santitos*. Index.

Pettit, Florence H., & Robert M. Pettit. (1978). *Mexican folk toys: Festival decorations and ritual objects*. New York: Hastings House Publishers.
Well illustrated. Has sections describing festival decorations and ritual objects, most of them derived from the blend of Spanish Christianity and

Native Indian religions. Alphabetical section on methods and materials involved in their construction. Calendar of traditional Mexican holidays. More prominent days rate longer descriptions. In addition, there is a list of market days and market places, as well as lists of museums and shops. Good for teaching units. Bibliography and index.

Temko, Florence. (1976). *Folk crafts for world friendship.* Garden City, NY: Doubleday.
Juvenile book. Among other things, shows how to make Colombian *bambulina* weavings, Mexican *posada* clay figures, and Spanish tin lanterns. Bibliography and index.

Toor, Frances. (1947). *A treasury of Mexican folkways: The customs, myths, folklore, traditions, beliefs, fiestas, dances, songs of the Mexican people.* New York: Bonanza Books.
Reprinted in 1985, this book is still probably the best single English-language source for information about specific regional fiestas and ceremonies, their cultural aspects, their music, and their dance. This classic discusses all that was, and much of what still is, unique to Mexico. Also discusses living habits, folk arts, family, government, and religion. Includes words, both Spanish and English, and music to over 100 songs. Bibliography, glossary, and index.

FOOD

Cadwallader, Sharon. (1980). *Savoring Mexico: A travel cookbook.* New York: McGraw-Hill.
Notable for its travelogue descriptions accompanying the recipes. Lack of a glossary might present problems to the new user. Index.

Dooley, Eliza B. K. (1948). *Puerto Rican cookbook.* Richmond, VA: The Dietz Press.
Discusses background of Puerto Rican cooking. Ranges from cocktails to coffee, soups, fish, meat and fowl, fruits, vegetables, and desserts. Index.

Ortiz, Elizabeth Lambert. (1979). *The book of Latin American cooking.* New York: Alfred A. Knopf.
Substantial (357 pages) book; introduction gives background on blends of cultures and materials that developed the unique foods of Latin America. Continues with definitions of ingredients foreign to Americans, with hints about where to find them. Book begins with hors d'oeuvres and continues with soups, fish, meats, poultry, "substantial" main dishes, vegetables, salads, breads, desserts, and drinks. Short list of vendors in selected cities. Index.

———. (1983). *The complete book of Caribbean cooking.* New York: M. Evans.
Long (448 pages) cookbook by experienced and popular author.

Sunset Mexican cookbook: Simplified techniques, 155 classic recipes.
(1978). Menlo Park, CA: Lane Publishing Co.
Introduction gives little-known facts about Mexican food: e. g., it doesn't
have to be spicy, and Mexicans don't eat such things as tacos and
tostadas daily. Gives recipes for appetizers and snacks, soups and salads,
tacos, burritos and sandwiches, main dishes, tamales and enchiladas,
vegetables, beans and rice, tortillas and breads, and desserts and drinks.
It nicely compromises by allowing authentic-tasting results with much
less bother than real Mexicans often go through. Index and metric chart.

Valldejuli, Carmen A. (1977). *Puerto Rican cookery.* Gretna, LA:
Pelican.
Reprinted source whose author was born in Puerto Rico.

Wolfe, Linda. (1970). *Recipes: The cooking of the Caribbean islands.*
Foods of the World. New York: Time-Life Books.
Reprinted in 1979, this book gives recipes for appetizers, soups, fish,
meat and poultry, vegetables, relishes and sauces, breads, desserts, and
drinks. Each recipe is identified by country. Indexes to recipes by names
in English and by the other names given them in the Caribbean. Glossary.

MUSIC AND DANCE

Cordry, Donald, & Dorothy Cordry. (1968). *Mexican Indian costumes.* The Texas Pan American Series. Austin, TX: The University of Texas Press.
Classic English-language work on the subject. Lavishly illustrated and
well-documented, this book depicts the peoples studied, providing much
useful background information on them. It lists descriptive details along
with pictures of items of clothing, one description per picture. Provides
panorama of the diverse peoples of Mexico and the country's geographical contrasts. The reader should be aware that the typical everyday dress
of most townspeople, and many country people, is western. This book
does depict some costumes that are no longer used. Black-and-white
photographs and illustrations. Bibliography and index.

Covarrubias, Luis. (1978). *Mexican native costumes.* Mexico:
Fishgrund.
Reissued several times, this thin book has many colorful plates of
individuals of different tribes wearing native costumes, one full illustration per leaf. Accompanying text gives background information. Color
gives this book an essential element missing from the Cordrys' book. No
index.

Dow, Allen, & Mike Michaelson. (1980). *The official guide to Latin
dancing.* Northbrook, IL: Domus Books.
Brief background identifying dances and countries of origin. Basically
this book consists of step-by-step instructions, shown in a series of
black-and-white photographs for the rumba, cha-cha, merengue, mambo,
samba, tango and paso doble. Should a teacher or librarian decide to

present these in a program, it would be wise to consult local Latin Americans about which of these dances are still being performed in their countries, and whether they are danced as regular ballroom dances or as curiosities. Index.

Geijerstam, Claes. (1976). *Popular music in Mexico.* Albuquerque, NM: University of New Mexico Press.
Discusses various types of popular music in their context. Gives biographical information on some musicians. Source for composers or artists. Documentation and index.

Paredes, Americo. (1976). *A Texas-Mexican cancionero: Folksongs of the lower border.* Music in American Life Series. Urbana, IL: University of Illinois Press.
Gives ample background. Includes melody, words, and English translations of many, many songs. Large section devoted to songs of border conflict. Provides insight into problems peculiar to border people. Glossary; bibliography; and index.

Pholeric, Janet J. (1980). *Folk dances around the world: The United States and Mexico.* San Diego, CA: A.S. Barnes.
Instructional book describes patterns and movements of various dances, including *corrido* and *jarabe tapatio.* Glossary, bibliography, and descriptive index chart, listing formation, difficulty, steps, and page number of text.

Roberts, John Storm. (1979). *The Latin tinge: The impact of Latin American music on the United States.* New York: Oxford University.
Definitive, analytic English-language work on Latin and Chicano music. Details how the various types evolved and cross-fertilized one other, particularly in the United States. Details histories of important recordings and important artists from both Latin American countries and the United States. Glossary, discography, bibliography and index.

Schwendener, Norma, & Averil Tibbels. (1934). *How to perform the dances of old Mexico: A manual of their origins, legends, costumes, steps, patterns and music.* New York: A.S. Barnes.
Reprinted in 1975, this book gives step-by-step instructions for dances such as the *huapango, los moros, los viejitos,* and others. These dances are performed in diverse regions of Mexico, usually only on special occasions. Best used as a resource for performances, with explanation about their regional origin. Toor's *Treasury of Mexican Folkways* might be useful for researching those origins. No index.

Toor, Frances. (1947). *A treasury of Mexican folkways: The customs, myths, folklore, traditions, beliefs, fiestas, dances and songs of the Mexican people.* New York: Bonanza Books.
See annotation for this book under "Culture, Customs, Folklore and Holidays" section of this chapter.

Appendix
Publishers and Distributors of Spanish-Language and Hispanic-Oriented Materials

Addison-Wesley
2527 Sandhill Road
Menlo Park, CA 94025

Alfadil Ediciones, S.A.
Apdo. 50-304
Caracas 1050, Venezuela

Alianza Editorial
Calle Milan 38
Madrid 33, Spain

Argos Vergara, S. A.
Aragón 390
Barcelona 13, Spain

Arte Público Press
Houston University
Central Campus
Houston, TX 77004

El Ateneo
Patagones 2463
Buenos Aires 1005, Argentina

Baker and Taylor
Books in Spanish
380 Edison Way
Reno, NV 89564

Bilingual Educational Services,
   Inc.
2574 South Grand Avenue
Los Angeles, CA 90077-2688

Bilingual Review/Press
1966 Broadway
New York, NY 10023

Bilingual Review/Press
Office of the Graduate School
SUNY Binghampton
Binghampton, NY 13901

Books from Mexico
812 West Figueroa Street
Santa Barbara, CA 93101

Los Californianos
788 Second Street W.
Sonoma CA 95476

Centro de Documentación e
   Información del Banco del
   Libro
1a. Av. Altamira Sur
Cruce con Av. Libertador
Caracas 1010-A, Venezuela

Chicano Studies Library
Publication Unit
3404 Dwinelle Hall
University of California
Berkeley, CA 94720

Children's Book Press
1461 Ninth Avenue
San Francisco, CA 94122

Children's Press
1224 W. Van Buren Street
Chicago, IL 60607

Colegio de México
Depto. de Publicaciones
Camino al Ajusco No. 20
México 10740, D. F.

Cordillera Press
4 Marshall Road
Natick, MA 01760

Departamento Ecuménico de
   Investigaciones
Apdo. 339
2050 San Pedro de Montes de
   Oca
San José, Costa Rica

Donars Spanish Books
PO Box 24
Loveland, CO 80439-0024

EDAMEX
Calle Angel Urraza 1322
México 03100, D. F.

Ediciones CEDEL
Apdo. 5326
Barcelona 8, Spain

Ediciones de la Flor
Anchoris 27
Buenos Aires 1280, Argentina

Ediciones de Norte
Dept. C, Box A130
Hanover, NH 03755

Ediciones Garza, S.A.
Numancia 73, 30. A
Barcelona 29, Spain

Ediciones Universal
PO Box 450353
Miami, FL 33145

Editores Mexicanos Unidos,
   S.A.
L. González Obregón 5-B
Apdo. Postal 45-671
México 1, D. F.

Editorial A.T.E.
Rda. General Mitre 90
Barcelona 21, Spain

Editorial Alhambra
Caludio Coello, 76
Madrid 1, Spain

Editorial Avante, S.A.
Luis González Obregón 9, Altos
1
06020 Delegacion Cuauhtemoc
México, D. F.

Editorial Diana
Roberto Gayol 1219
Apdo. 44-986
México 12, D.F.

Editorial Font, S.A.
López Cotilla No. 440
Guadalajara, Jalisco, México

Editorial Fontalba
Valencia 359, 6o 1a
Barcelona 9, Spain

Editorial Juventud
Provenza 101 Apdo. 3
Barcelona 29, Spain

Editorial Lidiun
Patagones 2463
Buenos Aires 1005, Argentina

Editorial Limusa, S.A.
Balderas 95 Primer Piso
Esq. Ayuntamiento
México 06040, D.F.

Editorial Losada
Moreno 3362
1209 Capital Federal, Argentina

Editorial Lumen
Ramón Miguel Y Planas 10
Barcelona 34, Spain

Editorial Miñon
Vásquez de Menchaca 10
Apdo. 28
Valladolid 8, Spain

Editorial Nueva Imagen
Apdo. Postal 600
México 1, D. F.

Editorial Paidos
Defensa 599
Buenos Aires 1065, Argentina

Editorial Patria
Canoa 521, Primer Piso
Colonia Tizapan
México 01090, D.F.

Editorial Sigmar
Belgrano 1580, 7o piso
Buenos Aires 1093, Argentina

Editorial Sin Nombre, Inc.
Apdo. de correos 4391
San Juan, PR 00905-4391

EDUCA
Nicolas Bravo 81
Morelia, Michoacan, México

Encuentro Ediciones
Alcalá 117, 6o izq.
Madrid 9, Spain

Garrett Park Press
Garret Park, MD 20896

Gisbert y Cia., S.A.
Calle Comercio 1270
Casilla Postal 195
La Paz, Bolivia

Grupo Editorial Mitre
Copérnico 2
Barcelona 21, Spain

Haymarket, S.A.
Travesera de Gracia 17-21, 1o
3o
Barcelona 21, Spain

Heffernan School Supply
2111 West Avenue
PO Box 5309
San Antonio, TX 78201

Hesperia
26-05 Ditmaria Blvd.
Astoria, NY 11105

Hispanic Books
240 East Yvon Drive
Tucson, AZ 85704

Imported Books
PO Box 4414
Dallas, TX 75208

Instituto Panamericano de
   Geografía y Historia
Secretaria General
EX-Arzobispado 29
México 18, D.F.

Ladybird Books
Chestnut Street
Lewiston, ME 04240

Larousse and Co., Inc.
572 Fifth Avenue
New York, NY 10036

Latin American Jewish Studies
   Association
2104 Georgetown Blvd.
Ann Arbor, MI 48105

Lectorum Publications
137 West 14th Street
New York, NY 10011

Librería Cosmos, S.A.
López Cotilla 440
Guadalajara, Jalisco, México

Librería La Latina
2548 Mission Street
San Francisco, CA 94110

Librería Latinoamericana
37 East Speedway
Tucson, AZ 85705

Libros de Hispanoamerica
Libreria Editorial
Talcahuano 452, Primer Piso,
   ofic. 2 y 3
Buenos Aires 1013, Argentina

Libros Rio Nuevo
Ediciones 29
Mandri 41
Barcelona 22, Spain

Mexican American Studies and
   Research Center
Modern Languages Building
University of Arizona
Tucson, AZ 85721

Monte Avila Editores, C.A.
Av. Ppal de la Castellana con
1a. Transv. Qta. Cristina
Apdo. Postal 70712
Zona 1070
Caracas, Venezuela

Montesinos Editores, S.A.
Ronda San Pedro 11, 6o.
Barcelona 10, Spain

National Textbook Co.
4255 West Touhy Avenue
Lincolnwood, IL 60646-1975

Newbury House Publishers
54 Warehouse Lane
Rowley, MA 01969

Novelas Populares
Box 104
Yonkers, NY 10710

Organización Editorial Novaro
Calle 5, No. 12
Naucalpan, Edo. de México,
   México

Paisano Books
13306 Bexhill
Houston, TX 77065

Pedeca (Revista Clave)
María Auxiliadora 5
Madrid 20, Spain

Plaza & Janes, S. A., Editores
Virgen de Guadalupe 21-33
Espulgas de Llobregat
Barcelona, Spain

POLIMAG
1031 Bay Blvd., Ste. W
Chula Vista, CA 92011

Prodace, S.A.
Ferraz 11
Madrid 8, Spain

Puvill Libros S.A.
Boters, 10 y Paja 29
Barcelona 2, Spain

SALALM Secretariat
Memorial Library
University of Wisconsin
Madison, WI 53706

Santillana
942 South Gerhart
Los Angeles, CA 90022

Santillana Publishing Co.
12111 Front Street
Norwalk, CA 90650

Silver Burdett
250 James Street
CN-1918
Morristown, NJ 07960-1918

SLUSA (Spanish Literature in
   the U.S.A.)
PO Box 832, 88 Eastern Avenue
Somerville, NJ 08876-0832

Southwestern Publishing Co.
5101 Madison Road
Cincinnati, OH 45227

Timun Mas Editorial, S. A.
Via Layetana 17
Barcelona 3, Spain

Trinity University Press
715 Stadium Drive, Box 97
San Antonio, TX 78284

Tusquets Editores
Iradier 24 Bajos
Barcelona 17, Spain

University of California-Irvine
Department of Spanish and
    Portuguese
Irvine, CA 92714

University of Texas at Austin
    Publications
The General Libraries
PO Box P
Austin, TX 78713-7330

El Virrey
Miguel Dasso 141
Lima 27, Peru

Western Continental Book, Inc.
2120 South Ash
Suite No. 2
Denver, CO 80222

Index

Compiled by Linda Webster